Inspire English International

Year 8 Student Book

T0346062

David Grant

Overview contents

Detailed contents

Unit 1: Heroes and villains

Unit 2: Safe and sound

Detailed contents

Detailed contents

Unit 5: A moment in time

Unit 6: Dramatic!

About the Student Book

Welcome to Inspire English International! We hope you will find this book useful (and inspiring!) as you develop your skill and knowledge in written English. Through explicitly addressing the areas needed to excel in this subject, you should gain mastery of the subject and make excellent progress.

This Student Book provides a clear structure to your learning. Each unit is based around a theme and uses a range of engaging texts to help you focus on the mastery of key skills. These skills are set out at the start of each unit, along with a clear explanation of what you will be able to do by the end of that unit.

Within each unit, the theme is broken down into sections designed to help you master those key skills in a clear learning progression. Activities and Boosts (covering skills, grammar, spelling and punctuation) all build towards your learning.

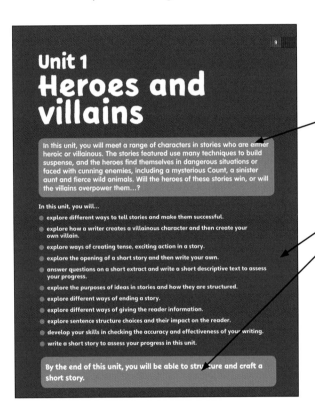

Each unit is based around a theme – at the start you will find a description of this theme and an idea of some of the texts you will explore.

Learning objectives are listed here, as well as a clear outcome – so that you understand what you will learn by following the unit.

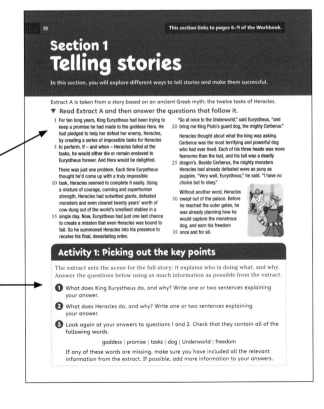

Each section begins with an engaging text on the unit's theme.

Activities throughout each unit focus on key skills and help structure your learning.

About the Student Book

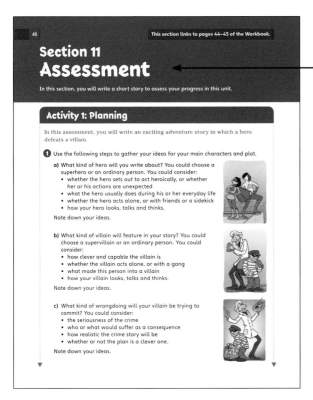

Assessment units help take the stress out of testing by giving you tools and structure and by walking you through the steps needed to produce outstanding answers every time.

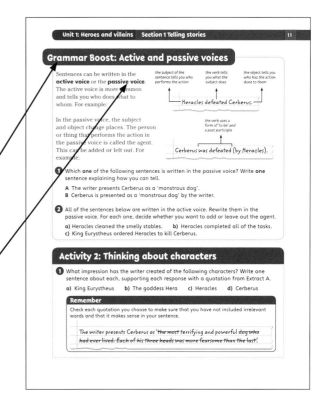

Boost boxes will develop your key skills further to help support you.

Key technical terms are in blue. You will find the definitions of these terms in the complete glossary at the end of the book.

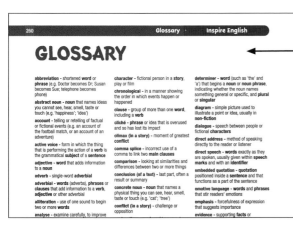

The glossary at the end of the book contains the key terms identified across all years of the course, along with clear definitions.

Unit 1
Heroes and villains

In this unit, you will meet a range of characters in stories who are either heroic or villainous. The stories featured use many techniques to build suspense, and the heroes find themselves in dangerous situations or faced with cunning enemies, including a mysterious Count, a sinister aunt and fierce wild animals. Will the heroes of these stories win, or will the villains overpower them…?

In this unit, you will...

● explore different ways to tell stories and make them successful.

● explore how a writer creates a villainous character and then create your own villain.

● explore ways of creating tense, exciting action in a story.

● explore the opening of a short story and then write your own.

● answer questions on a short extract and write a story opening to assess your progress.

● explore the purposes of ideas in stories and how they are structured.

● explore different ways of ending a story.

● explore different ways of giving the reader information.

● explore sentence structure choices and their impact on the reader.

● develop your skills in checking the accuracy and effectiveness of your writing.

● write a short story to assess your progress in this unit.

By the end of this unit, you will be able to structure and craft a short story.

Section 1
Telling stories

In this section, you will explore different ways to tell stories and make them successful.

Extract A is taken from a story based on an ancient Greek myth: the twelve tasks of Heracles.

▼ Read Extract A and then answer the questions that follow it.

1 For ten long years, King Eurystheus had been trying to keep a promise he had made to the goddess Hera. He had pledged to help her defeat her enemy, Heracles, by creating a series of impossible tasks for Heracles
5 to perform. If – and when – Heracles failed at the tasks, he would either die or remain enslaved to Eurystheus forever. And Hera would be delighted.

There was just one problem. Each time Eurystheus thought he'd come up with a truly impossible
10 task, Heracles seemed to complete it easily. Using a mixture of courage, cunning and superhuman strength, Heracles had outwitted giants, defeated monsters and even cleared twenty years' worth of cow dung out of the world's smelliest stables in a
15 single day. Now, Eurystheus had just one last chance to create a mission that even Heracles was bound to fail. So he summoned Heracles into his presence to receive his final, devastating order.

"Go at once to the Underworld," said Eurystheus, "and
20 bring me King Pluto's guard dog, the mighty Cerberus."

Heracles thought about what the king was asking. Cerberus was the most terrifying and powerful dog who had ever lived. Each of his three heads was more fearsome than the last, and his tail was a deadly
25 dragon's. Beside Cerberus, the mighty monsters Heracles had already defeated were as puny as puppies. "Very well, Eurystheus," he said. "I have no choice but to obey."

Without another word, Heracles
30 swept out of the palace. Before he reached the outer gates, he was already planning how he would capture the monstrous dog, and earn his freedom
35 once and for all.

Activity 1: Picking out the key points

The extract sets the scene for the full story: it explains who is doing what, and why. Answer the questions below using as much information as possible from the extract.

1 What does King Eurystheus do, and why? Write one or two sentences explaining your answer.

2 What does Heracles do, and why? Write one or two sentences explaining your answer.

3 Look again at your answers to questions 1 and 2. Check that they contain all of the following words.

goddess | promise | tasks | dog | Underworld | freedom

If any of these words are missing, make sure you have included all the relevant information from the extract. If possible, add more information to your answers.

Grammar Boost: Active and passive voices

Sentences can be written in the **active voice** or the **passive voice**. The active voice is more common and tells you who does what to whom. For example:

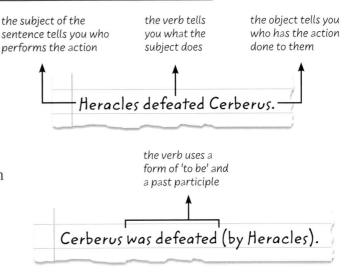

the subject of the sentence tells you who performs the action

the verb tells you what the subject does

the object tells you who has the action done to them

Heracles defeated Cerberus.

In the passive voice, the subject and object change places. The person or thing that performs the action in the passive voice is called the agent. This can be added or left out. For example:

the verb uses a form of 'to be' and a past participle

Cerberus was defeated (by Heracles).

1 Which **one** of the following sentences is written in the passive voice? Write **one** sentence explaining how you can tell.

  A The writer presents Cerberus as a 'monstrous dog'.
  B Cerberus is presented as a 'monstrous dog' by the writer.

2 All of the sentences below are written in the active voice. Rewrite them in the passive voice. For each one, decide whether you want to add or leave out the agent.

  a) Heracles cleaned the smelly stables. **b)** Heracles completed all of the tasks.
  c) King Eurystheus ordered Heracles to kill Cerberus.

Activity 2: Thinking about characters

1 What impression has the writer created of the following characters? Write one sentence about each, supporting each response with a quotation from Extract A.

  a) King Eurystheus **b)** The goddess Hera **c)** Heracles **d)** Cerberus

Remember

Check each quotation you choose to make sure that you have not included irrelevant words and that it makes sense in your sentence.

The writer presents Cerberus as 'the most terrifying and powerful dog who had ever lived. Each of his three heads was more fearsome than the last'.

Extract B is the beginning of a story that is also about Heracles' final challenge, but it is written in a different style. Heracles has just come ashore from the River Styx, which separates the Underworld from the living world.

▼ Read Extract B and then answer the questions that follow it.

1   The air of the Underworld was cold and thick with an ancient silence. The only sound came from the oars of the wooden boat as it retreated across the night-black river, leaving Heracles alone on the riverbank. He shivered. Was he the only living thing in this deserted
5   kingdom of the dead?

Huge gates loomed ahead of him. Torches set high on either side of them flickered dimly in the dank air.

Stone grated roughly on stone as Heracles shouldered the mighty palace gates aside. As he stepped through, every corner of the
10 courtyard shook with a frenzy of baying fury.

For a moment, Heracles stood as if dazed. Then in the deep darkness by a distant door, a terrifying shape began to emerge: a mighty hound, chained to a massive stone pillar, its three heads raised to the moonless sky, howling and monstrous in its rage.

15 Before Heracles could gather himself, a darkly shadowed figure stepped out into the courtyard. It silenced the beast with a bloody hunk of meat, and turned its dead white eyes to Heracles.

"I know why you are here," said the figure.

"I am here," said Heracles, steadying his shaking voice, "because King Eurystheus sent me. It is my final challenge:
20 to bring your dog to him. So I would be –"

Heracles' voice was lost in a blast of mocking laughter that echoed through the courtyard. In its dying echoes, the figure bent and released the chains that bound the dog.

Activity 3: Comparing two texts

1 Answer the questions below with reference to Extract B only.
   a) Where is Heracles at the start of this story?
   b) Why has Heracles come to this place?

2 Extract B contains less background information than Extract A. As Extract B goes on, the writer will have to give the reader all the important information they will need to understand the story.
   a) Which pieces of information will the writer of Extract B need to include later in the story? Look again at your answers to Activity 1 for support.
   b) Extract B describes a part of the story that comes after the events described in Extract A, but it also reveals things about Heracles' thoughts and feelings. Do you think Extract A would be improved if it revealed these things too? Write one or two sentences to explain your answer, giving the information you think could be included in Extract A.

Activity 4: Comparing intention and response

Think about how the writer of each extract tells the story.

1 Look at the following summary of the whole story of Heracles and Cerberus.

A   *Eurystheus sets Heracles impossible tasks, including capturing Cerberus.*

B   *Heracles enters the Underworld and faces Cerberus.*

C   *Heracles captures Cerberus and delivers him to Eurystheus.*

D   *Eurystheus begs Heracles to return the terrifying hound to the Underworld and gives Heracles his freedom.*

a) At what point in the plot does the writer of Extract A on page 10 begin the story?
b) At what point in the plot does the writer of Extract B on page 12 begin the story?
c) Why might the writers of the two extracts have made these different decisions?

2 What impression has the writer created of the following characters? Write one sentence about each, supporting each response with a quotation from Extract B.

a) Heracles   **b)** The darkly shadowed figure   **c)** Cerberus

3 In what ways are your impressions of Heracles in Extract B different from your impressions of Heracles in Extract A? Write one or two sentences explaining your ideas.

In Extract A, Heracles is presented as   *Whereas in Extract B, the writer*

4 Look again at the following descriptions of Cerberus in the two extracts.

Extract A	**Extract B**
Cerberus was the most terrifying and powerful dog who had ever lived. Each of his three heads was more fearsome than the last, and his tail was a deadly dragon's.	Then in the deep darkness by a distant door, a terrifying shape began to emerge: a mighty hound, chained to a massive stone pillar, its three heads raised to the moonless sky, howling and monstrous in its rage.

Both versions create a similar impression. How has each writer done so?

5 Do you prefer Extract A or B? Write **two or three** sentences explaining your choice.

Section 2
Building a character

In this section, you will explore how a writer creates a villainous character, and then create your own villain.

In this extract, Walter Hartright has come to challenge his enemy, the villainous Count Fosco. Walter knows an important secret about the Count – a mark on his arm proves he was a member of a secret group called the Brotherhood, but he betrayed them. The Count has been keeping this secret because if the Brotherhood find him again, they will kill him.

▼ **Read the extract and then answer the questions that follow it.**

1 He slipped by me with the quickness of thought, locked the door, and put the key in his pocket.

"You and I, Mr. Hartright, are excellently well acquainted with one another by reputation," he said. "Did it, by any chance, occur to you when you came to this house that I was not the sort of man you could trifle with?"

"It did occur to me," I replied. "And I have not come to trifle with you. I am here on a matter of life and death."

5 "On a matter of life and death," he repeated to himself. "Those words are more serious, perhaps, than you think. What do you mean?"

"What I say."

The perspiration broke out thickly on his broad forehead. His left hand stole over the edge of the table. There was a drawer in it, with a lock, and the key was in the lock.

10 "So you know why I am leaving London?" he went on. "Tell me the reason, if you please." He turned the key, and unlocked the drawer as he spoke.

"I can do better than that," I replied. "I can SHOW you the reason, if you like."

"How can you show it?"

"You have got your coat off," I said. "Roll up the shirt-sleeve on your left arm, and you will see it there."

15 The same livid leaden change passed over his face which I had seen pass over it at the theatre. The deadly glitter in his eyes shone steady and straight into mine. He said nothing. But his left hand slowly opened the table-drawer, and softly slipped into it.

My life hung by a thread, and I knew it.

"Wait a little," I said. "You have got the door locked – you see I don"t
20 move – you see my hands are empty. Wait a little. I have something more to say."

"You have said enough," he replied, with a sudden composure so unnatural and so ghastly that it tried my nerves as no outbreak of violence could have tried them. "I want one moment for my own
25 thoughts, if you please. Do you guess what I am thinking about?"

"Perhaps I do."

"I am thinking," he remarked quietly, "whether I shall add to the disorder in this room by scattering your brains about the fireplace."

Activity 1: Inferring character

1 What clues in the extract on page 14 reveal that Count Fosco is a villain?

2 Look again at the way Count Fosco speaks at the end of the extract:

> "You have said enough," he replied.

> "I am thinking," he remarked quietly, "whether I shall add to the disorder in this room by scattering your brains about the fireplace."

What does the writer suggest or reveal about Count Fosco's character through his speech? Note down the effect of each example.

3 Look at what Count Fosco says earlier in the extract. What further things can you infer about his character from what he says? Choose quotations as evidence to support your ideas.

> ### How do I do that?
> Look carefully through the relevant part of the text for a sentence, phrase or word that is particularly powerful in creating the effect you are describing. For example, if you wanted to prove that a character is presented as polite, you might select a sentence in which they say 'please' and 'thank you' several times.

4 a) What information can you find in the extract about Count Fosco's actions?
b) What can you infer about his character from his actions?

5 In your opinion, which reveals most about the character of Count Fosco: his speech or his actions? Write one or two sentences explaining your ideas.

6 a) What information can you find in the extract about Walter Hartright?
b) What can you infer about his character from what he says and does?

Activity 2: Responding to character

1 How do you respond to the character of Count Fosco? Note down some words to express your response. You could choose from the vocabulary below, or use your own ideas.

intrigued | frightened | disturbed | excited | revolted

2 Write **two or three** sentences explaining your response and how it was formed, using one or two quotations from the extracts to support your ideas.

Activity 3: Revealing a villain

1 In the extract, sometimes Count Fosco seems more powerful, and at other times Walter Hartright seems to hold more power. Look again at the sections of dialogue below from the extract on page 14. Which character seems most powerful in each section? How is this shown in their speech?

A 'So you know why I am leaving London?' he went on. 'Tell me the reason, if you please.' He turned the key, and unlocked the drawer as he spoke.

'I can do better than that,' I replied. 'I can SHOW you the reason, if you like.'

'How can you show it?'

'You have got your coat off,' I said. 'Roll up the shirt-sleeve on your left arm, and you will see it there.'

B 'Wait a little,' I said. 'You have got the door locked – you see I don't move – you see my hands are empty. Wait a little. I have something more to say.'

'You have said enough,' he replied, with a sudden composure so unnatural and so ghastly that it tried my nerves as no outbreak of violence could have tried them. 'I want one moment for my own thoughts, if you please. Do you guess what I am thinking about?'

2 The author varies the length of the sentences when writing dialogue. For example, short sentences can add pace, and longer sentences interrupted by dashes could suggest the character is nervous or panicking. Why do you think the author varies the sentences in this way? What effect does it have?

Skills Boost: Speech punctuation

1 Look again at the sections of dialogue in Activity 3. Use them to help you complete the rules of speech punctuation below. Select one option to complete each sentence.

The rules of speech punctuation

a) The words spoken are always enclosed in <u>commas / speech marks / capital letters</u>.

b) There is always <u>a full stop / a comma / some punctuation</u> before the closing speech mark.

c) When the words spoken are followed by an identifier, there is never <u>a comma / a question mark / a full stop</u> before the closing speech mark.

d) When the words spoken are **not** followed by an identifier, there is never <u>a comma / a question mark / a full stop</u> before the closing speech mark.

> **Remember**
>
> An identifier gives information about who is speaking. For example: *she said*.

2 Now check that all of the rules you have written are true of the examples of dialogue in Activity 3.

Activity 4: Building your own villain

You are going to build a villainous character that could appear in a story. Imagine that your teacher has left the school and has been replaced by a villainous teacher.

Choose your intention

1 How do you want readers to respond to the character of the villain you are creating?
You could choose from the vocabulary below, or use your own ideas.

amused | frightened | disturbed | excited | revolted

> ### Remember
> All the choices you make in this activity should help you to achieve your intention.

Imagine

2 Picture the scene at the start of the story: students are sitting in a classroom. The teacher enters. What is the first impression you want to create of this character? Write one or two sentences summarising your ideas.

Develop your ideas

3 Think about speech that will show the reader what your villainous character is like. Write down **two or three** things the teacher could say in the classroom.

4 Think about the actions that will show the reader what your villainous character is like. Note down **two or three** things the teacher could do in the classroom.
Ask yourself:
- How does my villain move around the classroom?
- How does my villain treat the students?
- What might my villain do with objects in the classroom, such as tables and books?

5 Think about your description of this villainous character's appearance. Choose **two** key features that you could describe. You could describe your character's:

hair | nose | eyes | ears | teeth | smile | shoes

6 Finally, give your villainous character a name. Aim to choose a name that suits his or her villainous nature.

This section links to pages 14–17 of the Workbook.

Section 3
Creating danger

In this section, you will explore ways of creating tense, exciting action in a story.

This is an extract from a short story. Fourteen-year-old Alex Ryder is investigating the car crash in which his uncle is thought to have died. Alex finds his uncle's car in the local breaker's yard – a junkyard where old cars are crushed. As Alex tries to inspect the car for clues, he hears voices.

▼ Read the extract and then answer the questions that follow it.

1 Without thinking, Alex threw himself into the only hiding place available: inside the car itself. Using his foot, he hooked the door and closed it. At the same time, he became aware that the machines had started again and he could no longer hear the men. He didn't dare look up. A shadow fell across the window as the two men passed. But then they were gone. He was safe.

2 And then something hit the car with such force that Alex cried out, his whole body caught in a massive shock wave that tore him away from the steering wheel and threw him helplessly into the back. The roof buckled and three huge metal fingers tore through the skin of the car like a fork through an eggshell, trailing dust and sunlight. One of the fingers grazed the side of his head … any closer and it would have cracked his skull. Alex yelled as blood trickled over his eye. He tried to move, then was jerked back a second time as the car was yanked off the ground and tilted high up in the air.

3 He couldn't see. He couldn't move. But his stomach lurched as the car swung in an arc, the metal grinding and the light spinning. The car had been picked up by the crane. It was going to be put inside the crusher. With him inside.

4 He tried to raise himself up, to wave through the windows. But the claw of the crane had already flattened the roof, pinning his left leg, perhaps even breaking it. He could feel nothing. He lifted a hand and managed to pound on the back window, but he couldn't break the glass. Even if the workmen were staring at the car, they would never see anything moving inside.

5 His short flight across the junkyard ended with a bone-shattering crash as the crane deposited the car on the iron shelves of the crusher. Alex tried to fight back his sickness and despair and think of what to do. Any moment now the operator would send the car tipping into the coffin-shaped trough. The machine was a Lefort Shear, a slow-motion guillotine. At the press of a button, the two wings would close on the car with a joint pressure of five hundred tons. The car, with Alex inside it, would be crushed beyond recognition. And the broken metal – and flesh – would then be chopped into sections. Nobody would ever know what had happened.

6 He tried with all his strength to free himself. But the roof was too low. His leg was trapped. Then his whole world tilted and he felt himself falling into darkness. The shelves had lifted. The car slid to one side and fell the few yards into the trough. Alex felt the metalwork collapsing all around him. The back window exploded and glass showered around his head, dust and diesel fumes punching into his nose and eyes. There was hardly any daylight now, but looking out of the back, he could see the huge steel head of the piston that would push what was left of the car through the exit hole on the other side.

Activity 1: Tracking key events

Answer the questions below to make sure you understand the key events in the extract on page 18.

1 What **two** dangers does Alex face in the extract?

2 At the end of the first paragraph, Alex thinks he is safe. Why does he think this?

3 In the second paragraph, Alex realises he is **not** safe. Using your own words, explain what happens in this paragraph. Make sure you include details of what happens to the car and to Alex himself.

4 Carefully reread the rest of the extract, from the third paragraph to the end. Copy and complete a graph like the one below to show how safe Alex is as the story develops.

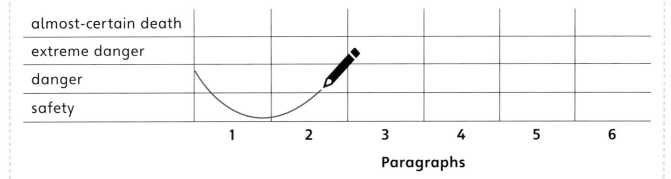

Activity 2: Identifying elements

There are some important elements you could use to create a gripping action scene in a story:
- Tell the reader what is happening.
- Tell the reader what is going to happen soon.
- Tell the reader how the main character is feeling.
- Tell the reader about the main character's five senses: what they can see, hear, smell, taste or touch.

1 Identify **one** example of each element in the extract on page 18.

2 Which element is used most often?

3 Which element is used least often?

Skills Boost: Word classes

Word classes are groups of words that have similar roles in sentences.

1 Nouns name a person, place or object. The words 'chair', 'movement' and 'idea' are examples of nouns. Note down **five** different nouns that could replace the **?**.

I can see the ?.

2 Adjectives are words that add information about nouns. They describe the things named by the nouns. The words 'happy', 'green', and 'close' are examples of adjectives. Note down **five** different adjectives that could replace the **?**.

She has bought a ? car.

3 Verbs express an action or situation. They can be preceded by a **pronoun** such as *I, you* or *it*. The words 'had', 'walk', and 'believes' are examples of verbs. Note down **five** different verbs that could replace the **?**.

I ? in the park.

4 Adverbs are words that add information about verbs, adjectives or other adverbs. The words 'quickly', 'soon' and 'often' are examples of adverbs. Note down **five** different adverbs that could replace the **?**.

He did his homework ?.

Activity 3: Exploring vocabulary

The writer of the extract on page 18 uses vocabulary to create a dramatic sense of danger. Look again at the following action-packed sentences from the extract.

> The roof buckled and three huge metal fingers tore through the skin of the car like a fork through an eggshell, trailing dust and sunlight.

> The back window exploded and glass showered around his head, dust and diesel fumes punching into his nose and eyes.

1 Focus on the writer's choice of verbs in the sentences above.
   a) Note down verbs that help the writer to create drama.
   b) Which verb do you find the most dramatic? Write one or two sentences explaining your choice.

2 Look again at the sentences above and find the simile the writer has used.
   a) Identify the **two** things described in the simile, and the **two** things with which they are compared.
   b) What does this simile suggest about the car and the car crusher?

Remember

A simile is a comparison made using the words *like* or *as*.

Activity 4: Facing danger

You are going to write an extract from a story. You will write two paragraphs of action-packed drama in which the hero of the story faces extreme danger.

Imagine

- You are the hero of the story. You have escaped from a group of villains. They are chasing you through a tunnel.

- You see daylight ahead. If you can reach the daylight, you will be safe!

- You emerge from the tunnel and find yourself on a narrow ledge of rock, on a cliff, high above the sea, with only a weak bridge in front of you.

- You have two options: cross the bridge, or jump...

Plan

1 Think about the elements you will include in your writing to tell the story to the reader. Use the plot above and lots of your own ideas to complete a table like the one below.

What is happening?	
What is going to happen soon?	
How is the main character feeling?	
What is happening to the main character's five senses: what can they see, hear, smell, taste or touch?	

2 Think about how the plot could introduce a feeling of apparent safety before even worse danger presents itself.

Write

3 Write **two** paragraphs, using all your ideas to tell the story of your heroic escape. Choose your verbs carefully, to create a dramatic sense of danger.

This section links to pages 18–23 of the Workbook.

Section 4
Openings

In this section, you will explore the opening of a short story and then write your own.

This extract is the opening of a short story.

▼ **Read the extract and then answer the questions that follow it.**

The tiger in the snow

1 Justin sensed the tiger as soon as he reached the street. He didn't see it, or hear it. He simply sensed it. Leaving the warm safety of the Baxters' porch light behind him, he started down the sidewalk that fronted State Street, feeling the night swallow him in a single hungry gulp. He stopped when he reached the edge of the Baxters' property line and looked back wistfully toward their front door.

2 Too bad the evening had to end. It had been just about the finest evening he could remember. Not that Steve and he hadn't had some fine old times together, the way best friends will; but this particular evening had been, well, magical. They had played *The Shot Brothers* down in Steve's basement while Mr and Mrs Baxter watched TV upstairs. When the game had been going well and everything was clicking, Justin could almost believe that Steve and he really were brothers. And that feeling had never been stronger than it had been this evening.

3 When Mrs Baxter had finally called down that it was time to go, it had struck Justin as vaguely strange that she would be packing him off on a night like this, seeing how he and Steve slept over at one another's homes just about every weekend. But this evening was different. Despite the snow, home called to him in sweet siren whispers.

4 Mrs Baxter had bundled him up in his parka, boots and mittens, and then, much to his surprise, she had kissed his cheek. Steve had seen him to the door, said a quick goodbye, then hurried away to the den. Funny thing, Steve's eyes had seemed moist.

5 Then Justin had stepped out into the night, and Mrs Baxter had closed the door behind him, leaving him alone with the dark and the cold and ... the tiger.

6 At the edge of the Baxters' property, Justin glanced around for a glimpse of the beast; but the street appeared deserted save for the houses and parked cars under a downy blanket of fresh snow. It was drifting down lazily now, indifferent after the heavy fall of that afternoon. Justin could see the skittering flakes trapped within the cones of light cast by the street lamps, but otherwise the black air seemed coldly empty. The line of lamps at every corner of State Street gave the appearance of a tunnel of light that tapered down to nothingness; and beyond that tunnel, the dark pressed eagerly in.

7 For a moment, Justin felt the urge to scurry back to the Baxters' door and beg for sanctuary, but he knew he should be getting home. Besides, he wasn't some chicken who ran from the dark. He was one of the Shot Brothers. Rough and ready. Fearless. Hadn't he proven that to stupid Dale Corkland just the other day? "You scared?" old zit-faced Corkland had asked him. And Justin had shown him.

Activity 1: Reading between the lines

1 Reread the first two paragraphs of the extract on page 22.
   a) How is Justin feeling as he leaves the Baxters' house?
   b) How is Justin feeling when he thinks about the time he has spent with Steve?

2 Look again at the third and fourth paragraphs of the story.
   a) Justin finds a number of things about this evening unusual or surprising. Note down as many of them as you can find.
   b) What do you think the writer is trying to suggest in these paragraphs?

3 Reread the final two paragraphs of the extract.
   a) What do you think might have happened between Justin and Dale Corkland?
   b) What do you think might happen next in the story?

Activity 2: Responding to the opening

A story opening should engage the reader so they want to keep reading.

| It can create excitement, interest or humour that appeals to the reader. | It can introduce a subject or character about which the reader wants to find out more. | It can make the reader ask questions they hope the story will answer. |

1 Which method is used most effectively in the extract on page 22? How is it used, and why is it effective? Write a short paragraph explaining your ideas.

How do I do that?

An effective response to a text needs to identify what the writer has done, and how they have done it.

1) Write one or two sentences, summing up your response to the story opening.

The writer engages the reader's interest by

2) Select **one** short quotation as evidence to prove your point.

For example, the writer describes

3) Finally, write one or two sentences explaining how the evidence you have selected proves the point you made at the beginning of your paragraph.

This suggests that   *The reader is given the impression that*

Skills Boost: Choosing tense and person

When you write a story, your choice of tense and person should be one of the first decisions you make. This table shows how they can be used in a story.

Tense	Present tense	Events are happening as they are being narrated: *I walk in the woods.*
	Past tense	Events happened at some point in the past: *I walked in the woods.*
Person	First person	Events are written from the narrator's point of view: *I was walking in the woods.*
	Third person	Events are written as though the narrator is watching the action: *She was walking in the woods.*

1 Rewrite this story extract in the third person and past tense.

> I walk through the darkness and I stop every time I hear a noise. As I go around a corner, I realise I can hear footsteps. They are getting faster and closer. I start to run. I have no idea where I am going — I just know I have to get away.

Activity 3: Choosing the first sentence

1 Look at the sentences below from the extract on page 22. Sentence A is the first sentence of the story and sentences B–E are other key sentences which set the scene for the reader. Any of these sentences could have been the first sentence in the story, although some would need one minor change.

A   Justin sensed the tiger as soon as he reached the street.

B   Leaving the warm safety of the Baxters' porch light behind him, ~~he~~ Justin started down the sidewalk that fronted State Street, feeling the night swallow him in a single hungry gulp.

C   ~~They~~ Justin and Steve had played *The Shot Brothers* down in Steve's basement while Mr and Mrs Baxter watched TV upstairs.

D   ~~When~~ Mrs Baxter had finally called down that it was time to go...

E   ~~Then~~ Justin had stepped out into the night, and Mrs Baxter had closed the door behind him...

a) Order the sentences to show the order in which the events actually took place.
b) Which sentence(s) tell the reader about one of the characters' thoughts or feelings?
c) Which sentence(s) tell the reader about an event that happened?
d) Which sentence(s) create a sense of danger or tension?
e) Which sentence(s) make the reader want to find out what will happen next?

2 Do you think the writer chose the most effective opening sentence? Why is this? Write one or two sentences to explain your ideas.

Activity 4: Writing an opening

You are going to write the first paragraph of an engaging story opening.

Imagine

Before you begin writing your story, you need to gather some ideas about the events that take place.

- The story begins in a place you know well. Where is it? It could be your home, your school, a friend or relative's house, or somewhere else.
- You decide to leave that place, to go somewhere else you know well. Where is it?
- As you make your way to the second place, something strange or disturbing happens. What is it? It could be something you notice using any of your senses.

Write

1 You are going to write the first **five** sentences of your story in chronological order. Write your sentences in the first person and the past tense.

a) Write a sentence describing the weather and the time of day when this story takes place.

b) Write a sentence telling the reader where you were at first, and why you were there.

c) Write a sentence telling the reader where you decided to go, and why.

d) Write a sentence telling the reader about the strange or disturbing thing that happened on the way there.

e) Write a sentence telling the reader how you felt when it happened. Try to give a detailed description.

Sequence

2 Look again at the five sentences you wrote in response to question 1.

a) Which sentence would make the most engaging first sentence of your story?

b) In what order will you sequence the other four sentences? Experiment with sequencing them in two or three different ways before choosing which way is the most effective.

Revise

3 a) Rewrite your story opening in the third person.

b) Which version do you prefer – the first-person version or the third-person version? Why is this? Write one or two sentences to explain your choice.

Section 5
Assessment

In this section, you will answer questions on a short extract and write a story opening to assess your progress.

Marcus and Cleo live with their parents at 52 Willow Gardens. When their parents travel overseas to a business conference, the children's Great Aunt arrives to look after them.

▼ **Read the extract and then answer the questions that follow it.**

1 "She's only staying a week," Mother had said; but from the moment Great Aunt Jampot arrived, Marcus and Cleo feared she would never leave.

They bitterly recalled
5 the morning she appeared on their doorstep. The children had gone to answer the loud
10 insistent knocking and were confronted by a tall, thin woman in a vast, rustling, purple dress. She had a nest of silver hair on her head, and what appeared to be a
15 dead badger draped about her shoulders. She pushed past them into the house, without any explanation, calling over her shoulder in a commanding voice, "My luggage is on the path…be careful with it!"

Marcus went to pick up the small, delicate-looking
20 bag in one quick movement – and almost fell over. It was much heavier than it looked. Carefully now, he wrapped his arms around it and lifted with all his strength. It clanked and the weight seemed to shift. He was sure he could hear his bones groaning under the
25 weight – what could be in there? His suspicions were further aroused when he discovered his Aunt a week later, crouching with her ear to the door of the safe in the study. Seeing Marcus staring, she straightened up and removed her black leather gloves. "I heard a
30 mouse. What are you doing creeping around, child?" she exclaimed.

It was the first of many **sinister**[1] clues the children observed about their unwelcome babysitter. Although the reason for her visit was to care for them, the twins
35 glumly reflected that "caring" was the last thing Great Aunt Jampot was inclined to do. That first evening, the children had been sitting in the dining room as usual when a shrill voice had called them to the kitchen. There, they'd been ordered to sit at a bare, grubby
40 table. In front of each of them sat a chipped bowl and a crudely carved wooden spoon. In the centre of the table sat a huge, rusty, black pot and in it a thick, grey liquid. Strange black misshapen lumps floated to the surface of the liquid, then sank quickly with a 'gloop'.
45 "Eat your stew, you need your strength – this house is disgusting!" said Aunt Jampot.

The children tried to protest, but they soon learnt that the new diet was only the first of a series of **draconian**[2] rules, forcing them to constantly scrub
50 the house, clean the windows, mow the lawn, and spend any free time they had left wiping fingerprints off the furniture in her room.

Aunt Jampot herself did not share the children's meals, and fed herself in an altogether more
55 luxurious manner. She was rarely to be seen without a cake clasped between her fingers, but for all her **gluttony**[3], she remained **gaunt**[4] and thin – her sharp, angular nose protruding like a shark's fin from her bony face. Sometimes, while working, they would
60 look up to see her glittering eyes boring into them, seeming to read every thought in their minds.

One day, when Cleo dared to suggest that they might take a day off from the endless round of chores, Aunt Jampot fixed her with those eyes, and smiled,
65 exposing steel-grey teeth like a snare. "Children…", she rasped, "must work for their delicious stew."

Key vocabulary

sinister[1]: suspicious
draconian[2]: strict
gluttony[3]: greed
gaunt[4]: starved

Activity 1: Reading

1 Identify **four** things you learn from the extract on page 26 about Great Aunt Jampot.

2 The writer implies **one** reason why Great Aunt Jampot has come to stay. What is it? Support your ideas with a quotation from the extract.

3 Look again at the following passage from the extract.

> Aunt Jampot fixed her with those eyes, and smiled, exposing steel-grey teeth like a snare.

What does this simile suggest about Great Aunt Jampot's thoughts and feelings at this point in the story?

4 In your opinion, will the twins be happy while Great Aunt Jampot looks after them? Write a short paragraph in which you:
- explain how the writer has given you this impression throughout the extract
- comment on why the writer might want to give this impression
- use evidence from the extract to support your ideas.

Activity 2: Writing

1 Write the opening to a story in which you describe meeting someone for the very first time.

Before you start writing
- Imagine the character you will meet, for example, a new teacher or a new neighbour.
- Decide where, how and why you meet this person.
- Think about the first impression you want to create of this person – and how you will create that impression. Think particularly about what effect you want to create with your opening sentence.
- Note down all your ideas and decide how you will begin your story to engage the reader's interest.

As you write
- Choose your vocabulary carefully, aiming to create interest and drama.
- Consider how you might create effects of both worry and relief.

When you have finished writing
- Check that your first sentence and the rest of your story opening will engage the reader's interest.
- Check to see if any of your vocabulary choices could be improved.
- Check that your spelling and punctuation are accurate, especially your speech punctuation.

This section links to pages 24–27 of the Workbook.

Section 6
Story structure

In this section, you will explore the purposes of ideas in stories and how they are structured.

This is a summary of the short story *The Brazilian Cat* by Arthur Conan Doyle, which was first published in 1898.

▼ **Read the summary and then answer the questions that follow it.**

1   Marshall King will one day inherit a fortune from his uncle, Lord Southerton. Until then, Marshall has very little money and no job.

Marshall needs money, so he's very pleased when his wealthy cousin, Everard King, invites him to stay at his house for a few days. Marshall hopes Everard will lend him some money.

5   Everard had been living in Brazil and returned with lots of wild animals and birds, which he keeps in his large country house and gardens.

Marshall arrives at Everard's house. Everard is very friendly, kind and hospitable. Everard's wife, however, is very unfriendly and unwelcoming. She even suggests Marshall should go home immediately.

Everard invites Marshall to inspect his collection of wild animals. One of them – a huge, black Brazilian cat – is kept
10   in a cage in a room with a heavy door and thick bars on the window. The cage can be opened by a lever, leaving only the top in place, so the cat can walk freely around the room. Everard is able to enter the room but warns Marshall it would be very dangerous if he entered.

One night, Marshall asks Everard for help with his money problems. Everard agrees. Everard says he must check on his animals before going to bed. He asks Marshall to go with him.

15   Everard and Marshall go to check on the Brazilian cat. Everard tricks Marshall and locks him in the room with the Brazilian cat while the cage is open.

Marshall realises that he will be safest if he climbs up on top of the cage. He lies still and silent in the darkness.

20   In the light of morning, the Brazilian cat sees and attacks Marshall. He is very badly wounded. The cat seems to think it has killed Marshall and so doesn't attack him again. However, when Everard comes to check that Marshall is dead, the cat attacks Everard and kills him.

25   Six weeks later, when Marshall has recovered from his injuries, he learns that Lord Southerton has died and that he's now very rich – and that, if the Brazilian cat had killed him, his cousin Everard would have inherited all of Lord Southerton's money.

Punctuation Boost: Apostrophes

Remember

Apostrophes have two jobs:

- They are used in contractions, to show that some letters have been missed out.
- They are used to show possession: that something belongs to someone or something.
  - When a word is a plural and ends –s, you do not need to add another 's' to show possession – you just add the apostrophe:
  - However, when a word is **not** a plural and ends –s, you usually **do** need to add another 's':

> do not ⟶ don't
>
> the cousin of my mum ⟶ my mum's cousin
>
> the favourite song of the boys ⟶ the boys' favourite song
>
> the hat of James ⟶ James's hat

1 Rewrite the sentences below, using as many apostrophes as you can. You can change the words and their order, but do not change the meaning of the sentences.

> Everard does not have any money. Marshall visits the house belonging to Everard. The wife of Everard does not like Marshall. Marshall wants to borrow some of the money belonging to Everard. Everard agrees and Marshall thinks he is very kind. Marshall is attacked by the Brazilian cat belonging to Everard. He is shut in the room containing the Brazilian cat and he cannot escape.

Activity 1: Exploring ideas and intentions

1 At the start of the summary on page 28, the reader is told about Marshall King's financial situation.
   a) Why is it important to the story that Marshall has very little money?
   b) Why is it important to the story that Marshall will inherit a fortune from his uncle?

2 For most of the story, the writer suggests that Everard King is kind and generous.
   a) How does the writer suggest this?
   b) Why does the writer suggest this?

3 Why do you think Everard King's wife is so unfriendly and unwelcoming to Marshall King?

4 Why do you think the writer decided that Everard King should have gone to Brazil to collect all his animals?

Activity 2: Story structure

One way to think about a typical story structure is to break it into four parts as shown in the table below.

Exposition	The **exposition** 'exposes' the situation at the start of the story, introducing characters and setting. For example: *Two friends learn that there will be a talent competition at school.*
Conflict	In a **conflict**, one or more of the characters has a problem. Conflicts could be disagreements, difficulties or challenges, for example. There could be more than one conflict in a story. For example: *The friends both want to win. They argue, and they try to stop each other practising.*
Climax	The **climax** of a story is often its most exciting moment. Characters attempt to solve their conflicts– for example, in a battle – and their challenges seem huge. For example: *The friends finally have a huge argument. While arguing, they learn they both want to impress their parents more than they want to win.*
Resolution	At the end of the story, a **resolution** to the conflict is found. Sometimes the conflict is resolved successfully, giving the story a happy ending – but not always! For example: *The friends make up, and decide to help each other do well.*

1 Think about how *The Brazilian Cat* fits into this structure. Copy and complete the table below with your answers to the following questions.

The exposition

a) What is Marshall King's situation at the start of the story?

The conflicts

b) What is the first problem that Marshall needs to solve?
c) How does Marshall think he might be able to solve the problem?
d) How is Marshall wrong about this?

The climax

e) What major event happens as a result of the problems?

The resolution

f) How are the problems resolved?

	The Brazilian Cat
Exposition	
Conflict	
Climax	
Resolution	

Activity 3: Planning a story

You are going to plan a short story using the four-part story structure from Activity 2.

1 Note down your answers to the following questions.

a) In *The Brazilian Cat*, the hero Marshall King faces a problem: he has no money. What problem could the hero of your story face? Perhaps they need to get, do or escape something.

b) Marshall King tries to solve his problem by visiting his cousin and asking to borrow money. How will your hero try to solve their problem? Can they solve it by themselves or do they need someone to help them?

c) Everard King is the villain in *The Brazilian Cat*. Could there be a villainous character who makes things worse in your story? Perhaps it could be someone who seems like a friend at first.

d) Everard King makes Marshall King's problems much worse in *The Brazilian Cat*. How might your villainous character make things worse for your hero? They could make the first problem harder to solve or introduce a new problem.

e) How could your hero eventually solve the problems they are facing?

f) At the end of *The Brazilian Cat*, Everard is killed by the animal that he thought would kill Marshall. How will the villain in your story end up?

2 Look over your answers to questions 1a–1f. Use them to complete a table like the one below, considering which ones should make up each part of the story.

	Put the title of your story here
Exposition	
Conflict	
Climax	
Resolution	

This section links to pages 28–31 of the Workbook.

Section 7
Endings

In this section, you will explore different ways of ending a story.

A **synopsis** is a summary of a story.

▼ **Read each synopsis and then answer the questions that follow.**

Story A

- A homeless orphan lives in misery and poverty in a workhouse.
- He escapes from the workhouse and is tricked into joining a gang of criminals.
- He is forced to take part in the burglary of a house and is injured.
- The owner of the house takes pity on him, nurses him back to health and reunites him with his family – and the criminals are punished.

Story B

- A town is infested with rats. A man arrives in the town saying he can rid the town of rats. The mayor promises to pay him in gold.
- The man plays strange and beautiful music on a pipe, and the rats all follow him. The piper lures the rats into a river and they drown.
- Now the rat problem is solved, the mayor refuses to pay the piper.
- The piper plays his music again and the town's children all follow him. He lures them into a cave and neither the children nor the piper are ever seen again.

Story C

- A man picks up a hitch-hiker in his new car. The man boasts about how quickly his new car can go.
- The car is stopped by a police officer, who says the man has been driving over the speed limit.
- The officer writes all the man's details down in his notebook and says he will soon hear from the police.
- The man and the hitch-hiker drive off. The man says he is worried.
- The hitch-hiker reveals that he is a pickpocket, which worries the driver even more.
- The hitch-hiker then reveals that he has taken the officer's notebook – meaning that the driver's details won't reach the police station.

Activity 1: Identifying endings

There are lots of different types of endings a story could have. For example:
- a happy ending
- a sad ending
- a 'twist': an unexpected ending
- a 'cliffhanger': an unresolved ending that leaves the reader wondering what happened.

1 **a)** What kind of ending does Story A have?
b) What kind of ending does Story B have?
c) What kind of ending does Story C have?

Activity 2: Responding to endings

1 What impression is created of each of the key characters in the three story synopses on page 32? You could choose from the suggestions below, or use your own ideas.

good | perfect | bad | cruel | clever | cunning | funny
kind | lucky | unlucky | foolish | mysterious

a) In Story A: **i)** the orphan **ii)** the criminals **iii)** the owner of the burgled house
b) In Story B: **i)** the piper **ii)** the mayor **iii)** the children
c) In Story C: **i)** the driver **ii)** the hitch-hiker **iii)** the police officer

> Story C gives the impression that the driver of the fast car is

> Story C gives the impression that the hitch-hiker is

2 Think again about the different characters in the stories and your response to them.
a) Which characters in which of the three stories do you feel sympathy for?
b) Which characters in which of the three stories do you feel happy for?
c) Which characters in which of the three stories do you feel got what they deserved?

Punctuation Boost: Colons and semi-colons

When you link two ideas or pieces of information in a sentence, you usually use a conjunction:

The Mayor was foolish because he thought he did not have to pay the piper.

Alternatively, you can link clauses using a colon or a semi-colon.

- Use a colon if the first clause is more important, and the second clause adds a reason, explanation or example:

The Mayor was foolish: he did not pay the piper.

- Use a semi-colon if the clauses are of equal importance. This is often where you could use 'and' or 'but':

The piper played a new tune; he led the children away.

1 Copy the sentences below, replacing each conjunction with a colon or semi-colon.
    a) The police officer stopped the driver because he was driving too fast.
    b) The piper lured the children into a cave and they were never seen again.
    c) The orphan hoped life will be better outside the workhouse but he was wrong.

2 Read the sentences you have rewritten using a colon or semi-colon to be sure they make clear sense.

Activity 3: Exploring the writer's intention

A writer chooses the ending of their story depending on how they want the reader to respond. For example, a story ending can make the reader feel...

- positive: 'Life can be difficult, but it usually turns out well in the end.'

- surprised and entertained: 'I wasn't expecting that to happen!'

- that justice has been done: 'The good have been rewarded and the bad have been punished.'

1 Look again at the story synopses on page 32. For each story, write one or two sentences explaining how you might feel at the end of the story.

Activity 4: Writing an ending

Look at one student's unfinished plan for a story:

	The Jewellery Shop
Exposition	A mean old man owns a jewellery shop and lives above it with his son. Every day, the old man tells his son he is useless.
Conflict	One night, the old man is woken by noises from the shop below. He tiptoes downstairs in the darkness.
Climax	As he peers into the dark shop, the old man sees a shadowy figure moving about. Is it a thief stealing all the rings, necklaces and watches from his shop?
Resolution	

1 You are going to think of some different ways in which the story could end. For each of the following questions, write one or two sentences explaining your answer.

a) How could the story end happily, making the reader feel positive?

b) How could the story end sadly, making the reader feel sympathy for one or more of the characters?

c) How could the story end with a twist, to make the reader feel surprised?

d) How could the story end so that the reader feels justice has been done: the good characters are rewarded and the bad characters are punished?

2 Which ending would you choose to use? Write one or two sentences explaining your choice.

3 Now look at the whole story, including the ending you have chosen. How do you think the reader will feel about the different characters by the time they have read the whole of the story? Write one or two sentences about each character, explaining your ideas.

This section links to pages 32–35 of the Workbook.

Section 8
Ways of telling stories

In this section, you will explore different ways of giving the reader information.

This is an extract from a story set in the United States of America in the early twentieth century. A cowboy named Givens is on his way home, and has stopped to spend the night camping by a water hole (a pond or pool of water).

▼ Read the extract and then answer the questions that follow it.

1 In the grass lay an empty fruit can. Givens caught sight of it with a grunt of satisfaction. In his coat pocket tied behind his saddle was a handful or two of ground coffee.

5 In two minutes he had a little fire going clearly. He started, with his can, for the water hole. When

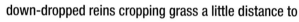

10 within fifteen yards of its edge he saw, between the bushes, a side-saddled pony with down-dropped reins cropping grass a little distance to

15 his left. Just rising from her hands and knees on the brink of the water hole was Josefa O'Donnell. She had been drinking water, and she brushed the sand from the palms of her hands. Ten yards away, to her right, half concealed by a clump of **sacuista**[1], Givens saw

20 the crouching form of the Mexican lion. His amber eyelids glared hungrily; six feet from them was the tip of the tail stretched straight.

Givens did what he could. His six-shooter was thirty-five yards away lying on the grass. He gave a loud

25 yell, and dashed between the lion and the girl.

The "rucus", as Givens called it afterward, was brief and somewhat confused. When he arrived on the line of attack he saw a dim streak in the air, and heard a couple of faint cracks. Then a hundred pounds

30 of Mexican lion plumped down upon his head and flattened him, with a heavy jar, to the ground. He remembered calling out: "Let up, now!" and then he crawled from under the lion like a worm, with his mouth full of grass and dirt, and a big lump on the

35 back of his head where it had struck the root of a **water elm**[2]. The lion lay motionless.

Josefa was standing in her tracks, quietly reloading her silver-mounted **.38**[3]. It had not been a difficult shot. The lion's head made an easier mark than a

40 tomato can swinging at the end of a string. There was a provoking, teasing, maddening smile upon her mouth and in her dark eyes.

"Is that you, Mr. Givens?" said Josefa. "You nearly spoiled my shot when you yelled. Did you hurt your

45 head when you fell?"

"Oh, no," said Givens, quietly; "*that* didn't hurt." He stooped **ignominiously**[4] and dragged his best Stetson hat from under the beast. It was crushed and wrinkled. Then he knelt down and softly stroked the

50 fierce, open-jawed head of the dead lion.

"Poor old Bill!" he exclaimed, mournfully.

"What's that?" asked Josefa, sharply.

"Of course you didn't know, Miss Josefa," said Givens. "Nobody can blame you. I tried to save him, but I

55 couldn't let you know in time."

"Save who?"

"Why, Bill. I've been looking for him all day. You see, he's been our camp pet for two years."

Key vocabulary

sacuista[1]: tall grass
water elm[2]: tree
.38[3]: gun
ignominiously[4]: with embarrassment

Activity 1: Exploring the extract

These questions will help you check your understanding of the extract on page 36.

1 Why does Givens go down to the water hole at the beginning of the extract?

2 What does he see as he approaches the water hole?

3 What does he observe about the lion?

4 How does Givens say he feels at the end of the extract?

5 Do you think he really feels this way? Write one or two sentences explaining your ideas.

Activity 2: Identifying ways of telling stories

You are now going to look at some of the ways in which the writer tells the story.

1 The sentences below give information about the character Givens: what he sees, does, says and thinks or feels.

A   His amber eyelids glared hungrily; six feet from them was the tip of the tail stretched straight.

B   "Nobody can blame you. I tried to save him, but I couldn't let you know in time."

C   He gave a loud yell, and dashed between the lion and the girl.

D   There was a provoking, teasing, maddening smile upon her mouth and in her dark eyes.

Which sentence gives the reader information about:
a) what Givens can see?
b) Givens's actions?
c) what Givens says?
d) what Givens thinks?

2 Look again at this part of the extract from page 36.

Josefa was standing in her tracks, quietly reloading her silver-mounted .38. It had not been a difficult shot. The lion's head made an easier mark than a tomato can swinging at the end of a string. There was a provoking, teasing, maddening smile upon her mouth and in her dark eyes. "Is that you, Mr. Givens?" said Josefa.

Which word, phrase or sentence gives descriptive information about:
a) Josefa?
b) Josefa's actions?
c) what Josefa says?
d) what Josefa is thinking?

Activity 3: Using different ways of telling stories

Look at the following extract from one student's story. In the story, Jem and Tad are lost in the desert.

> In every direction, all they could see was sand stretching to the horizon. Jem realised she had no idea where they were or how to get home again. Jem was worried that they were lost. Tad wished they had brought some food and water with them.

1 In this extract, all the information is given to the reader using the character's thoughts.

  a) Rewrite the **first two** sentences using speech. Think about what the characters could say to each other to give the reader the same information.

  b) Rewrite the **second two** sentences using description to give the reader the same information. Think about how to describe Jem and Tad to show how they felt.

Skills Boost: Identifiers and adverbs

An identifier is a phrase that tells the reader who is speaking. The writer of the extract on page 36 sometimes also uses adverbs to describe the ways in which the characters speak.

Identifier

"Poor old Bill!" he exclaimed, mournfully.

This adverb suggests Givens sounds sad.

Identifier

"What's that?" asked Josefa, sharply.

This adverb suggests Josefa is surprised by what Givens says.

1 The dialogue below shows a parent and their child talking to each other.

> Parent: "Could you please go and tidy your room?"   Child: "Do I have to?"
> Parent: "Yes!"   Child: "But I tidied it only a
> Parent: "Go and tidy your room!"   few months ago!"

Rewrite the dialogue, adding the following elements:

- some simple identifiers: he said | she asked | Jonathan muttered
- an adverb for each identifier: quietly | angrily | quickly
- **two** more-precise verbs to
  replace **two** verbs and their adverbs: she ~~said loudly~~ shouted

Activity 4: Choosing different ways of telling stories

You are going to write an extract from a story. Your story should be engaging, exciting and entertaining.

Imagine

Imagine that two characters are looking at a computer screen.

1 Think about who they are.
- What are their names?
- What is their relationship to each other?
- Do they like or dislike each other? Why?

2 Think about why they are looking at a computer screen. You could choose one of the reasons below or use your own ideas.

looking at an online map | breaking a secret code | trying to prevent a disaster

Write

You are now going to write sentences that will become your story extract.

3 Write one or two sentences using description to set the scene. You should describe:
- your characters
- where they are
- what they are looking at.

4 Write one or two sentences using action. You could give information about:
- what the characters do
- what happens on the computer screen.

5 Write one or two sentences using speech. You could give information about:
- what the characters are doing and why
- what the characters think of each other.

6 Write one or two sentences using thoughts. You could give information about:
- how the two characters are feeling
- what they think, hope or worry will happen next.

7 Look at the sentences you have written. Sequence some or all of them to create an extract from a story.

8 Check that your speech punctuation is accurate.

Remember
- All the words that are spoken should be inside speech marks.
- There should always be a punctuation mark before the closing speech mark.

Section 9
Structuring sentences

In this section, you will explore sentence structure choices and their impact on the reader.

This extract is the opening of a short story.

▼ Read the extract and then answer the questions that follow it.

1 Ella had witnessed it three times. Each time she would hear the rev of an engine, the smell of the petrol, and watch as the motorbike drove furiously towards a terrified individual, disappearing before anyone had
5 time to think. Shopping bags, wallets and briefcases were taken: people standing at bus stops were ideal targets, the thief worked quickly, and the innocent passers-by were visibly surprised and shocked.

Occasionally, the thief would give a little wave before
10 speeding off with the stolen goods. Ella heard others say it was like the thief was laughing at the whole town, and she was sure that once she had seen a faint smirk through the helmet's dark visor before the engine roared off. As a child, Ella had always avoided
15 any sort of argument or conflict, she preferred to stay out of it. But here, something wasn't right, this thief was mocking everyone.

Waiting patiently for her bus home, before anyone could react, Ella had watched as the woman next to
20 her had her child's birthday present snatched from her hands. She had seen the mother's face in shock, and then witnessed her tears.

The next day, in the same queue, the thief went for Ella's bag. Something changed. Before there was time
25 to speed off, the normally shy, quiet, 20-year-old PE teacher grabbed the thief's arm. She sprang onto the back of the bike. She chained her arms around the rider's waist, and, after some restraint, grabbed hold of the controls and steered the bike down the street.

30 Glancing at the building to her left, Ella squeezed the brake on the handle and brought the bike to an abrupt stop. The rest was a blur as she grabbed the ignition key, pulled the rider off the bike and used an **armlock** to stop the thief from escaping.

35 "Get off!" shouted the thief angrily, but Ella held on tighter.

Ignoring her nerves, Ella tugged the helmet off the thief's head and saw that she had long hair. She couldn't believe it. It was Henrietta Buckingham! Even
40 when they were kids at school together, Henrietta was a thief and a bully.

"Let. Me. Go," said Henrietta, angrily, wriggling to break free.

"Do you think it's funny to steal from all those
45 people?" demanded Ella, becoming braver by the minute.

"Who cares?" said Henrietta, laughing.

"You could have run someone over," replied Ella.

"So what?" said Henrietta.

50 In a quick motion, she tried to push Ella away, but somehow Ella flipped her down flat onto the ground.

"You're not getting away again," said Ella, and
55 she watched Henrietta's face drop as she pulled her to her feet in a double-arm
60 lock and headed towards the police station's steps.

Key vocabulary

armlock: holding someone's arm firmly behind their back so that they cannot escape.

Activity 1: Exploring short sentences

Some sentences in the extract on page 40 are very short, and some are very long.

1 Look again at the very short sentences on lines 47–49 of the extract.
  a) How would you describe the pace that these short sentences create? Write one or two sentences explaining your ideas.

> ### How do I do that?
> Read the sentences aloud. Think about whether or not it sounds like the two characters are talking particularly quickly or slowly.

  b) Why do you think the writer chose to create this pace? Think about how the two characters are feeling at this point in the story, and how they might be talking to each other. Write one or two sentences explaining your ideas.

Activity 2: Exploring longer sentences

1 Look again at the following sentence from the fifth paragraph of the extract on page 40.

> Glancing at the building to her left, Ella squeezed the brake on the handle and brought the bike to an abrupt stop.

The sentence above contains three clauses. The writer could have chosen to give this information in three single-clause sentences instead:

> Ella glanced at the building to her left. She squeezed the brake on the handle. She brought the bike to an abrupt stop.

Read both versions aloud. Which version has more impact? Which version would you choose? Write one or two sentences explaining your choice.

2 Look again at the following sentence from the first paragraph of the extract.

> Shopping bags, wallets and briefcases were taken: people standing at bus stops were ideal targets, the thief worked quickly, and the innocent passers-by were visibly surprised and shocked.

  a) The sentence above contains **four** clauses. Rewrite the sentence as **four** single-clause sentences.
  b) Which version would you choose? Write one or two sentences explaining your choice.

Activity 3: Building sentences

Look again at the following sentence from the fifth paragraph of the extract on page 40.

> The rest was a blur as she grabbed the ignition key, pulled the rider off the bike and used an armlock to stop the thief from escaping.

The writer has listed three events, using a comma between the first two and the conjunction 'and' before the third.

1 Write **one** multi-clause sentence using a comma and the conjunction 'and' to link the following three events.

> He tripped. He fell over. He scraped his arm.

2 Link the same three events in another multi-clause sentence, using **one or two** different conjunctions.

Conjunction bank

and	until
but	because
when	so that
as	although
before	if
after	

3 Think of **three** things you did when you got to school this morning.
   a) Write the three things you did as **three** single-clause sentences.
   b) Rewrite the three things you did as **one** multi-clause sentence, linking them with a comma and the conjunction 'and'.
   c) Rewrite the three things you did as another multi-clause sentence, linking them with **one or two** different conjunctions.

Grammar Boost: Linking with adverbials

Adverbials can help to make a clear connection between sentences. You can use adverbials to show connections of time, contrast and consequence.

Adverbials of time	Firstly	Then	Afterwards	Next	Still	Eventually	Later	Finally
Adverbials of contrast and consequence	Nevertheless	Instead	However	Besides	Moreover As a result	Consequently

1 Look at the three single-clause sentences you wrote in your response to Activity 3, question 3a.
   a) Rewrite them, beginning each sentence with an adverbial of time.
   b) Rewrite the short passage below to begin each sentence, except the first one, with an adverbial of contrast or consequence.

> Stef was desperate to play football. Nita said she did not want to. She wanted to watch television. She had hurt her foot. Stef begged and sulked and begged again. Nita would not change her mind.

Activity 4: Experimenting with structure

You are going to write a story extract in which a superhero stops a major crime.

Imagine and write

1 It is 1.00 p.m. on a Wednesday afternoon in a busy city. Write one or two sentences describing the scene.

2 A superhero is eating lunch in the busy city when he or she sees a villain escaping from a bank with bags full of money. Write **two or three** sentences describing what the superhero sees.

3 The superhero decides to catch the villain. It takes only a minute! What happens in the 60 seconds? Note down **five** things that happen, and then use them to write **two or three** sentences.

4 What do the superhero and the villain say to each other? Write a dialogue in which each character says at least **two** things. Remember to use accurate speech punctuation.

5 What happens next? Write one or two sentences to finish off this story extract.

Review your structure

6 Look at each of the sentences you have written in your story extract. Ask yourself:
- Are any of my sentences too long? Would they have more impact as shorter sentences?
- Could I link some single-clause sentences using conjunctions?
- Could I add an adverbial to the opening of any sentences to make my meaning clearer?

7 Decide how to group your sentences into paragraphs. Ask yourself: Could I add an adverbial to the opening of any paragraphs to make my meaning clearer?

Evaluate

8 Write **two or three** sentences explaining some of sentence structures you have chosen, and the impact you want them to have on your reader. For example:
- Did you use conjunctions to build multi-clause sentences linking events? Why or why not?
- Did you break down any very long sentences into shorter sentences? Why or why not?
- Did you choose to use longer or shorter sentences in the conversation between the superhero and the villain? Why or why not?

Section 10
Reviewing, revising and proofreading

In this section, you will develop your skills in checking the accuracy and effectiveness of your writing.

Spelling Boost: Homophones

Homophones are words that sound alike but have different spellings and meanings.

1 The words below are some of the most common homophones in English. Using the hints to help you, match each homophone to its correct definition.

a) their	(i) belonging to them	
b) there	(ii) that place or position	Hint: 'Here' and 'there' have similar spellings.
c) too	(i) a number	
d) two	(ii) an excessive quantity	Hint: There are a lot of letter 'o's in 'too'.
e) no	(i) a negative	
f) know	(ii) understand	Hint: You have to understand about the silent letter.
g) hear	(i) this place or position	
h) here	(ii) sense with your ears	Hint: There is a word hidden in 'hear'.

2 Use the given homophones to complete each of the following sentences.
   a) their/there: I'm walking over to visit my cousins – _____ house is over _____.
   b) too/two: We have to complete _____ pages of maths questions, _____.
   c) no/know: I _____ that there is _____ cricket training tonight.
   d) hear/here: The music is so loud that I can _____ it from _____.

Activity 1: Irregular past tenses

Verbs often have the suffix '–ed' added when they are in the past tense. However, some verbs have irregular past-tense forms, as shown in the table below.

Change of vowel sound	came | woke | spoke | broke | chose | ate | found | wrote | began | knew
Lose a vowel and add 't'	slept | kept | felt | lost | swept
Completely different word	bought | brought | caught | fought | taught | thought

1 Look carefully at each of the past-tense forms above. Write them out, adding the present-tense form of each verb. For example:

came – come	woke – wake

Activity 2: Proofreading

Look at the following extract from one student's writing. It contains **fifteen** mistakes.

- To find punctuation mistakes, look closely at the use of apostrophes and speech punctuation.
- To find spelling mistakes, look closely at any homophones and past-tense verb forms to make sure the correct spelling has been used.
- To find grammar mistakes, look closely at each pronoun and verb to make sure that:
  - the text is written in the same tense and person throughout
  - the correct verb forms have been used.

> Their were only two people who could possibly no Doctor Dooms evil plans – and now he had taken one of them prisoner. The other one was me. I knowed I had to do something. Doctor Doom had to be stopt.
>
> I keeped myself hidden in the bushes opposite the Doctors enormous house. As I watch and waited, she was begining to worry. After an hour, the front door opened. It was the Doctor and a short, dark-haired man in a suit. I could here everything they said, but they couldnt see me.
>
> "I will be back in too hours" said the Doctor.
>
> "Yes, sir, said the other man.

1 Copy and correct the text. As you correct each mistake, label it to show the kind of mistake the writer has made.

2 How many mistakes of each kind (punctuation, spelling, grammar) did you find? There were five of each in the text. Take note of the kinds of mistakes that you had most difficulty finding. Set yourself proofreading targets using the scorecard below.

How did you score?

5/5 or 4/5 – Well done! You are good at spotting this kind of mistake.

3/5 or 2/5 – Well done, but you need to check twice for this kind of mistake.

1/5 or 0/5 – You need to look very closely at your writing for this kind of mistake.

Activity 3: Reviewing vocabulary

Synonyms are words that have the same or very similar meanings.

1 Look at the short passage below. Using the synonyms beneath (or your own ideas), rewrite the sentences to make the verb choices as dramatic and exciting as possible.

> I walk up to the house and look in through the window. I try the window but it won't move. Sweat is running down my face. Then, without warning, I hear someone shouting. "Hey, you!" I realise they mean me. I stop.

walk	shout	look	stop	run
step	yell	peer	wait	pour
creep	scream	glance	pause	trickle
tiptoe	bellow	stare	freeze	drip

Grammar Boost: Conjunctions and relationships

A conjunction can signal the relationship between two pieces of information. Conjunctions can, for example, signal time information (e.g. *when*), contrasting information (e.g. *but*), and conditional information (e.g. *if*).

1 For each pair of sentences below, choose one conjunction that could link the action and the information that follows it in a multi-clause sentence.

Conjunction bank

until	as
unless	although
because	as long as
before	even though

a) Information about time:

> I often read at night.

> I go to sleep.

b) Contrasting information:

> I often read at night.

> I am sometimes too tired.

c) Conditional information:

> I often read at night.

> I am not too tired.

Activity 4: Reviewing sentence structure

Think about the different ways in which you could restructure the sentences in this paragraph:

> I started walking and I soon heard footsteps behind me. I walked more quickly. The footsteps were getting nearer. I was starting to feel frightened.

1 Look at the multi-clause sentence.
   a) Rewrite it by breaking it down into **two** single-clause sentences.
   b) Rewrite it using a different conjunction to make the connection between the clauses clearer.

2 Look at the single-clause sentences.
   a) Link the **first two** single-clause sentences with a conjunction.
   b) Link the **last two** single-clause sentences with a conjunction.
   c) Link all **three** single-clause sentences with two different conjunctions.

3 Look at all the sentences you have written. Choose the versions you think are the most effective and write a final improved draft of the paragraph above.

Activity 5: Reviewing and proofreading writing

1 Look at the following extract from one student's story. It contains some mistakes.

> My lungs hurt and my legs hurt and I couldnt run anymore. I fell on the pavement and hit my head on the cold, hard concrete. I tried to get up and two hands taked hold of me and I was lookking into the face of a woman I had never seen before. "Are you OK," she asked.

   a) Copy down the extract and then find, circle and correct the mistakes. Check first for punctuation mistakes, then for grammar mistakes and then for spelling mistakes.
   b) Underline **three** vocabulary choices that you think could be improved.
   c) Create a vocabulary bank for each word you have underlined, and then choose the best word to replace it.
   d) Look carefully at the structure of the sentences in the extract. Would you choose to restructure any of them? Write out one or two using your preferred structure.

This section links to pages 44–45 of the Workbook.

Section 11
Assessment

In this section, you will write a short story to assess your progress in this unit.

Activity 1: Planning

In this assessment, you will write an exciting adventure story in which a hero defeats a villain.

1 Use the following steps to gather your ideas for your main characters and plot.

a) What kind of hero will you write about? You could choose a superhero or an ordinary person. You could consider:
- whether the hero sets out to act heroically, or whether her or his actions are unexpected
- what the hero usually does during his or her everyday life
- whether the hero acts alone, or with friends or a sidekick
- how your hero looks, talks and thinks.

Note down your ideas.

b) What kind of villain will feature in your story? You could choose a supervillain or an ordinary person. You could consider:
- how clever and capable the villain is
- whether the villain acts alone, or with a gang
- what made this person into a villain
- how your villain looks, talks and thinks.

Note down your ideas.

c) What kind of wrongdoing will your villain be trying to commit? You could consider:
- the seriousness of the crime
- who or what would suffer as a consequence
- how realistic the crime story will be
- whether or not the plan is a clever one.

Note down your ideas.

2 Use the following steps to plan your story's structure, noting down your ideas in a table like the one below.

	Put the title of your story here
Exposition	
Conflict	
Climax	
Resolution	

a) Think about the opening of your story. Consider:
- How will you engage the reader from the very first sentence?
- How will you set the scene and introduce your characters?

b) Think about the ending of your story. Consider:
- Will it end happily, sadly or with a twist?
- Will your characters get what they deserve?

Activity 2: Writing

1 Write your story. As you write, try to make your story as dramatic, engaging and exciting as possible. You can do this by using:
- suitable language styles for your characters' speech
- precise, varied and interesting vocabulary
- a variety of sentence lengths, with a variety of conjunctions
- adverbials to link sentences and paragraphs.

Activity 3: Reviewing and revising

1 Read through your story. As you read, ask yourself:
- Is my plot interesting and engaging?
- Is my vocabulary dramatic and exciting?
- Are my sentences clear and easy to understand?

Check that:
- the registers you have chosen suit your content
- you have made effective vocabulary choices
- you have used a variety of single- and multi-clause sentences
- you have consistently used the same tense and person throughout your writing
- your spelling, punctuation and grammar are accurate.

Unit 2
Safe and sound

In this unit, you will explore a range of non-fiction texts that are written to inform their readers about dangers and problems in their lives, such as smoking, fake news and mental health problems. These texts are written to persuade readers to take steps to reduce the risks posed by these problems, using persuasive vocabulary and key pieces of evidence. Can you spot when a text is trying to persuade you?

In this unit, you will...

- identify key points of information and vocabulary choices the writer has used to persuade you.

- explore further how writers' choices of ideas and language can make a text more persuasive

- develop your skills in responding to texts.

- explore ways of organising a response to a text.

- answer questions on a short extract and write a short response to it, to assess your progress.

- explore paragraph structure in a persuasive instruction text.

- explore the structure of a persuasive text.

- explore how the writer's choices of ideas, vocabulary and sentence structure can make texts more persuasive.

- explore how a variety of rhetorical devices can make a text more persuasive.

- develop your skills in identifying relevant features of a text and planning your response to it.

- answer questions on a text to assess your progress in this unit.

By the end of this unit, you will be able to analyse and respond to a persuasive text, exploring the writer's choices and their impact on the reader.

This section links to pages 46–49 of the Workbook.

Section 1
Spotting persuasive techniques

In this section, you will identify key points of information and vocabulary choices the writer has used to persuade you.

▼ Read the poster and then answer the questions that follow it.

You can live for WEEKS without food.
But only a few DAYS without water.

1   Water makes up three-quarters of your body weight.
It keeps your temperature stable.
It flushes out waste.
It's the solvent in which all your food is digested.
5   It keeps all your body functions working.

Drink at least 2 pints of water every day.
Drink more when it's hot, or if you're exercising,
playing sport, dancing, or on a long flight.

The best source of water is your tap.
10   Tap water contains useful minerals, such as calcium and magnesium.
Bottled waters are unlikely to be better for you than tap water.
Fruit juices, fruits and vegetables are also useful sources of water.
Isotonic sports drinks and fancy fizzes are not as good for you as water.
Even if they don't contain much sugar (and many do), they're very acid
15   and can damage your teeth by eating into the enamel.

Water tastes even better cold.
Keep some in the fridge.
Water – the best drink for your body and every body.

Remember

When you are asked to read a text, it can help to read it twice:

• The first time, read it quickly so you get a general idea of what the text is about.

• The second time, read it more slowly, to make sure you understand every part of the text.

Activity 1: Beginning to explore the text

When you first explore a text, begin by thinking about:
- the writer's intention: the reason the writer has written the text
- the writer's key ideas: the points the writer has used to try to achieve their purpose.

1 What is the writer of the poster on page 52 persuading the reader to do or think? Give your answer by completing the following sentence in **five** words or fewer.

The writer is trying to persuade the reader to

2 **a)** Which of the following ideas are included in the poster?
- what to do   • why you should do it   • how you should do it

b) Identify **one** example from the poster for each of the above ideas that are included.

Activity 2: Identifying, linking and comparing ideas

Linking and comparing ideas can help you to work out which ideas are key, and why the writer has chosen to include them.

Identifying ideas

1 Identify **five** pieces of information in the poster on page 52 that suggest drinking water is important.

> **How do I do that?**
>
> Looking at each sentence in turn, ask yourself: Does this sentence make me realise why drinking water is important, or is it doing a different job?

Linking ideas

2 Look again at the five pieces of information you have selected. What **one** point are they all making? Complete the following sentence in **ten** words or fewer.

The writer suggests it is important to drink water because

Comparing ideas

3 Look once more at the five pieces of information you have selected.
a) Which one is the most persuasive? Label it 'MOST'.
b) Which one is the least persuasive? Label it 'LEAST'.
c) Write a sentence explaining each of your choices.

Grammar Boost: Imperative verbs

Imperative verbs are also known as commands. This is because they give the reader or listener an instruction: they tell them what to do. A verb usually has a subject. Imperative verbs do not. For example:

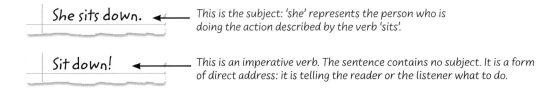

She sits down. ← This is the subject: 'she' represents the person who is doing the action described by the verb 'sits'.

Sit down! ← This is an imperative verb. The sentence contains no subject. It is a form of direct address: it is telling the reader or the listener what to do.

1 Identify the imperative verb in each of the following sentences.
   a) Turn left at the end of the road.   **b)** Chop up the onions.
   c) Quickly, tell me the answer!

Activity 3: Thinking about the writer's vocabulary choices

Persuasive texts often use:
- imperative verbs, to tell the reader what they should do
- positive vocabulary, to make the writer's point of view sound more appealing
- negative vocabulary, to make other points of view sound less appealing.

1 Look again at lines 13–18 of the poster on page 52.
   a) Copy and complete the table below, adding words from lines 13–18 as examples of the three categories.

Imperative verb	Positive language	Negative language

   b) Look again at the whole of the poster. Identify at least **two** other examples of persuasive vocabulary and add them to the table.

2 Look again at the most persuasive sentence you chose in response to Activity 2 in the previous lesson.
   a) Identify examples of persuasive vocabulary in the sentence.
   b) What made the sentence so persuasive? Was it the information it gave, the words the writer used, or both? Write one or two sentences to explain your ideas.

Grammar Boost: Parts of speech

When you comment on a writer's choices of vocabulary or sentence structure, you should try to correctly name the part of speech.

Noun	A noun describes a person, place, object or idea. For example: *The writer repeats the noun 'water' to emphasise its importance.*
Adjective	An adjective adds information to a noun. For example: *The adjective 'useful' suggests the practical benefit of water.*
Verb	A verb describes and action, event or state. For example: *The verb 'flushes' creates a familiar feeling in the reader's mind.*
Adverb	An adverb adds information to a verb or adjective. For example: *The adverb 'very' strengthens the impact of the adjective 'acid'.*

1 Copy the table below, and complete it with all the nouns, adjectives, verbs and adverbs in the following sentences.

> Ayo filled her glass with cold water and drank it slowly. It was an extremely hot day.

Nouns	Adjectives	Verbs	Adverbs
Ayo		filled	

Activity 4: Writing persuasively

You are going to write your own short persuasive paragraph encouraging people to drink water rather than fizzy, sugary drinks.

Plan

1 Select **three** key persuasive ideas for your argument. You could choose from the suggestions below or use your own ideas.

- Fizzy drinks contain sugar.
- Fizzy drinks are high in calories.
- Sugary drinks damage your teeth.
- Tap water is not expensive.
- Water is a healthy choice.
- Water tastes nice.

2 Look at each of the key ideas you have chosen. Note down vocabulary you could use to make your chosen ideas more persuasive. Consider using:
- positive language to make water sound more appealing
- negative language to make fizzy drinks sound less appealing
- imperative verbs to tell the reader what to do.

Write

3 Using the ideas you have chosen and the vocabulary you have gathered, write **three** persuasive sentences encouraging people to drink water, not fizzy drinks.

Section 2
Persuasive vocabulary

In this section, you will explore further how writers' choices of ideas and language can make a text more persuasive.

▼ **Read the webpage and then answer the questions that follow it.**

● ● ● Search...

Teens' teeth

1 **Why is a healthy smile important?**

An attractive and healthy smile is important. It can boost your confidence and help you feel good about yourself.

If you don't look after your teeth and gums properly you could suffer from a
5 number of different conditions that will make you stand out from the crowd for all the wrong reasons:

- Bad breath
- Gum disease
- Stained teeth
- Tooth loss
- Tooth decay
- Dental erosion

Why is a healthy diet important for my oral health?

10 Every time you eat or drink anything sugary, your teeth are under acid attack for up to one hour. This is because the sugar reacts with the bacteria in plaque and produces harmful acids. Plaque is a build-up of bacteria which forms on your teeth. It is better to have three or four meals a day rather than lots of snacks.

15 **What is dental erosion?**

Dental erosion is the gradual loss of tooth enamel caused by acid attacks. Enamel is the hard, protective coating of the tooth. If it is worn away, the dentine underneath is exposed and your teeth can look discoloured and become sensitive.

20 **Top tips for teens**

- Brush your teeth last thing at night and at least one other time during the day.
- Use a toothbrush with a small- to medium-sized brush head with soft to medium bristles, and brush for two minutes.
- You should use a pea-sized amount of toothpaste that contains 1350 ppm
25   to 1500 ppm (parts per million) fluoride.
- Have sugary food and drinks just at mealtimes.
- Visit your dental team at least once a year or as often as they recommend.
- Wait for at least one hour after eating or drinking anything acidic before you brush your teeth.

Drink up

Acidic foods and drinks, and fizzy drinks cause dental erosion.

Still water and milk are the best things to drink. Tea without sugar is also good for teeth as it contains fluoride.

Snacks

Avoid sugary snacks. If you need to eat between meals, try these foods instead:

- Plain popcorn
- Nuts
- Plain yogurt
- Raw vegetable pieces
- Fresh fruit

Activity 1: Identifying key ideas

Persuasive texts often highlight the positive consequences of doing what they say, and the negative consequences of ignoring them. They tell the reader:
- what to do
- what not to do
- why they should or should not do those things.

1 Look again at the first section of the webpage on page 56:

> **Why is a healthy smile important?**

    a) Identify **two** positive consequences of looking after your teeth, according to the webpage.

    b) Identify **two** negative consequences of not looking after your teeth, according to the webpage.

2 Identify **three** things that the webpage recommends you should do, one from each of the following other sections:

    a) **Why is a healthy diet important for my oral health?**

    b) **Snacks**

    c) **Top tips for teens**

Activity 2: Inferring key ideas

Sometimes writers imply what you should do, or not do, and why. This means that the reader has to infer the writer's meaning.

1 Look at the following sentence from the webpage on page 56.

> If you don't look after your teeth and gums properly, you could suffer from a number of different conditions that will make you stand out from the crowd for all the wrong reasons.

    a) In this sentence, the writer does not state clearly what you, the reader, should do. What is the writer implying you should do?

    b) What does the writer state will happen if you do not do this? Give the exact phrase the writer uses.

    c) Look at your response to **1b**. What is the implied meaning of this phrase?

2 What is the writer implying you should or should not do in the following sentence from the webpage?

> Every time you eat or drink anything sugary, your teeth are under acid attack for up to one hour.

Skills Boost: Connotations

The connotations of a word are the ideas that a word suggests or creates in a reader's mind.
- Some words suggest positive ideas. These are words with positive connotations.
- Some words suggest negative ideas. These are words with negative connotations.

1 Look at the pairs of words below. Each one could be used to complete the following sentence.

Computers can be

A useful | valuable   **B** addictive | fascinating   **C** harmful | deadly

The words in each pair have similar meanings but different connotations. Select one pair (A, B or C) for each sentence below describing the relationship between the words.
a) One word has positive connotations and the other has negative connotations.
b) Both words have positive connotations but one is more positive than the other.
c) Both words have negative connotations but one is more negative than the other.

Activity 3: Considering connotations

The writer of the webpage on page 56 uses the word 'bacteria'. This word has some very negative connotations, as shown in this spidergram:

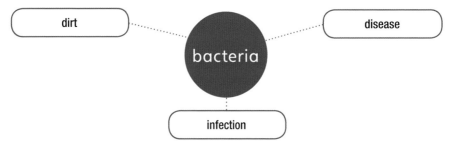

dirt   disease   bacteria   infection

1 Copy the spidergram above and complete for the following words, taken from the webpage:
a) acid
b) attack

2 Consider the phrase 'acid attack' again. How positive or negative are the connotations of this phrase?

Activity 4: Persuasive vocabulary

1 Look again at the second section of the webpage on page 56:

> **Why is a healthy diet important for my oral health?**

a) Identify **one** phrase or sentence in this section that suggests what you, the reader, should do.

b) Identify **one** phrase or sentence in this section that the writer uses to explain why you should do it.

c) Select the **one** word or phrase in this section that you find most persuasive.

d) Write one or two sentences explaining why that word or phrase is persuasive.

> I found this word persuasive because it has connotations of

> This phrase makes the reader think that   It suggests that

Activity 5: Writing persuasively

You are going to write some persuasive sentences about computer use.

1 Choose one side of the following argument.

> Time spent on a computer is time well spent.

> You should turn off the computer and get some exercise instead.

Note down one or two key ideas that you think support your chosen argument.

2 a) Write one sentence telling your readers what you think they should do.

b) Write **one** sentence explaining the benefits of doing this.

3 a) Write **one** sentence telling your readers what you think they should **not** do.

b) Write **one** sentence explaining the consequences if they ignored your advice.

4 Look again at the words you have used in your responses. Circle the words you have used that have positive or negative connotations.

5 Review your sentences. Could any of your vocabulary choices be made more persuasive? If so, revise your sentences.

This section links to pages 54–57 of the Workbook.

Section 3
Responding to a text

In this section, you will develop your skills in responding to texts.

▼ **Read the webpage and then answer the questions that follow it.**

● ● ● Search...

Ready for social networking?

1 Want to stay in touch with your friends online? You'll know there are lots of 'social networking' websites and mobile apps that people use to chat, comment, share pictures and game with their friends.

You probably also know that for most of these sites you need to be at least 13 years old to sign up. For some, you need to be even older. If you're under 13, you shouldn't be using them – you'll be breaking their rules
5 and could be putting yourself at risk.

Why?

There are lots of reasons why these sites can be unsafe for young people, even those over 13, so it's important that you don't use them until you know how to do so safely.

If you're already using social networks, make sure you know what the risks are and what you can do to be safer.

10 ### 5 top tips for safer social networking

If you use social networks, always think about who can see the things you post and what they reveal about you.

1 Know who your friends are.
It's really tempting to accept as many friend requests or follows as possible. It can make us feel popular. But remember, they could be anyone. Do you really want them seeing your pictures, videos or comments?

15 **2 Share with care.**
Once you've put something online you've lost control of it – it can be copied, shared or edited. It could turn up anywhere. You might be happy showing a funny picture to your friends but would you want your parents or teachers to see it?

3 Use privacy settings.
20 Most social networks let you limit what you share to friends or followers you've OKed. It's always a good idea to let only people you know and trust see your stuff. Learn how to use privacy settings and how to block people who are bothering you.

4 Know how to report.
Most social networks let you report to them if you have a problem on their site. So, if someone's shared an
25 embarrassing picture or is being nasty to you, you need to know how to get help. Learn how to report on any site or app you use by visiting their 'safety' pages.

5 Know how to get help.
If someone's bullying you on a social network, you should talk to an adult you trust. If someone's being weird or making you feel uncomfortable, you should report it. You won't be in trouble.

Activity 1: Identifying the message

When you first explore a persuasive text, try to identify the key message it is trying to convey to the reader.

1 Look again at each of the three sections of the webpage on page 60.
   a) What key point is the writer is making in the first section?
   b) What key point is the writer is making in the second section?
   c) What key point is the writer is making in the third section?

How do I do that?

- Read the whole of the section and then look at each of its sentences in turn.

- After reading each sentence, ask yourself: Does this sentence, or a phrase in this sentence, sum up everything else the writer has written in this section? If not, keep looking until you find a sentence or phrase that does.

Activity 2: Identifying intention and audience

Some persuasive texts are aimed at a very specific audience. For example, the writer of a persuasive text might be aiming their ideas at readers of a specific age or of a specific interest group, such as people who like gardening, football or reading.

1 At what audience is the writer of the webpage on page 60 aiming their message?

2 Identify **one** sentence from the webpage that shows clearly who is the writer's intended audience.

Remember

Put your chosen sentence inside quotation marks to show that it is a quotation. It does not matter if you use single or double quotation marks, as long as you are consistent.

3 Why has the writer aimed the webpage at this audience? Write one or two sentences explaining your ideas.

4 Imagine you have been asked to create a poster that gets this website's message across to the same intended audience. Write **two or three** sentences describing the words and images that would appear on your poster.

Skills Boost: Punctuating quotations

If you choose a short quotation, you can use it inside a sentence. For example:

> The writer points out that social networking sites may be 'unsafe' for young people.

If you need to use a longer quotation that cannot be embedded in a sentence, introduce it with a colon. For example:

> The writer reassures the reader : 'You won't be in trouble.'

1 Copy the sentences below, adding the correct punctuation. You may need to use capital letters, full stops, quotation marks or colons.

a)
> the writer points out the dangers of social networking for example
> Once you've put something online you've lost control of it

b)
> the writer lists all the things you can do on social networks
> chat, comment, share pictures and game.

c)
> the writer warns young people they are at risk if they use social
> networks when they are too young

Activity 3: Choosing quotations

When you are looking for a quotation, make sure you choose a sentence, phrase or word that best supports the point you are making. Try not to include any sentences, words or phrases that do not support that point.

1 Look again at the following sentences from the webpage on page 60.

> It's really tempting to accept as many friend requests or follows as possible. It can make us feel popular.

a) Which sentence best supports the point that young people want to have as many online friends as they can?

b) Choose **one** word from either sentence that best shows why young people want to have lots of online friends.

c) Use the word you chose in **1b** as a short quotation to help you complete the following sentence.

> The writer suggests that young people want to have lots of online friends because

Activity 4: Exploring vocabulary choice

1 Look again at the following sentences about social networking websites and apps.

> If you're under 13 you shouldn't be using them – you'll be breaking their rules and could be putting yourself at risk.

> If you're already using social networks, make sure you know what the risks are and what you can do to be safer.

a) Choose **three** words or phrases that suggest you should be careful.

b) Look again at the words or phrases you have chosen. What do they suggest about the reason you should be careful?

Activity 5: Commenting on the writer's choices

You are going to use all the skills you have been practising in this section to write a paragraph responding to the webpage on page 60. An effective paragraph of critical response should contain three key elements, carefully linked:

- a key point about what the writer has done
- evidence to support this point
- an explanation of how the evidence demonstrates what the writer has done and supports your point.

1 Write **one** sentence making a point about something the writer has done in the webpage. For example, you could focus on one of the writer's key messages or their target audience.

> The writer is trying to persuade readers to

> The text is aimed at

2 Add **one** quotation to support your point about what the writer has done. Aim to choose only the sentence, phrase or word that best supports your point.

> This is shown when the writer states

> This is achieved by the writer's use of

3 Finally, write one or two sentences commenting on how your chosen quotation demonstrates what the writer has done. For example, you could explain how a word or phrase has helped the writer to emphasise the key message or appeal to its target audience.

> The writer has used the words _____ to suggest that

This section links to pages 58–61 of the Workbook.

Section 4
Organising your response

In this section, you will explore ways of organising a response to a text.

▼ **Read the webpage and then answer the questions that follow.**

● ● ● Search...

Hazards around the home

1 Statistics have shown that the most common place for babies and young children to be injured, often seriously, is at home. Children aged 0–4 years old are most at risk from hazards in the home
5 because they spend a lot of time there, before starting school, and are curious to explore their surroundings.

So, what can we do to protect children in our care from some everyday, but often extremely
10 dangerous, home hazards? The type and number of potential dangers will vary from home to home, but here are some tips to help you make your home safer for little ones.

Falls

15 Doctors report that falls are the most common home injury. By three months old, babies are strong enough to roll over, which means they can easily fall off beds, sofas and other surfaces.

- Fit window stops to prevent windows from
20 opening further than 10 centimetres or fit window guards to the bottom of windows. Did you know that most children under five can squeeze through openings of 15 centimetres?
- Install safety gates at the top and bottom of
25 staircases, and do not leave **clutter**[1] on the stairs which you could trip over while carrying your child.
- Always use the safety straps on baby equipment such as high chairs and changing tables, and place any portable equipment on the floor rather
30 than on tables or other furniture.

Key vocabulary
clutter[1]: items lying about in an untidy way
scald[2]: to injure with hot liquid or steam
fatally[3]: in way that leads to death

Burns

Burns are the second most common home injury. Medical staff report that they see babies and small children who have hurt themselves by touching
35 kettles and hot pans, or who have had hot drinks accidently spilled on them.

- Use the back rings/burners of your cooking appliance. Handles of pans at the front of cooking appliances are very tempting for small
40 children to reach up and grab.
- Keep hot drinks and hot kettles (including cords) well out of reach. Remember, a hot drink can still **scald**[2] a baby's delicate skin 15 minutes after it was made.

45 ## Choking

Food is the most common choking danger for babies, but crawling babies and young children can put *any* small object into their mouth and choke, sometimes **fatally**[3].

50 - Encourage your child to sit while eating. Children are more likely to choke on food while eating lying down, running around or playing.
- Watch out for small objects on the floor that could be choking hazards. Get down to child
55 height and look around.

Activity 1: Identifying intentions

This activity will help you to work out the writer's intentions for the webpage on page 64.

1 Every text has a target audience.
   a) Who is the target audience for this webpage?
   b) Identify **two or three** quotations that suggest this target audience.

2 What is the writer's intention in providing this information and advice? Write one or two sentences explaining your answer.

The writer is trying to persuade _____ so they will

3 Identify **three** ways in which the writer has tried to achieve their intention and write one or two sentences explaining your answer.

You could think about:
- the ideas the writer has chosen to include in the webpage
- the vocabulary the writer has chosen to use
- the structure of the text or sentences.

Activity 2: Choosing the best evidence

1 Look at the following three quotations from the extract. Each one could be used as evidence of a key idea in the text.

   A   Watch out for small objects on the floor that could be choking hazards.

   B   Statistics have shown that the most common place for babies and young children to be injured, often seriously, is at home.

   C   Use the back rings/burners of your cooking appliance. Handles of pans at the front of cooking appliances are very tempting for small children to reach up and grab.

   a) Which quotation would be the best evidence that the home generally can be dangerous? Identify **one** word or phrase from your chosen quotation that emphasises the danger.
   b) Which quotation would be the best evidence that parents must be careful? Identify **one** word or phrase from the quotation that emphasises the danger.
   c) Which quotation would be the best evidence that small children do not understand these dangers? Identify **one** word or phrase from your chosen quotation that emphasises the danger.

Skills Boost: Structuring a paragraph of critical response

An effective paragraph of critical response should contain three key elements, carefully linked:

- A **key point** about what the writer has done.

    > The writer uses lots of imperative verbs throughout the text.

- **Evidence** to support this point.

    > "Keep", "Watch out for", "Fit"

- An **explanation** of how the evidence demonstrates what the writer has done, supporting your key point.

    > Imperative verbs tell the reader what they must do and make advice sound important and urgent.

1 What do you think would be the best order to sequence the three example elements above? You could try experimenting with different sequences to help you decide which one is most effective.

2 Write out the paragraph in your chosen sequence, using full sentences and linking all the elements in the paragraph together. You could use some of the following phrases to help you:

> One way in which the writer persuades the reader is by

> For example

> The writer has done this because

Activity 3: Exploring emotive and dramatic vocabulary choices

Emotive and dramatic vocabulary choices can make a text more persuasive.

Remember

Emotive words create an emotional response in the reader.

1 Look at the writer's vocabulary choices in the following quotations from the webpage on page 64. Which are the most emotive and dramatic words or phrases in each of them?

a) a hot drink can still scald a baby's delicate skin 15 minutes after it was made.

b) crawling babies and young children can put any small object into their mouth and choke, sometimes fatally.

Activity 4: Writing your response

You are going to write two paragraphs in response to this question: How has the writer tried to persuade the reader to follow the advice in the webpage on page 64? Copy the following planning table, and then use the steps below to complete it.

	Paragraph 1	Paragraph 2
Key point		
Evidence		
Explanation		

1 Look again at your answer to Activity 1, question 3 in the previous lesson. Choose **one** of the techniques the writer has used to persuade the reader. In your table, add it to the 'Key point' row for Paragraph 1.

2 You now need to select evidence to support the key point you have chosen.
   a) Identify **one** sentence from the webpage that demonstrates your key point.
   b) Identify **one** word or phrase in that sentence that provides a clear example for your key point. Add it to the 'Evidence' row for Paragraph 1.

3 You now need to explain the writer's choices in your quotation, and the effect they have on the reader. You might be able to explain the effect of:
   • the idea or information the writer has included
   • the writer's use of an imperative verb
   • the writer's choice of emotive or dramatic vocabulary.

4 Select a different technique from your answer to Activity 1, question 3. Repeat questions 1–3 in relation to this second example to complete your planning for Paragraph 2.

5 Use your planning notes to write **two** paragraphs in response to the question above. Think about:
   • the best order in which to sequence the elements in your paragraphs
   • how you will link the elements in each paragraph.

This section links to pages 62–63 of the Workbook.

Section 5
Assessment

In this section, you will answer questions on a short extract and write a short response to it, to assess your progress.

▼ Read the leaflet and then answer the questions that follow it.

RIDE SAFELY ON THE ROAD

1 Cycling is a fun way to exercise and an easy way to get around by yourself. But **statistics**[1] show that young riders and teenagers are more likely to be killed or seriously injured in road accidents than any other age group. So, before you get on your bike, make sure you know how to keep yourself safe on the road.

PROTECT YOUR HEAD

5 Cycling safety organisations agree that cycling helmets are the most **effective**[2] piece of safety equipment to reduce head injury and death from road bicycle accidents.
   - **ALWAYS** wear a helmet.
   - Make sure your helmet fits well and is securely fastened under your chin.

BE AWARE AND BE SEEN

10 Most cycling accidents occur in daylight because this is when most cycling takes place. However, cycling accidents in the dark are more likely to be **fatal**[3].
   - Wear **reflective**[4] clothes if you ride at night, so that drivers can see you on the road.
   - Make sure you stay alert to your surroundings and **NEVER** wear headphones.

RIDE SAFELY

15 Accidents involving younger cyclists are often the result of the cyclist riding too fast or losing control.
   - Keep **both hands** on the bike's handlebars.
   - Carry schoolbooks or other items safely in a backpack.

FOLLOW THE RULES OF THE ROAD

20 Reports show that most cyclists who are killed or seriously injured were involved in **collisions**[5] at or near road junctions.
   - Always ride in a straight line in the **same direction** as other traffic.
   - Respect traffic signals: stop at stop signs and obey traffic lights in the same way as cars.

SIGNAL YOUR MOVES

25 Sudden changes in direction are the cause of many collisions.
   - **Do not** change direction without first looking behind you.
   - **Signal** what you intend to do.

> ### Key vocabulary
>
> **statistics**[1]: number facts about how often something happens
> **effective**[2]: works well and gives results
> **fatal**[3]: results in death
> **reflective**[4]: sends back light and so is more easily seen
> **collision**[5]: two or more things crashing together

Activity 1: Reading

1 What is the writer's intention in the leaflet on page 68? Write one or two sentences to explain your answer.

2 Identify **three** things that can increase the chances of a road accident, according to the leaflet.

3 **a)** What, in your opinion, are the **three** most important pieces of advice in the leaflet?

   b) Write **one** sentence that explains all three of the important pieces of advice you identified.

4 Who do you think is the target audience for this leaflet? Select **one** piece of evidence to support your answer.

5 The writer gives the reader lots of facts and lots of advice. Identify **one** way in which the writer's vocabulary choice makes the facts or advice more persuasive.

Activity 2: Writing

1 Write **two or three** paragraphs in response to the following question: How has the writer tried to persuade the reader to follow the advice given in the leaflet on page 68? You could comment on, for example, the writer's intention, their vocabulary choices or the ideas they have chosen to include in the leaflet. Ensure that you support each of your ideas with evidence from the text.

Before you start writing

Plan your ideas. Think about:
- the key point you will make in each paragraph
- what evidence you will use to support each point
- how you will explain what the writer has done in your chosen quotations.

As you write
- Choose your vocabulary carefully, aiming to be clear and to use correct **terminology**.

When you have finished writing
- Check that your spelling and punctuation are accurate.
- Check to see if you have used each of the three key elements in each of your paragraphs.

Section 6
Persuasive paragraphs

In this section, you will explore paragraph structure in a persuasive instruction text.

> **DO NOT READ the webpage below!**
> **Go straight to Activity 1 and follow the instructions.**

● ● ●   Search...

Fake news, and how to spot it

1   We all like to share news stories with our friends on social media, but do any of us check if the stories are actually true?

Sharing news and stories with our friends on social
5   media can be fun. When we learn an interesting fact, or something makes us laugh, many of us will send it around to other people who might be interested. We can't be doing anything wrong, can we?

Well, in recent years there has been an increase
10   in the number of made-up stories and false news reports being posted on the internet. If we share these made-up stories and treat them as true, we could actually be causing people to make misinformed decisions. We need to know how
15   to not become influenced by this 'fake news'.

What is fake news?

Fake news articles are simply stories and news reports that aren't true, and there are thousands of them around. Now that everyone has access to
20   technology like website-building and image-editing software, they are much easier to create than before.

How can you spot fake news?

Here are some questions to ask yourself when reading a news story:
25   • Is the story being reported anywhere else?
  • Are the supporting sources reliable?
  • Does it have a correct date?
  • Is it a well-known site or author that is trusted?
  • Do the photos and videos look realistic?
30   • Is it a believable story?
  • Is the website address normal (e.g. ending in '.com' or '.co.uk')?

If the answer to one of these questions is 'no', it may be a fake news story.
35   • Type the story into a search engine and check if a well-known news station mentions it.
  • Look up any facts that you don't know are true.
  • Ask an adult or trusted friend for their opinion.

Fake or real?

40   Some people don't want others to read the real news as it contains facts that disagree with their personal viewpoints. Some of them even tell others on social media that the real news is actually fake news! However, they are just sharing their opinion, and not
45   the facts.

In order to identify the real news stories, go back to the seven questions. Work out how many of the questions answer 'yes' and then decide logically if it should be true. If you are still unsure, do some more
50   research on well-known websites.

Activity 1: Reading the opening

1 Look at the title and the first line of the webpage on page 70.
   a) What do you think the webpage is going to be about?
   b) Who do you think is the writer's target audience?
   c) What do you think the webpage will try to persuade readers to do?

2 Now read the webpage. Check your answers to question 1. Would you change any of them? If so, note down your new answers.

3 Look again at your answers to all the questions in this activity so far. Write a short list of the things that an effective opening should do.

Activity 2: Exploring elements of persuasion

Paragraphs or sections in persuasive texts often contain:
- a key point that the writer wants to make
- evidence or examples that support the key point – perhaps facts or statistics
- a suggestion of how the reader should change their opinions or their actions.

1 Look carefully at the first section of the webpage on page 70: the three paragraphs under the main heading.
   a) Which sentence makes the writer's key point?
   b) Which sentence includes examples?
   c) Which sentence implies a way the reader should react to the problem?
   d) What does the writer imply the reader should do?

2 Look at the third section of the webpage:

How can you spot fake news?

   a) In your own words, explain the writer's key point in this section.
   b) Write **one** sentence that summarises what the writer suggests readers should do.
   c) There are no major examples to support the ideas in this section. The writer could have included two news stories: a fake one and a real one, for example:

President opens new shopping centre
Incredbal health drinks cures all disease. You be amazed!!

Do you think this section would be more effective if the writer had included examples like this? Why? Write one or two sentences explaining your ideas.

Activity 3: Giving orders and conditions

1 Look again at lines 33–36 of the webpage on page 70. Each sentence includes an imperative verb.

> ### Remember
> Imperative verbs give commands or orders: they tell the reader or listener what to do.

   a) Identify **two** more examples of imperative verbs in the webpage.

   b) Do you think these verbs are effective? Write one or two sentences explaining your ideas.

2 On the webpage, the writer uses several multi-clause sentences linked with the conditional conjunction 'if'. For example:

> If you are still unsure, do some more research on well-known websites.

   a) Identify two more examples of conditional clauses in the extract.

   b) What effect do these conditional clauses have?

3 Answer each of the following questions using a sentence that uses an imperative verb to give a command. Follow it with a multi-clause sentence using the conjunction 'if'.

   a) Should I trust news articles online?   **b)** Should I worry about fake news?

Grammar Boost: Demonstrative pronouns

You can refer back to a previous sentence using a pronoun. This helps to link your ideas and make your meaning clear.

1 Look at this example sentence: *Mwaka read a news story. He believed it..*

   a) Which noun does the pronoun 'he' represent?

   b) Which noun does the pronoun 'it' represent?

2 The words 'that', 'this', 'those' and 'these' can be used as pronouns that represent ideas or collections of ideas in whole sentences.

   a) What does the pronoun 'that' represent in the following sentences?

> *I believe fake news is a problem. That seems to be clear.*

   b) What does the pronoun 'this' represent in the following sentences?

> *You should not believe everything you read. This is the first rule of the internet.*

   c) What does the pronoun 'those' represent in the following sentences?

> *Every news story should be true and honest. Those are the key things.*

Activity 4: Writing persuasive paragraphs

You are going to write three paragraphs for an article about how to deal with rumours.

Plan

1 Note down **one** piece of advice about how someone should react when they first hear a rumour.

2 Note down **two** specific pieces of advice you would give someone about checking the truth of a rumour.

3 Give your article a heading, and write an attention-grabbing first line. You could refer to Activity 1 in the previous lesson to remind yourself of what makes an opening effective.

Write

4 In your first paragraph, introduce the subject of your text.
   a) Begin your first paragraph with a sentence that makes a key general point about rumours.
   b) Add one or two examples of kinds of rumours, or where they may be heard.
   c) Using imperative verbs, add one or two sentences that tell your reader what to do when they first hear a rumour.

5 In your second paragraph, give one of your specific pieces of advice about checking the truth of a rumour.

   a) Begin your second paragraph with a key point. This could be in the form of an instruction that uses an imperative verb.
   b) Add one or two sentences giving examples or evidence that support your key point.
   c) Add one or two sentences giving further suggestions about how the reader should act. Include at least **one** multi-clause sentence using the conjunction 'if' or 'when'.

6 In your third paragraph, give your second specific piece of advice.
   a) Start your paragraph by giving examples or evidence that will lead your reader to your second key point.
   b) Make your second key point. This could be in the form of an instruction that uses an imperative verb.
   c) Add one or two sentences giving further suggestions about how the reader should act.

This section links to pages 68–71 of the Workbook.

Section 7
Persuasive structures

In this section, you will explore the structure of a persuasive text.

▼ **Read the webpage and then answer the questions that follow it.**

 Search...

How to improve your mental wellbeing

1 Mental wellbeing describes your mental state – how you are feeling and how well you can cope with day-to-day life. Our mental wellbeing is dynamic. It can change from moment to moment, day to day,
5 month to month or year to year. If you have good mental wellbeing you are able to:
- feel relatively confident in yourself and have positive self-esteem
- feel and express a range of emotions
10 • build and maintain good relationships with others
- feel engaged with the world around you
- live and work productively
- cope with the stresses of daily life
- adapt and manage in times of change
15 and uncertainty.

Below we look at steps you can take to manage your mental wellbeing.

Think about what is affecting your mental wellbeing

20 We're all different. What affects someone's mental wellbeing won't necessarily affect others in the same way. Common life events that can affect your mental wellbeing include:
- loss or bereavement
25 • loneliness
- relationship problems.

Build positive relationships

Connecting with others can help us to feel a greater sense of belonging and can help to
30 challenge feelings of loneliness.
- Make time for the people you love. Keeping regular contact with friends and family, whether it's face-to-face, on the phone or by text, can strengthen your relationships.
35 • Join a group. Think of the things you like to do, such as drawing, gardening or sport and look for local groups. Meeting others with a shared interest can increase your confidence and build your support network.
40 • Talk about the way you feel. Opening up can help you to feel listened to and supported. Just acknowledging your feelings by saying them out loud can help.

Take time for yourself

45 At times you may feel guilty for spending time on yourself. But it's essential for your wellbeing and can help you to be more resilient.
- Learn something new. Learning new skills can help boost your confidence and give you a sense
50 of achievement. You could learn a new language, sign up for an art class or try a new recipe. It doesn't have to be something big.
- Do something you enjoy. Whether it's taking a long walk, playing an instrument or going to
55 the cinema, it's positive for your wellbeing to do something that makes you feel good.

Activity 1: Reading the text

1 The webpage on page 74 contains the following features:

| paragraphs | bullet points | a heading | subheadings |

a) What is the webpage about? Summarise it in **five** words or fewer.
b) Which feature of the webpage tells you most clearly what it is about?
c) Note down **three** ways in which the webpage suggests you can help your mental wellbeing.
d) Which feature of the webpage tells you this most clearly?

2 a) Imagine you are trying to identify something that, according to the webpage, could affect your mental wellbeing. Under which subheading would you look for the answer?
b) Identify **one** thing that, according to the webpage, could affect your mental wellbeing.

How do I do that?

Look at all the subheadings. Which one suggests that the section will contain information about things that could affect your mental wellbeing?

3 a) Imagine you are trying to identify something that, according to the webpage, you could do to create positive relationships with other people. Under which subheading would you look for the answer?
b) Identify **two** things that, according to the webpage, you could do to create positive relationships with other people.

Activity 2: Exploring the text's structure

1 What is the purpose of the following features in the webpage on page 74?
a) the introduction
b) the subheadings
c) the bullet-pointed lists

For each one, write one or two sentences to explain your ideas. You could choose from the ideas below or use your own.

to make the ideas clearer and easier to follow | to explain what the webpage is about

to explain what a phrase in the heading means | to tell the reader what each section is about

to guide the reader through the ideas | to make the webpage easier to read

Grammar Boost: Determiners

Determiners are words such as:

this | that | these | those | the | a | some | his | her | their

They add information to nouns about quantity, definiteness and belonging, as shown in the table below.

You can refer back to a previous sentence using a determiner. This helps link your ideas and make your meaning clear.

1 Compare the following pairs of sentences. Which one (A or B) makes it clearer that both sentences are about the same man? Write one or two sentences explaining your answer.

  A A man walked into a clothes shop. A man bought a new shirt.

  B A man walked into a clothes shop. The man bought a new shirt.

2 Rewrite the following sentence, making its meaning clearer by replacing the highlighted determiner.

> Hania smelled food. A smile appeared on a face.

Activity 3: Responding to the text

The writer of the webpage on page 74 has tried to create a variety of responses in the reader. Look again at the subheading 'Build positive relationships' and lines 28–43.

1 Sentences A–C below are examples of responses that the writer of the webpage intended to achieve.

  A   to encourage the reader to think about their mental wellbeing

  B   to encourage the reader to take action

  C   to explain how taking action could help the reader's mental wellbeing

Which of the sentences above is the intended response of:
a) the subheading 'Build positive relationships'?   **b)** lines 28–30?   **c)** lines 31–43?

Activity 4: Planning a text

You are going to write a text persuading young people to spend less time on their mobile phones or computers, and to advise them about other ways in which they could spend their time.

Gather ideas

1 Your text should point out why spending all day on a mobile phone or computer is a bad idea, and why spending more time doing other things is a good idea. Note down **two or three** reasons why this might be.

2 Your text should also advise young people about other ways they could spend their time. Note down **four or five** suggestions. You could choose from the suggestions below or use your own ideas.

reading | cooking | exercising | drawing

Plan

3 Choosing a heading or title for your text will help you focus your ideas. Write a title to tell readers what your text will be about.

4 Look again at the ideas you gathered in response to question 1. Use them to plan an introduction to your text. In your introduction, you could introduce the problem and explain why it is a problem.

5 Look again at the ideas you gathered in response to question 2.
   a) Choose and note down **three** different ways in which young people could spend their time.
   b) For each activity, write a subheading. Use an imperative verb to encourage the reader to take action.

> **Remember**
> An imperative verb gives an order or an instruction.

6 In a paragraph under each subheading, your text should explain the benefit of each of the activities suggested. Note down **two or three** details describing at least **two** benefits for each activity. You could choose from the suggested descriptions below or use your own ideas.

relaxing | interesting | exciting | useful | healthy

Section 8
Exploring the writer's choices

In this section, you will explore how the writer's choices of ideas, vocabulary and sentence structure can make texts more persuasive.

▼ **Read the webpage and then answer the questions that follow it.**

  Search...

Sleep matters!

1   Sleep may be the last thing on your mind but here are some reasons why you should give it a little more thought:
   • The right amount of sleep will make it easier to maintain a healthy weight.
   • Sleep deprivation can make it hard to concentrate and remember things – the last thing you need when you are in an exam situation!
5   • You are more likely to feel down when you are tired.
   • Growth hormones are released when you are asleep.
   • Getting a good night's sleep can help you to cope better with the stresses of life.
   • Lack of sleep can cause havoc with your skin and result in spots
10   and pimples.
   • Learning to drive is great but driving when sleep-deprived is seriously dangerous.
   • Bedtime routines aren't just for young kids! Everyone benefits from having a routine in the run-up to bedtime – even your parents.
15   • Try to do the same things at around the same time each night so that your body has time to prepare for sleep and to relax.

Why is sleep so difficult?

Do you find nodding off hard work? If you struggle to stop your brain going round at 100 miles an hour, here are a few possible
20   reasons why:
   • Your body clock alters in your teen years, which means that waking and sleeping times get later and later. You will probably find that you prefer to stay up late at night but struggle to get up in the morning. This is normal. Getting into a good routine can help with this.
   • According to some research, using 'screens' before you go to bed can double the length of time it takes you
25   to fall asleep as it suppresses the production of your sleep hormone, melatonin. Ditch your phone or tablet in the hour leading up to your bedtime.
   • The school day may start early for you, which means that you have to get up before your body has had enough sleep. However, being overtired makes it even more difficult to fall asleep. Unfortunately we can't change the time that school starts but what you can do is have a regular sleep and wake-up time to help
30   your body to cope better with the early mornings.

Activity 1: Identifying persuasive ideas

1 What is the writer's intention in the webpage on page 78? Write **one** sentence to summarise it.

2 The writer of the webpage lists advice that can help you sleep better. Using your own words, explain **three** pieces of advice the writer gives about getting more sleep.

3 The writer makes their advice more persuasive by highlighting how important it is to sleep well.
   a) Using your own words, explain **three** of the benefits of sleep that the writer describes.
   b) Look again at your answers to question 3a. Are you persuaded to follow the writer's advice? Write one or two sentences explaining your answer.

Activity 2: Considering the effects of vocabulary

The writer has used some emotive, dramatic vocabulary choices to make their writing more persuasive.

1 Look again at the following sentences from the webpage on page 78.

   a) Lack of sleep can cause havoc with your skin and result in spots and pimples.

   b) Learning to drive is great but driving when sleep-deprived is seriously dangerous.

   c) If you struggle to stop your brain going round at 100 miles an hour, here are a few possible reasons why:

For each example, write a sentence in which you state the emotive words and identify the problem that the writer's vocabulary choices is highlighting.

   In this sentence, the writer uses the word '_____' to highlight the problem of

2 In some sentences, the writer does not use such emotive and dramatic vocabulary choices. For example:

   You are more likely to feel down when you are tired.

   a) Rewrite the sentence above, replacing the highlighted words with more dramatic choices.
   b) Do you think your version of the sentence above is more persuasive than the original version? Write one or two sentences explaining why.

Grammar Boost: Sentence types

Sentences can contain:

- just one clause. These are called single-clause sentences. For example:

  I go to bed at 9pm every night.

- two or more clauses. These are called multi-clause sentences. For example:

  I go to bed at 9pm every night and get up at 7am every morning.

Remember

A clause must contain a verb and gives the reader information about one event or action. Clauses are often linked with conjunctions.

Conjunction bank

and	but
when	as
before	after
until	because
so that	although
if	

1. Look at each of the sentences below. Are they single-clause or multi-clause sentences?
   a) Go to bed early.
   b) Read a book in bed so you relax before you try to sleep.
   c) Get lots of rest.
   d) You will feel better and you will look healthier.

2. Look again at each of the multi-clause sentences in question 1. Note down the number of clauses each one contains, and the conjunctions used to link them.

Activity 3: Explaining yourself

Persuasive texts often tell the reader to think or act in a certain way. Explaining **why** the reader should think or act in that way makes the text more persuasive.

1. Look again at the following example sentences from the webpage on page 78. Each sentence gives the reader an instruction and explains why they should follow it.

   a) The right amount of sleep will make it easier to maintain a healthy weight.

   b) Getting a good night's sleep can help you to cope better with the stress of life such as exams, parents and relationships.

   c) Try to do the same things at around the same time each night so that your body has time to prepare for sleep and to relax.

   For each example, write a sentence in which you identify what the reader should do and why.

2. Look again at Sentence C above. How has the writer linked the instruction and the explanation in this multi-clause sentence?

Activity 4: Developing a response

You are going to write a developed response to the webpage on page 78, answering the following question: How does the writer persuade you that sleep is important? In each of the paragraphs in your response, include:

- a key point about what the writer has done
- evidence to support this point
- an explanation of how the evidence demonstrates what the writer has done.

Copy the table below and complete it by answering the questions that follow.

Paragraph 1	Paragraph 2
Quotation:	Quotation:
Key point:	Key point:
Explanation:	Explanation:

Identify evidence

1 Choose **two** key quotations from the webpage that you find particularly persuasive. They could be sentences, phrases or even single words. Add these to the top row of your table.

Plan your points

2 For each of the quotations you selected, write a sentence stating what persuasive techniques the writer has used. Add these to the middle row of your table.

Plan your explanations

3 For each quotation, write one or two sentences explaining how the writer's choices make the webpage more persuasive. Add these to the bottom row of your table.

This suggests that   This gives the impression that

Write

4 Use your notes to write **two** paragraphs in response to the question at the top of this page. Consider the clarity of your response as you write, using carefully selected vocabulary and a variety of single- and multi-clause sentences.

Section 9
Rhetorical devices

In this section, you will explore how a variety of rhetorical devices can make a text more persuasive.

This extract is from a fact sheet about the importance of not smoking.

▼ **Read the extract and then answer the questions that follow it.**

STAYING SMOKE-FREE

1 Smoking is anti-social, addictive and deadly. In fact, the more we learn about the effects of smoking, the more harmful we know it is. Staying smoke-free is much smarter, healthier and easier than having to
5 quit in later life, when you will have felt the effects first hand.

REASONS NOT TO SMOKE

- Tobacco contains nicotine, which is an extremely addictive chemical. Nicotine has a similar habit-
10 forming effect on the body to that of heroin: it makes your body and mind think they need the drug just to feel normal.

- Smoking dramatically increases your risk of developing cancer, **emphysema**, heart disease
15 and asthma.

- By not smoking, you will save a lot of money, keep your teeth a lot whiter, your breath a lot sweeter, your skin a lot clearer, and your whole body a lot fitter.

- By not smoking, you will help not only your own health but also the health of people around you. Smokers make everyone around them breathe in their smoke – this is called passive smoking.

20 Which would you choose: poisoning your friends, your family and yourself – or living a longer, fitter, more comfortable life?

REASONS TO SMOKE

There aren't any.

Key vocabulary

emphysema: a disease that destroys the tissue of your lungs.

Remember

In persuasive texts, writers select ideas that they think will persuade the reader. The vocabulary and sentence structure the writer uses to express those ideas can make them even more persuasive.

Activity 1: Identifying persuasive ideas

1 Write **one** sentence to summarise the writer's intention in the extract on page 82.

2 Using your own words, explain **three** negative consequences of smoking that have been included in the extract.

3 Using your own words, explain **three** positive consequences of not smoking that have been included in the extract.

Activity 2: Identifying rhetorical devices

Rhetorical devices are language techniques that writers use to present ideas persuasively. The following techniques are rhetorical devices:

- **Rhetorical questions** are questions asked when an answer is not expected.
- A **triple structure** is a persuasive pattern of three ideas.
- **Repetition** is doing or saying something more than once.
- **Lists** are sequences of connected items written one after another.
- **Direct address** is a method of speaking directly to the reader or listener.

1 Which rhetorical devices can you spot in each of the following persuasive sentences?
   a) It's fast, fun and free!
   b) Do you want to live a happy life?
   c) It makes no difference if you're male, female, old, young, rich, poor, a beginner or a professional.
   d) Never give up; never stop trying; never stop believing.

2 Identify the examples of these rhetorical devices in the extract on page 82. Copy the table below and complete it by adding **one** example of each device.

Rhetorical device	Example
Rhetorical question	
Triple structure	
Repetition	
List	
Direct address	

Punctuation Boost: Commas in lists

Commas are used to separate items in a list, apart from the last two items: these are linked with a conjunction such as 'and' or 'or' instead. Lists can include individual items or events. For example:

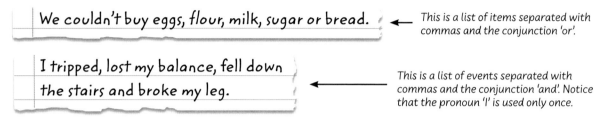

We couldn't buy eggs, flour, milk, sugar or bread. ← This is a list of items separated with commas and the conjunction 'or'.

I tripped, lost my balance, fell down the stairs and broke my leg. ← This is a list of events separated with commas and the conjunction 'and'. Notice that the pronoun 'I' is used only once.

1 Rewrite the following bullet-pointed lists as sentences. Remember to use commas.

My favourite subjects:
• English
• maths
• science

Things I do every morning:
• I get up
• I get dressed
• I eat breakfast
• I clean my teeth

Activity 3: Exploring rhetorical devices

Different rhetorical devices have different impacts on a reader:
- Rhetorical questions engage readers and involve them in the argument.
- Repetition can add emphasis to ideas.
- Lists and triple structures can be used to highlight range and variety.
- Direct address gives the impression the writer is talking directly to the reader.

1 Compare the following pairs of sentences. Which sentence in each pair is more persuasive? In each case, write **one** sentence explaining why.

a) Smoking shortens your life.   Do you want to shorten your life?

b) Smoking is expensive: it can cost you your life.

Smoking is expensive: it can cost people their lives.

c) Smoking harms your whole body.

Smoking harms your heart, brain, lungs, skin and circulation.

2 Look again at your answers to Activity 2, question 2. For each of the rhetorical devices you identified, write **one** sentence explaining what effect each one creates.

Activity 4: Creating rhetorical devices

Imagine you have been asked to write a text that persuades young people to eat healthily. Look at the ideas and information below.

People should eat a healthy diet.	Eating a healthy diet can make people feel better and live longer.	Your body will be fitter and you will have more energy.	You will look good and feel great.
A healthy diet can be just as filling as an unhealthy diet.	Healthy food tastes delicious.	Reduce: • sugar • salt • fat	Increase: • fruit • vegetables • water

Follow the steps below to write **four** persuasive sentences on the topic of healthy eating. Use direct address in all of them.

1 Write a persuasive rhetorical question. Make it a short sentence that catches the reader's attention.

How do I do that?

Try starting your question with one of these phrases:

Do you want to… | How could you… | Should you…

2 Write a persuasive sentence featuring a triple structure.

How do I do that?

You could use a pattern of three verbs to highlight the benefits of a healthy diet, or three adjectives to highlight three reasons why readers would enjoy a healthy diet.

3 Write a persuasive sentence featuring a list. This is likely to be a long sentence, as it should show the range and variety involved in a subject.

How do I do that?

You could list some of the things to do, or not do, in order to eat a healthy diet.

4 Write a persuasive sentence featuring repetition.

How do I do that?

• Choose a key noun phrase (for example, 'healthy diet'), a key adjective (such as 'better') or a key verb (like 'eat' or 'feel').
• Write a sentence in which you use that key word or phrase twice or more.

5 Look at each of the sentences you have written. Have you used direct address in all of them? If not, adapt them.

This section links to pages 80–83 of the Workbook.

Section 10
Getting ready to respond

In this section, you will develop your skills in identifying relevant features of a text and planning your response to it.

This webpage is taken from a website that gives advice about avoiding the dangers of very hot weather.

▼ **Read the webpage and then answer the questions that follow it.**

● ● ● Search...

Extreme heat: staying safe

1 Everyone likes hot weather, right? Wrong! Sunny days are nice, but when temperatures hit 35 degrees or higher, many people start to suffer. If you live or travel in areas that can experience sweltering heat, there are a few important things you need to know.

Look after yourself – and others

5 Stay aware of your body. Heat exhaustion occurs when someone is subjected to hot conditions for a long time and loses a considerable amount of bodily fluids. Untreated, it can lead to serious problems requiring medical attention like heatstroke, where the body's temperature soars and is no longer able to cool itself down. Anyone can get heatstroke, but older people and babies are the most vulnerable, so keep a special eye on them. Be alert for the symptoms that could suggest heat exhaustion:

10 • racing pulse
• dizziness
• headaches
• uncontrollable sweating.

The best remedy is to lie down somewhere as cool and shady as
15 possible, and drink lots of water. If you don't feel a bit better in half an hour, call for medical help.

Feeling cooler

There are many ways to cool down, even in roasting temperatures. Some are obvious, like drinking lots of water, wearing thin clothes,
20 opening windows, and using curtains and blinds to shut out the sun. But you can also try the following clever tricks:
• Wear white. Light-coloured clothes reflect the sun's rays, so some of the heat will bounce off you.
• If you've got an electric fan, put a bowl of ice in front of it. The ice will cool the air as it blows towards you.
• If it's too hot to sleep, try filling a bottle with cold water and popping it in the freezer before bedtime. The
25 frozen bottle should cool your bed down nicely, at least for a while!
• Run cold water over your wrists, feet and head. This will freshen you up quickly.

If you take these sensible steps, you'll remain safe even in blistering temperatures!

Activity 1: Checking understanding

Before you think about your response to a text, it's important to make sure that you:
- understand what the text is about
- understand the text's target audience: the people the writer expects to read it
- understand the writer's intention: how the writer wants the reader to respond.

1 Write down:
- a) three hot-weather symptoms that could be dangerous according to the webpage on page 86.
- b) two things you could do to relieve the symptoms.
- c) two ideas to help you keep cool.

2 Look again at your answers to question 1 and then write one or two sentences summing up the text's target audience and the writer's intention.
- who is the target audience for the webpage?
- what is the writer's intention?

Activity 2: Looking at structure and intention

When you are sure you understand the text and the writer's intention, look at its structure and how that helps the writer to achieve their intention.

1 Consider the following structural features.

| a heading or title | an introduction | subheadings | bullet points |

- a) Which of these structural features has the writer used in the webpage on page 86?
- b) Which of these structural features helps to guide the reader through the webpage? Write one or two sentences explaining your ideas.
- c) Which of these structural features helps to persuade the reader to do what the writer suggests? Write one or two sentences explaining your ideas.

Activity 3: Looking at vocabulary and intention

When you are sure you understand the text and have looked at its structure, look for any significant vocabulary choices the writer has made.

1 a) Which of these three words from the webpage on page 86 most powerfully describes the way very hot weather can feel?

extreme　　roasting　　sweltering

b) Identify two further examples of emotive language that the writer uses to highlight the way hot weather can make people feel.

Skills Boost: Selecting vocabulary in your response

When you write a response to a text, aim to choose the most precise vocabulary to convey it.

1 a) Look at the incomplete sentence below, taken from one student's response to the extract. Select **one** word to replace the **?**.

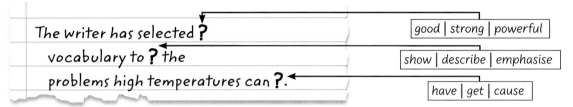

The writer has selected **?** vocabulary to **?** the problems high temperatures can **?**.

good | strong | powerful

show | describe | emphasise

have | get | cause

b) Look at the incomplete sentences below. Copy the sentences, selecting **one** word to fill each gap.

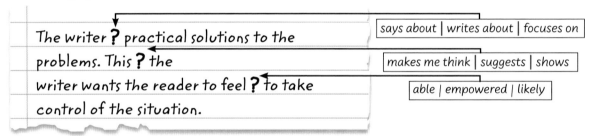

The writer **?** practical solutions to the problems. This **?** the writer wants the reader to feel **?** to take control of the situation.

says about | writes about | focuses on

makes me think | suggests | shows

able | empowered | likely

Activity 4: Looking at sentence structure, rhetorical devices and intention

When commenting on sentence structures and rhetorical devices, look out for unusual features, such as:
- direct address to engage the reader
- rhetorical questions to engage the reader
- very short sentences to add emphasis to a key idea
- very long sentences to highlight a range or variety.

1 Look again at the following paragraph from the webpage on page 86.

> Everyone likes hot weather, right? Wrong! Sunny days are nice, but when temperatures hit 35 degrees or higher, most people start to suffer. If you live or travel in areas that can experience sweltering heat, there are a few important things you need to know.

a) Which significant sentence structures or rhetorical devices can you identify in the paragraph above?

b) For each significant sentence structure or rhetorical device you identify, write a sentence explaining how it helps the writer to achieve their intention.

Activity 5: Putting it all together

Below is one student's response to the following question: How does the writer of the webpage on page 86 persuade the reader to follow their advice?

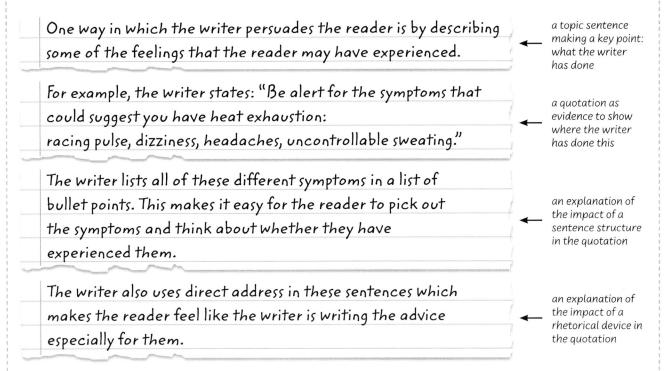

One way in which the writer persuades the reader is by describing some of the feelings that the reader may have experienced.

← a topic sentence making a key point: what the writer has done

For example, the writer states: "Be alert for the symptoms that could suggest you have heat exhaustion: racing pulse, dizziness, headaches, uncontrollable sweating."

← a quotation as evidence to show where the writer has done this

The writer lists all of these different symptoms in a list of bullet points. This makes it easy for the reader to pick out the symptoms and think about whether they have experienced them.

← an explanation of the impact of a sentence structure in the quotation

The writer also uses direct address in these sentences which makes the reader feel like the writer is writing the advice especially for them.

← an explanation of the impact of a rhetorical device in the quotation

1 Write another paragraph in response to the question at the top of this page. You could focus on one of the following topics or use your own ideas:

- the writer's use of subheadings

- the writer's use of rhetorical questions

- the writer's vocabulary choices.

To build your paragraph, follow the steps below.

a) Select a quotation that shows the aspect of the webpage you have chosen as your focus. It could be a word, a phrase or a sentence.

b) Write a topic sentence making a key point about what the writer has done in the quotation you have selected.

c) Write a comment explaining the impact of the writer's choices in the quotation. Look at your quotation again. Are there any other significant vocabulary choices, sentence structures or rhetorical devices on which you could comment?

This section links to pages 84–85 of the Workbook.

Section 11
Assessment

In this section, you will answer questions on a text to assess your progress in this unit.

▼ Read the newspaper article and then answer the questions that follow it.

TEN EASY STEPS TO HAPPIER LIVING

1 We're constantly bombarded with messages about what makes for a good life. Advertisers tell us it comes from owning and consuming their products. The media associate it with wealth, beauty or fame. But do any of these things really bring lasting happiness?

Scientists have found that a huge proportion of the
5 variations in happiness between us come from our choices and activities. So although we may not be able to change the circumstances in which we find ourselves, we still have the power to change how happy we are – by the way we approach our lives.

10 Action for Happiness has identified these keys to happier living.

1. Do things for others
Caring about others is fundamental to our happiness. Helping other people is not only good for them; it's good
15 for us too. It makes us happier and can help to improve our health.

Action ideas
- Do three extra acts of kindness today. Offer to help, give away your change, pay a compliment or make
20 someone smile.
- Reach out to help someone who's struggling. Give them a call or offer your support. Let them know you care.

2. Connect with people
25 Our relationships with other people are the most important thing for our happiness. People with strong relationships are happier, healthier and live longer.

Action ideas
- Make more time for the people who matter. Chat with
30 a loved one or friend, call your parents or play with the kids.

- Make three extra connections today. Stop to chat in the shop, wave at a neighbour, learn the name of someone new.

35 **3. Take care of your body**
Our body and mind are connected. Being active makes us happier as well as healthier. We can also boost our wellbeing by spending time outdoors, eating healthily, unplugging from technology and getting enough sleep.

40 **Action ideas**
- Be more active today. Get off the bus a stop early, take the stairs, turn off the TV, go for a walk – anything that gets you moving.
- Eat nutritious food, drink more water, catch up on
45 sleep. Notice which healthy actions lift your mood and do more of them.

Activity 1: Reading

1 Identify **three** things that the newspaper article on page 90 suggests advertisers and the media tell us will make us happy.

2 At the end of the first paragraph, the writer asks, 'But do any of these things really bring lasting happiness?' What do you think the writer is suggesting in this sentence? Write one or two sentences to explain your ideas.

3 The article is focused on how people can be happier. According to the writer, the suggestions in the article can also make people healthier and help them to live longer. Why do you think the writer has included these ideas?

4 The writer has used some structural features to guide the reader through the article, and to make it easier to understand. Identify **three** structural features that the writer has used for this reason.

5 Which of the suggestions in the article do you think are most likely to make people happy? Write **two or three** sentences explaining your choice.

Activity 2: Writing

1 Write **two or three** paragraphs in response to the following question:
How has the writer tried to persuade the reader to follow the advice given in the article on page 90?

You could comment on:
- the writer's intention
- the ideas the writer has chosen to include
- the writer's vocabulary choices
- the writer's choices of sentence structure.

Ensure that you:
- express your ideas clearly and fluently as you can
- use the three basic elements of a critical paragraph:
  - a key point
  - a supporting quotation
  - an explanation of the quotation's effect.

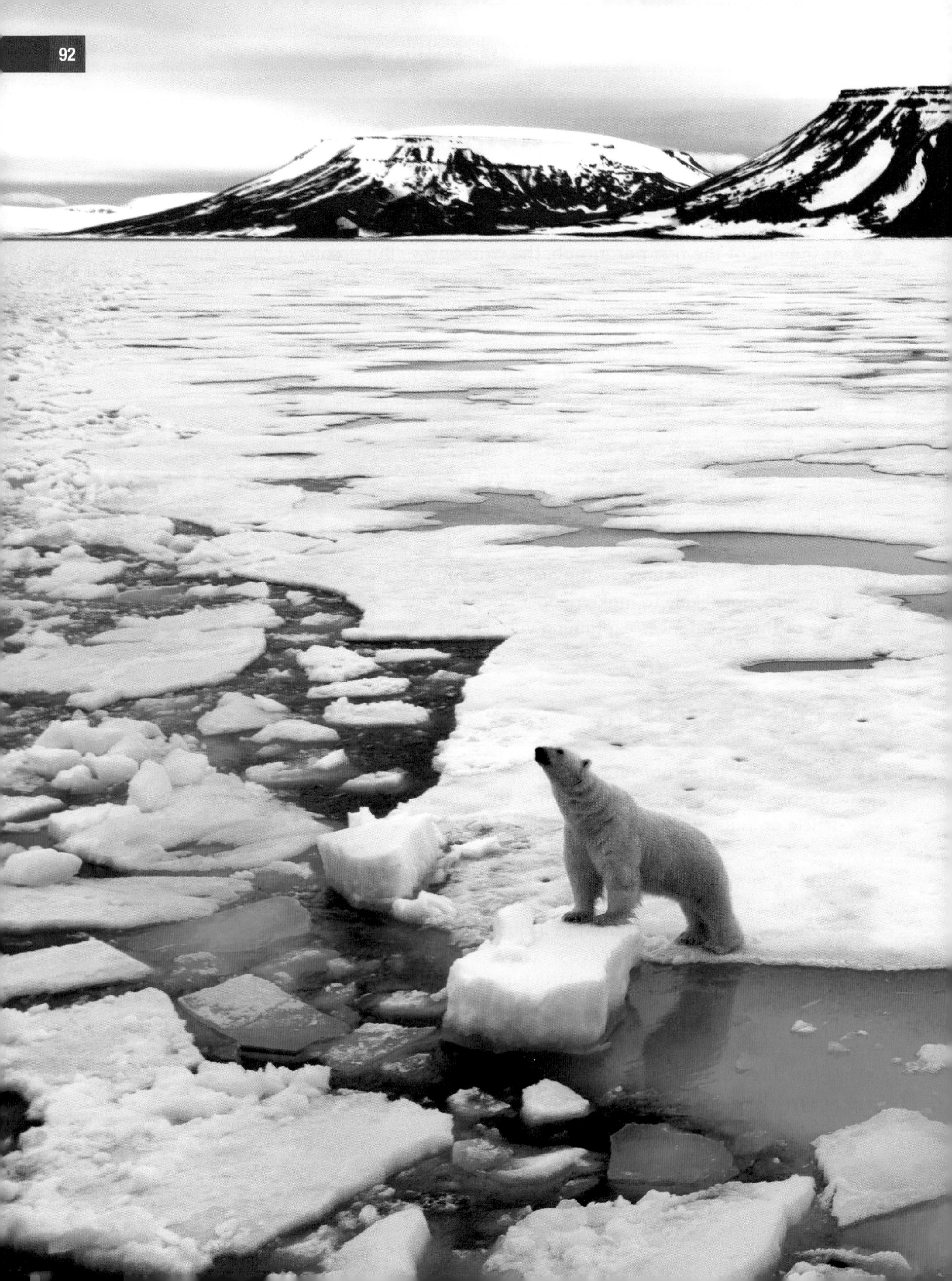

Unit 3
A perfect world

In this unit, you will read a variety of stories and non-fiction texts about the world around you. These texts explore potential threats to the planet and humanity, such as climate change and artificial intelligence, and present some of the ways in which these might be avoided. Reading and responding to these texts will help you learn how to craft an argument, supporting it with well-chosen vocabulary and relevant evidence.

In this unit, you will...

- explore how writers can engage their readers in an imaginary world.

- explore the structure of an argument text and plan your own.

- explore how writers imply ideas and select vocabulary to add impact to them.

- explore how nouns and verbs can be modified with adjectives and adverbs to add to their impact.

- answer questions on a short extract and write a short argument text to assess your progress.

- explore how writers support their ideas with evidence, examples and explanations.

- explore and experiment with the impact that different sentence structures can have on your writing.

- explore ways in which rhetorical devices can add impact to your ideas.

- explore the contribution that introductions and conclusions make to effective argument texts.

- explore ways of correcting and developing a response to give it as much impact as possible.

- write an article arguing your point of view.

By the end of this unit, you will be able to construct an effectively structured article, expressing a clear and compelling point of view.

Section 1
Exploring a fictional future

In this section, you will explore how writers can engage their readers in an imaginary world.

This is an extract from the first chapter of a novel. The story takes place in the future, after the Great Pollution. Owning luxury items is now a crime, and an order of knights has been created to enforce the laws of the New Society.

▼ Read the extract and then answer the questions that follow it.

1 Marco reined his horse to a halt and dismounted with ease. He paused, admiring the glossy saddle. The leather was beautiful – salvaged from the cabins of an abandoned luxury aircraft – it seemed incredible to him that such machines had ever existed. **Repurposed**[1] by skilled craftsmen, the leather saddle showed everyone Marco's status – a shining token that he was a Knight of the New Society – an achievement he wore with pride.

5 As he tied his horse to a tree nearby and approached the **ramshackle**[2] house, he thought back to his years of training at the Academy. Selected at nine for his gifts in logic and mathematics, he was taken away from his family and given the chance to fulfil his potential. In the twelve long years of training, he had only seen them once a year, on Founder's Day – his parents, tired and thin, and his elder sister, Anya, neat and plain in the grey uniform worn by the younger Commoners. Every year, Anya asked him kindly about his studies, and listened as he talked about the

10 laws he had learned. But as the years passed, their conversations became polite and insincere, and he wondered what feelings she hid behind her dutiful smile. The coldness which grew between them was a shame, but he accepted it. The Academy taught that feeling and emotion should be ignored if they were to deliver justice in cases of greed-crime.

The world was better now. Only those who had learned logic and wisdom achieved positions of influence. The role

15 of the Knight was clear – to preserve the world the Founders had built after the Great Pollution. It was the desire for the bigger house, the faster car, the sleeker phone and the mindless exploitation of the Earth's resources, which had brought humanity close to destruction. To survive they must live without the luxuries their ancestors had wanted. The Founders knew there would be resistance. The Commoners would fight to preserve the lives they remembered, but unless everyone accepted a simpler,

20 harder existence, the result would be **anarchy**[3]. Luxury was greed, and greed was a crime, the penalty of which was imprisonment.

Outside the house, he could he hear the faint sound of voices. He knocked softly on the door. Through the dirty

25 window he saw a tired-looking woman in a threadbare grey uniform. A report had reached him that the householder had bought a television on the black market.

Key vocabulary

repurposed[1]: recycled
ramshackle[2]: poor
anarchy[3]: chaos

Activity 1: Understanding and summarising ideas

When you summarise a text, you first need to identify and understand its key ideas.

1 Look at some key ideas you might expect to find information about in the first chapter of the novel from which the extract on page 94 was taken:

The characters: the relationship between Marco and Anya.	The setting: the place where Marco and Anya live.
What has happened before the story started.	What might happen next in the story.

    a) Which of the key ideas above do you learn something about from the extract on page 94?

    b) Look again at your answers to question 1a. Write down everything you learn about each one.

    c) Look at all the information you have gathered about the extract. Underline the four or five most important ideas and use them to write a summary of the extract in just one or two sentences.

2 It is important that the opening of a story or a novel engages the reader's interest. Which of the key ideas above would engage the reader in this novel, do you think? Write one or two sentences explaining your answer.

Activity 2: Inferring ideas

The extract on page 94 is taken from the beginning of a story. Not all the ideas in the story are explained. Some of them are left to the reader to try to work out.

1 What you can guess or work out about:

    a) When the story is set: is it in the past, the present or the future?

    b) What happened in the Great Pollution?

    c) The purpose of the Academy, the role of the Knights, the lives of the Commoners?

For each of your answers, write a sentence explaining how you worked it out – either using the clues you found in the extract, or the clues you got from the word itself.

> The clues I found in the extract were

> The word 'Academy' made me think that

Activity 3: Responding to the writer's ideas

The extract on page 94 is taken from a story which is set in the future.

1 In what ways is this imaginary world of the future different to the world in which you live? Add three ideas to a table like the one below.

	In the world where I live...	...but in the imaginary world of the story...
1		
2		
3		

2 Would you like to live in the imaginary future that the writer describes in the story? Give **three** reasons to support and explain your answer.

Grammar Boost: Subjects and verbs in Standard English

Remember

- The **verb** in a sentence describes the action or event that is taking place.
- The **subject** of that verb is the person or thing that is doing it.

Verb forms must agree with their subjects:

Verb: to have	I have	you have	she has	we have	they have
Verb: to go	I go	you go	he goes	we go	they go
Verb: to be	I am	you are	it is	we are	they are

1 Each **?** in the sentences below represents a missing verb in the present tense: a form of 'to have', 'to go', or 'to be'. Note down the correct verb and its correct form.
   a) They **?** the best players in the team.
   b) She **?** to school every day.
   c) The homework **?** due in on Tuesday.
   d) My mother **?** three sisters.
   e) My uncle **?** older than my father.

Activity 4: Planning and writing a story opening

You are going to plan and write the opening of a story set in the future. Your story could be set in:

- a **perfect** world where all the world's problems have been solved. This kind of setting is sometimes called a **utopia**.
- a very **imperfect** world where the world's problems have become far worse. This kind of setting is sometimes called a **dystopia**.

Gather ideas

1 You are going to gather ideas for a story set in a utopia: a perfect world of the future.

a) Write down three things you **do not like** about the world in which you live now.

b) How might the things you do not like get **better** in the future?

c) Write down three things you **like** about the world in which you live now.

d) How might the things you like get **even better** in the future?

Plan

2 You are going to write the opening paragraphs of a story in which your narrator is travelling to school or to work. Answer the questions below, noting down as many ideas as you can.

a) Where is your narrator travelling – through the city or through the countryside?

b) What does it look, sound and smell like?

c) How is your narrator travelling – on foot or in some kind of vehicle?

d) Who is your narrator travelling with – a friend, a family member, someone else or are they alone?

e) If your narrator is alone, what are they thinking about?

f) If they are with someone, what are they talking about? You could use their conversation to give the reader some clues about life in this imaginary world of the future.

g) What will your narrator find when they arrive at school or work? Note down some ideas for a school or workplace of the future.

Write

3 Use some or all of your ideas to write the opening paragraphs of your story.

Section 2
Building an argument

In this section, you will explore the structure of an argument text and plan your own.

Newspaper articles often draw attention to problems facing the world. They frequently argue that action needs to be taken, and sometimes suggest solutions that could make the world a better place.

▼ **Read the newspaper article and then answer the questions that follow it.**

EVEN OUR OWN BODIES NOW CONTAIN PLASTIC WASTE. IT'S TIME TO GET DRASTIC

1 **We are what we eat, and what we eat reveals something about what we are. So it shouldn't be all that surprising that humans are now apparently eating plastic.**

2 A small trial at the Medical University of Vienna found tiny shreds of it in the digestive systems of people from eight different countries including the UK. The study involved just eight people and doesn't tell us what effect eating plastic was having on their bodies, which means an awful lot more research is needed.

3 We already knew fish were **ingesting**[1] plastic. Did we really think that the consequences of our own actions couldn't return to haunt us? However, this goes beyond cleaning up the oceans. Six of the eight subjects of the study ate sea fish, but not all of them did. Other possible theories involve drinking out of plastic bottles, eating food that's been wrapped in plastic, or tiny plastic particles floating in the air which then land on our food. But our environment is so saturated now with plastic that it seems almost inevitable that we were going to absorb it somehow.

4 Does it actually matter? This study can't yet answer that question, because all it tells us is that **microplastics**[2] were found in human **faeces**[3]. If it's just passing through like an unwelcome guest before being expelled from the body, then perhaps there's no damage done. If there were evidence of plastics being absorbed and **accumulating**[4] in our internal organs, that would be a **red flag**[5]. But either way, finding something inside ourselves that we wouldn't have chosen to put there ought to put rocket boosters under efforts to tackle plastic pollution.

5 Solving plastic pollution is, it should be said, nowhere near as simple as some campaigners make it sound. There's a reason we got so reliant on plastic in the first place, and even if it were possible to phase the stuff out tomorrow, it would take up to 1,000 years for some of what's being produced right now to biodegrade6.

6 But just because it's difficult, doesn't mean we do nothing. There is something genuinely mad about a society that is obsessed with the quality of the food we put in our mouths, and yet also eats its own garbage. The war on plastic, it seems, just got personal.

Key vocabulary

ingesting[1]: eating
microplastics[2]: tiny particles of plastic
faeces[3]: waste (poo)
accumulating[4]: building up
red flag[5]: warning sign
biodegrade[6]: break down naturally

Skills Boost: Identifying features

Paragraphs in an argument text often contain three key features:
- a topic sentence that makes a key point
- evidence or an example that supports or proves that point
- an explanation of how the point is important and helps to build the writer's argument.

Look at the following two short paragraphs from two different argument texts: one argues for homework, the other argues against it.

	Paragraph 1		Paragraph 2
A	Some education professionals believe that homework is of no benefit to young children.	D	Every week at school, we would be given 20 spellings to learn by the next day.
B	In a recent survey, almost 30% of primary school teachers rated it as being 'of little or no value'.	E	I know for a fact that this homework improved my skills – I was transformed from a poor speller to an excellent speller within a year.
C	If these experts do not consider homework important, surely we should listen to them.	F	It may not be popular or fun, but homework can certainly make a difference to a student's learning.

1   a) Identify the topic sentence in each paragraph.
     b) Identify the evidence or example in each paragraph.
     c) Identify the explanation in each paragraph.

Activity 1: Identifying key ideas

A paragraph of writing often has a topic sentence: a sentence in which the writer makes the topic of the paragraph clear. The topic sentence is often the first sentence in a paragraph – but not always.

1   The first paragraph in the article on page 98 contains only two sentences. One sentence is the topic sentence: it makes a key point. The other sentence is a comment: it explains the relevance of this key point and helps to build the writer's argument.
     a) Which sentence is the topic sentence?
     b) Why do you think the writer used this sentence order for the first paragraph of the article? Write one or two sentences explaining your ideas.

2   Identify the first **three or four** words of the topic sentence in:
     a) paragraph two   b) paragraph three   c) paragraph four
     d) paragraph five   e) paragraph six

Activity 2: Exploring structure

Every argument begins with a problem. If there is no problem, there is no need for an argument! Argument texts often follow a structure like the one in the table below:

| 1. What the problem is | 2. Why it's a problem | 3. What we should do about it |

1 The article on page 98 begins by identifying a problem.
a) What fact is the problem that the article identifies?
b) In which paragraph or paragraphs does the writer identify the problem?

2 The article then goes on to explain **why** the fact is a problem.
a) Write a sentence in your own words to explain why it is a problem.
b) In which paragraph or paragraphs does the writer explain why it is a problem?

3 Finally, the article suggests what we should do about the problem.
a) Write a sentence to explain what the article suggests we should do.
b) In which paragraph or paragraphs does the writer suggest what we should do?

Activity 3: Which side are you on?

In Activity 4, you are going to plan an argument text: an article for a newspaper or news website in which you argue for or against giving students homework.

1 Do you think homework is a good idea or a bad idea? To help you decide, copy and complete the table below with as many ideas as you can find.

For:	Against:
I think homework is a good idea because:	I think homework is a bad idea because:
•	•

2 Look at all the points you have gathered. Will you plan an argument article for or against homework? Choose the side you find most convincing.

Activity 4: Planning an argument

You are going to plan your newspaper article that argues for or against homework, using the same three-stage structure you explored in Activity 3.

Create a table like the one below and use the questions beneath it to help you complete each row.

What is the problem?	
Why is it a problem?	
What should we do about it?	

1 What is the problem your argument will address? You could choose one of the suggestions below or use your own ideas.

*If you are arguing that homework is a **good** idea:*

- *Not having homework means no preparation can be done for lessons.*

- *Classroom lessons don't allow time for background research.*

*If you are arguing that homework is a **bad** idea:*

- *Students can't ask for guidance from teachers while doing homework.*

- *Homework means students have less time to rest.*

Note down your chosen problem in the first row of the table.

2 Why is this a problem? In the second row of the table, add **three** reasons. You may be able to use some of the ideas you noted during Activity 3.

3 What should be done about it? You could choose one of the suggestions below or use your own ideas.
- Schools should introduce or ban homework for every lesson.
- Schools should change how much and/or how often homework is set.
- Schools should provide more support when setting homework and/or planning lessons.

In the third row of the table, add one or two sentences explaining your ideas.

Section 3
Choosing vocabulary 1

In this section, you will explore how writers imply ideas and select vocabulary to add impact to them.

Theirworld is a charity that campaigns to improve the lives of young children around the world. This extract is a page from Theirworld's website.

▼ **Read the webpage and then answer the questions that follow it.**

● ● ●   Search...

#5for5 campaign

1   The first five years of your life has everything to do with how you turn out as an adult – literally. From brain development and good nutrition to play and imagination building, those early years set us up for success in later life. Which is why #5for5, Theirworld's
5   global campaign, is aiming to change how the world thinks about early childhood development, but we need your help!

What is #5for5?

By the time a child reaches five years old, 90% of their brain has already developed – which means the journey from birth to school is one of the most important of their lives.
10

And even though it's been scientifically proven that those early years are critical, world leaders still aren't giving it the attention it deserves. That's why as part of Theirworld's #5for5 early childhood development campaign, we are calling on everyone to help make early childhood development a top priority.

15   We believe all young children should have access to the care they need, including nutrition, health, learning, play and protection, so they stand the best chance of growing up to be, well, to be anything they want.

That's why our #5for5 campaign is all about taking small actions, which could have a big impact.

Please add your voice, and ensure 200 million children under five get the start in their schooling life that
20   they deserve.

Five key areas of quality care

- Nutrition
- Health
- Learning
- Play
- Protection

#5for5: Tell world leaders to invest in Early Childhood Development

World leaders must allocate the funds needed to establish quality early childhood development programmes so that
25   every child is given the best start in life.

Sign the #5for5 petition

Activity 1: Identifying key points and intentions

1 Theirworld's #5for5 campaign focuses on children's first five years of life. In your own words, write one or two sentences explaining why they think these years are so important.

2 Theirworld argues that children need **five** things to help them in their early lives. What are they?

3 On the webpage on page 102, Theirworld supports their ideas with statistics.

a) Identify **one** example of a statistic in the text.

> **How do I do that?**
> A statistic is a fact relating to numerical information. To find a statistic, scan the text for a number.

b) Look again at the statistic you have identified. What key point is the statistic being used to make?

4 On this webpage, Theirworld is trying to influence the reader's opinions and actions.
a) What is the reader intended to think and feel after reading the page?
b) What is the reader intended to do after reading the page?

Activity 2: Inferring ideas

1 The text on the webpage on page 102 both implies and clearly states that children's brains develop significantly during the first five years of their lives.
a) Identify **one** instance in which the writer states this.
b) Identify **one** instance in which the writer implies this.

2 Look again at the following sentences from the webpage.

> We believe all young children should have access to the care they need, including nutrition, health, learning, play and protection, so they stand the best chance of growing up to be, well, to be anything they want.

These sentences imply that access to care makes a difference to children's lives.
a) In your own words, write **one** sentence explaining what the writer is implying about how much of a difference this care can make.
b) In your own words, write **one** sentence explaining what the writer is implying about how children's lives are affected if they do not have the care they need.

Activity 3: Exploring nouns

A writer's choice of nouns can help them to achieve their intention. Look at the following phrases and sentences taken from the webpage on page 102:

> those early years set us up for success in later life

> the journey from birth to school is one of the most important of their lives

> they stand the best chance of growing up to be, well, to be anything they want

> That's why our #5for5 campaign is all about taking small actions, which could have a big impact.

1 Throughout the webpage, the writer implies that the #5for5 campaign will help to improve children's lives as they grow up.

a) Choose three nouns in the sentences above that help to create that impression.

b) Write a sentence about each of the nouns you have chosen to explain what it suggests.

Remember
A noun names a person, place, object or idea.

Spelling Boost: 'Silent' consonants

Some words are spelled with **'silent' letters** – letters that are not sounded independently when a word is spoken aloud.

1 Look at the words below. Each row contains five words that are missing the same silent letter. Copy out the words, adding the correct silent letter to each one.

a) sc_ool   w_at   w_ere   w_y   _onest

b) s_ience   mus_le   s_ene   s_ent   fas_inating

c) si_n   desi_n   forei_n   campai_n   _naw

d) _not   _nee   _nock   _now   _nowledge

e) thum_   crum_   com_   clim_   bom_

f) _rong   _rite   _reck   _riggle   _rinkle

'Silent' Letters
c | b | h | k | w | g

Activity 4: Arguing a point of view

You are going to write a letter presenting a point of view.

Imagine
You want to start a new club at your school. It could be a sports club or a hobby club. Choose a sport or hobby that you enjoy or think will appeal to people of your age.

Gather ideas
You are going to write a letter to your headteacher, arguing the opinion that a club like this would improve the lives of students at your school.

1 Note down **three** ways in which this club could improve the lives of students.

Write

2 Begin your letter by stating your intention. Write **one** short paragraph explaining to your headteacher what you want to do.

> Dear Mr Bannerjee,
> I am writing to ask you if it would be possible to set up a club for

3 Use the **three** ideas you noted above to form your argument. Explain why this club would make the lives of students at your school so much better. You could use some of the vocabulary suggestions in the **Vocabulary Bank**.

4 Finally, write a conclusion. Write **two** sentences summarising how much of a difference your idea would make to how many people's lives.

> Yours sincerely,

Vocabulary Bank

Positive nouns	Positive verbs
future	need
chance	deserve
dream	achieve
journey	call on
success	build
happiness	create
action	change
impact	improve

This section links to pages 98–101 of the Workbook.

Section 4
Choosing vocabulary 2

In this section, you will explore how nouns and verbs can be modified with adjectives and adverbs to add to their impact.

This extract is a page from the website of a charity that campaigns to save the orangutan from extinction.

▼ Read the webpage and then answer the questions that follow it.

● ● ●   Search...

Help us save the orangutan

1 The problem

The world's orangutan population is disappearing as you read this text. In fact, conservation charities have warned that orangutans will disappear completely
5 within ten years unless we take urgent action to save the rainforests of Borneo and Sumatra where they live.

Why they matter

Orangutans are gentle, intelligent creatures who use their long, powerful arms and **dexterous**[1] hands
10 and feet to move effortlessly through the rainforest **canopy**[2]. As they travel, they break branches and create gaps in the canopy. These gaps allow light to reach the forest floor and help the forest to regrow naturally. Rainforests play a vital role in keeping our
15 whole planet healthy.

Threats

Orangutans face many threats that mainly arise from human actions:
• **Deforestation:** Because orangutans spend their
20 lives in trees, deforestation is the greatest threat to their survival. Deforestation is the clearing of huge parts of the rainforest so it can be used for other things such as mining and farming to produce food for rapidly increasing human populations.
25 • **Palm oil production:** A massive amount of rainforest land is being cleared *every day* to produce palm oil on large-scale plantations. Palm oil is used in over 50 per cent of products on supermarket shelves and is an urgent, ever-growing threat to the future of
30 orangutans. It is estimated that over the last 30 years,

orangutans have lost over 80 per cent of their natural living space. This means that orangutans are forced to look more widely for food, leading to increased conflict with humans.
35 • **Illegal activity:** Other threats to orangutans are from hunting or the cruel pet trade. It is illegal to keep orangutans as pets but still hundreds of baby orangutans are taken every year. Illegal traders shoot the helpless mother and take a baby. Charities
40 estimate that, for every baby orangutan that is taken, another three or four babies are innocent victims because they fall from the trees when their mother is shot.

So, what can you do to
45 help? There are many ways you can help to ensure the survival of orangutans in the wild.

Click to donate	Click to join	Click to volunteer
Donate to help us fund our vital work.	Become a member to help us plan our projects.	Look at our exciting volunteering opportunities.

Key vocabulary

dexterous[1]: skilful with the hands
canopy[2]: overlapping high branches and leaves

Activity 1: Understanding the text

1 The writer is trying to influence the reader's opinions and actions.
   a) What does the writer want readers to think and feel when they have finished reading the webpage on page 106? Write one or two sentences to explain your ideas.
   b) What does the writer want readers to **do** when they have finished reading the webpage? Write one or two sentences to explain your ideas.

2 The webpage explains why orangutans 'are forced to look more widely for food, leading to increased conflict with humans'.
   a) In your own words, explain **one** reason why orangutans are coming into contact with humans more frequently.
   b) What do you think the writer is implying through the word 'conflict'? Write one or two sentences to explain your ideas.
   c) Why do you think the writer has implied this, instead of directly stating it? Write one or two sentences to explain your ideas.

3 The webpage highlights the problem of deforestation. In your own words, write one or two sentences explaining **two** reasons why deforestation is a threat to the survival of the orangutan.

Activity 2: Selecting adjectives and adverbs

Adjectives and adverbs add descriptive information to nouns and verbs. They can also add impact to the writer's ideas, to help a text achieve its intention.

1 Look at the underlined adjective and adverb in the following sentence from the webpage on page 106.

   In fact, conservation charities have warned that orangutans will disappear <u>completely</u> within ten years unless we take <u>urgent</u> action to save the rainforests of Borneo and Sumatra where they live.

   a) Which underlined word is an adjective?
   b) Which underlined word is an adverb?
   c) What do the adjective and adverb suggest about the orangutans' situation? Write **one** sentence explaining your ideas.
   d) Look again at your answers to Activity 1, question 1. How do the adjective and adverb in the sentence above help the writer to achieve their intention?

2 Look again at the section of text following the bullet point 'Illegal activity'. Identify **two** adjectives that the writer has chosen in order to highlight how harmful the illegal activity is.

Spelling Boost: Unspoken or 'silent' vowels

Some words are difficult to spell because they contain letters that are not sounded when the word is spoken.

1 Look at the table below. Each word contains an unspoken or unstressed vowel.

separate	vegetable	family	memorable	dictionary
library	interest	biscuit	history	different
miniature	jewellery	medicine	category	business

a) Write each word, separating the spoken syllables and the unspoken or unstressed vowel. For example:

sep – a – rate | veg – e – ta – ble | fam – i – ly

b) Read each word aloud, clearly sounding each syllable, and the unspoken or unstressed vowel. Read each word aloud three times.

2 Close this book and write down as many of the 15 words above as you can. Then come back to this page to see how many you spelled correctly.

Activity 3: Building a noun phrase

A noun phrase is a group of words containing a noun and all the other words that add description or information to it, such as adjectives and adverbs. For example:

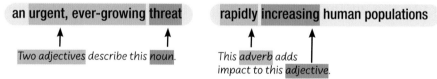

an urgent, ever-growing threat

Two adjectives describe this noun.

rapidly increasing human populations

This adverb adds impact to this adjective.

1 Create **five** different noun phrases using the suggestions below and your own ideas.

Adverbs	incredibly	surprisingly	disappointingly	extremely	particularly
Adjectives	large	beautiful	new	fascinating	exciting
Nouns	car	house	film	orangutan	city

2 Look at the noun phrase in the following sentence.

> In the distance, I saw <u>a fully grown and extremely large, very beautiful, terrifyingly wild and frighteningly powerful and softly hooting orangutan.</u>

a) Is this an effective noun phrase? Why is that?
b) Rewrite the sentence, making any changes you think would improve it.

Activity 4: Adding impact

You are going to write part of a short news article that argues your point of view.

Plan

1 Copy out a planning table like the one below.

What should change?	
Why is there a problem?	
What should we do about it?	

a) If you could change or improve one thing about your local area, what would it be?

Less litter! | More recycling! | Less pollution! | Better facilities!

Add your answer to the first row of your planning table.

b) In the second row of your table, note down **two or three** reasons explaining what problems your idea would solve.

c) In the third row of your table, note down **two or three** things that could be done to help solve this problem.

Write

2 Using your planning, write the first five or six sentences of your article, highlighting the problem in your local area and arguing that action needs to be taken.

Review

3 Look again at the short article you have written. As you respond to the following steps, you could use words from the **Vocabulary Bank** or your own ideas

a) Underline all of the verbs in your sentences.

b) Could you add impact to some of your verbs by adding adverbs? Note down the adverbs you could add.

c) Underline all of the nouns and noun phrases you have used in your sentences.

d) Could you add impact to some of your nouns and noun phrases by adding adjectives and more adverbs? Note down the adjectives and adverbs you could add.

e) Look again at the noun phrases in your sentences. Do any of them need to be edited?

Vocabulary Bank

Verbs			**Adjectives**			**Adverbs**	
need	want	demand	serious	vital	essential	desperately	urgently
must	should	become	necessary	important	dreadful	immediately	quickly
stop	change	improve	disastrous	dreadful	shocking	greatly	vastly
			appalling	terrible		dramatically	highly

Section 5
Assessment

In this section, you will answer questions on a short extract and write a short argument text to assess your progress.

This extract is a page from a website aimed at helping young people take action to protect the environment against global warming.

▼ Read the webpage and then answer the questions that follow it.

● ● ●   Search...

Global warming – take action!

Our planet's future is in our hands

1　Anyone who watches TV or uses the internet knows that the climate is changing due to global warming. Sometimes we feel inundated with depressing facts and alarming images – from
5　shrinking polar ice caps to devastating droughts and rising sea levels. It's tempting just to wish it would all go away.

But the truth is, global warming won't just go away. And if we don't act now, we face a worsening
10　future – for people, for animals, for plants and for the whole planet.

You might be thinking, "What can I do? I'm just a kid!" But don't despair. Here are three positive things that YOU can do to help reduce
15　global warming.

Spread the message

Talk to your parents and friends. If you're passionate about the environment, and genuinely committed to saving energy, you'll find it
20　surprisingly easy to convince others to join you!

Make good energy choices

If we all saved energy and used renewable sources where possible, it would make a real difference to global warming. You can be a climate hero if you:
25　• turn off lights whenever possible
• shut doors to stop heat escaping
• take short showers, not long baths
• turn off devices when you're not using them
• walk and cycle wherever you can.

30　## Learn, learn, learn!

Scientific knowledge about green energy is constantly evolving. One way of helping to tackle climate change is to educate yourself about the science and find out the facts from reputable
35　sources. This will help you answer people who suggest that global warming is a myth. And who knows, maybe one day you will be a scientist helping to solve this problem for our whole planet!

Activity 1: Reading

1 The writer of the webpage on page 110 is trying to influence the reader's opinions and actions.
a) What is the reader intended to think and feel after reading the page?
b) What is the reader intended to do after reading the page?

2 Look again at the first two paragraphs of the webpage. What does the writer imply about the future in these paragraphs? Write one or two sentences explaining your ideas, including **one** quotation from the extract to support your ideas.

3 Identify **two** things the writer suggests young people could do to influence other people's opinions about climate change.

4 How do the writer's vocabulary choices help to highlight the problem of climate change?
a) Identify **two or three** examples of powerful vocabulary choices.
b) Write one or two sentences explaining what is suggested by each choice and its impact on the reader.

Activity 2: Writing

1 Imagine that your school's headteacher is asking students for their views on how the school could be improved. Write a letter to your headteacher, arguing your views on **one** change that you feel could make a big difference. You could argue on one of the topics below or use your own ideas.

- what you learn or how you are taught

- how homework, school holidays or timetables are organised

- the school buildings or facilities

Before you start writing

Plan your ideas. Think about:
- the problem you want to solve
- why it is a problem
- how your suggestion will solve it.

As you write
- Choose your vocabulary carefully, aiming to be persuasive.

When you have finished writing
- Check to see if any of your vocabulary choices could be improved.
- Check that your spelling and punctuation are accurate.

Ms H. Goh
New International School
College Road

Dear Ms Goh,

Yours sincerely,

This section links to pages 104–107 of the Workbook.

Section 6
Supporting key points

In this section, you will explore how writers support their ideas with evidence, examples and explanations.

▼ Read the newspaper article and then answer the questions that follow it.

ARTIFICIAL INTELLIGENCE COULD MAKE US STUPID

1 Once upon a time, if I wanted to find my way to somewhere unfamiliar, I would have pulled out a map and plotted my route. These days I just put the destination into my smartphone and let it make all the decisions.

2 Is this a simple, practical thing to do or, by relying on increasingly smarter phones, are we allowing them to make us, day by day, a little bit dumber?

3 My worry is this: why would you bother to learn a new language or drive a car or even teach someone else something if a machine can do it for you?

4 We need to keep challenging ourselves mentally, if we are to keep our brains supple and nimble. It is very much a case of use it or lose it.

5 But is there any real evidence that the use of modern technology is actually making us dumber? I'm sorry to say that there is. It is called the Flynn Effect.

6 It is named after a psychologist called James Flynn who, in the 1990s, looked at the results of hundreds of studies done on **IQ**[1] and discovered, to his surprise, that scores had been rising in most industrialised countries by about three points every decade.

In other words, someone who scored 100 on an IQ test in 1930 would probably have scored 115 in 1990. When I met Dr Flynn a few years later, I asked him: 'Why?'

7 He thought it was the result of a combination of factors including improved nutrition, more time in school and a more demanding intellectual environment.

The disturbing thing is the Flynn effect has now stopped.

8 Not only are IQ levels no longer rising, they are falling. No one knows why but plausible reasons are the rise of junk food, computer games, social media, a fall in reading and less face-to-face communication.

9 So if you want to keep your brain in good shape as you get older, what should you do? I recommend that you limit your screen time, and eat a diet rich in vegetables, olive oil and oily fish.

10 You need to remain active, physically and mentally, and keep up with old friends. Social isolation and loneliness are almost as bad for the brain as having high blood sugar levels.

11 In the years ahead, **AI**[2] will have an extraordinary impact on our lives, from self-driving cars to robot surgeons, but we would be foolish to allow ourselves to become too reliant on them.

12 I like my smartphone. But I like my brain even more.

Key vocabulary

IQ[1] (intelligence quotient): number representing reasoning ability that is measured using problem-solving tests, worked out in relation to an average score of 100

AI[2] (artificial intelligence): computer systems able to perform tasks that usually rely on human intelligence

Activity 1: Evidence

One way to support your ideas in an argument is with evidence. To prove their point of view, writers often use evidence such as an expert's opinion, scientific research and statistics from surveys.

1 The writer of the article on page 112 gives the reader evidence to support the viewpoint that human beings may be getting less intelligent.
   a) What kind of evidence has the writer used?
   b) What does the evidence tell us?
   c) What does the evidence imply?

Activity 2: Points, examples and comments

As well as evidence, writers usually support their ideas with examples and comments. A typical section or paragraph of an argument text may include:
- a key point
- an example to support it (possibly from the writer's own experience)
- a comment that explains how the point and the example support the writer's argument.

1 Look at the ideas in the first four paragraphs of the article on page 112:

Paragraphs 1 and 2

A   I used to use a map but now I use a smartphone to find my way.

B   We are becoming more and more reliant on our smartphones.

C   Not making our own decisions could make us less intelligent.

Paragraphs 3 and 4

D   We need to keep using and challenging our brains.

E   Learning a new language and learning to drive a car are challenging for our brains.

F   If we don't use our brains, they will lose their power and not work so well.

a) Which ideas are the key points?
b) Which ideas are examples?
c) Which ideas are comments that the writer uses to express their point of view?

Activity 3: Sequencing points, examples and comments

A point, an example and a comment used to express a point of view can be sequenced in different ways. Look again at the following sentence from the article on page 112.

> In the years ahead, AI will have an extraordinary impact on our lives, from self-driving cars to robot surgeons, but we would be foolish to allow ourselves to become too reliant on them.

1 In what order has the writer sequenced these three different elements? Choose one answer.

A point–example–comment	**B** point–comment–example
C example–point–comment	**D** example–comment–point
E comment–point–example	**F** comment–example–point

2 The sentence could be rewritten with the elements in a different order. For example:

> We would be foolish to allow ourselves to become too reliant on AI, such as self-driving cars and robot surgeons, as it will have an extraordinary impact on our lives in the years ahead.

a) Rewrite **two** new versions of the sentence, putting the three elements in **two** more different orders.

b) Which version of the sentence do you prefer: the original version, the rewritten example above or one of the versions you have written?

Grammar Boost: Linking points with adverbials

Adverbials help to make a clear connection between sentences and paragraphs. They help the reader to understand your meaning. Two ways that adverbials can be used are to signal supporting or contrasting information.

1 Rewrite the sentences below, adding fronted adverbials from the **Adverbial Bank** to help signal the ideas in the second and third sentences.

> We rely on our smart phones far too much. The more we use technology, the harder it becomes to imagine life without it. It is not too late to take back control of our lives.

Adverbial Bank

Showing support	Showing contrast
In addition	On the contrary
Furthermore	However
Indeed	On the other hand

Activity 4: Building a paragraph

You are going to write **two** paragraphs of an article arguing that technology improves our lives. In each paragraph, ensure you include:
- a key point
- an example to support it (from your own or someone else's experience)
- a comment that explains how the point and the example support the argument.

Plan

1 Write a sentence summing up the positive view of technology that you will argue.

2 Think about the different types of technology you could focus on. Choose **two** types of technology. You could choose from the suggestions below or use your own ideas.

mobile phones   personal computers   medical technology   robotics

Write

3 Focus on the first type of technology you have chosen.
   a) Write **one** key point for your first paragraph: a sentence stating how this technology can be used.
   b) Write one or two sentences containing examples or evidence that support your point. You could use an example from your own experience, an expert view, or a statistic.

   | When my grandmother was in hospital, she | According to leading experts, |

   c) Finally, you need to add a comment, explaining how your point and example support your argument. How do they show that technology improves our lives?

   | This shows that | It is clear that |

4 Write a second paragraph for your article, repeating the steps in question 3 as you focus on the second type of technology you have chosen.

Review and revise

5 Read back through your two paragraphs. Use adverbials of addition to support or contrast your ideas.

This section links to pages 108–111 of the Workbook.

Section 7
Structuring sentences

In this section, you will explore and experiment with the impact that different sentence structures can have on your writing.

This extract is an article taken from a news website. In the article, the writer expresses his views about manners.

▼ **Read the article and then answer the questions that follow it.**

● ● ●   Search...

Two words we ought not take for granted

1   I was brought up to always say "please" and "thank you".

That lesson has lived with me from my early years and I did my best, with my wife's help, to instil the same basic decency in my own children. I think we did a reasonable job; our children are generally well-mannered and polite. But it's their children I fear for. Not because I think they will fail to teach them the same lessons but
5   because society seems to expect it less and less.

It was obvious when my children brought home schoolfriends that not all of them had had the same parental instruction or, at least, been willing to apply it. Handing out slices of pizza or soft drinks, for instance, would usually elicit "thank yous" from most of them but by no means all.

10   To a parent of my age, it just seems rude. They may not necessarily be ungrateful but they simply don't see or understand that another individual has gone out of his or her way to benefit them.

I blame much of it on peer pressure; it has become "uncool" to acknowledge the services a parent supplies for his or her child. So what
15   if your mum has spent hours cooking your dinner or ironing your clothes – it's her job, isn't it?

And if today's children don't even say "thanks" to the people they care about most, what hope is there for the future? A new study looked at more than 1,000 examples of how gratitude is expressed in everyday conversations between friends, families and neighbours in eight different languages. They found that people almost always
20   responded positively to small requests for help but were rarely rewarded with gratitude in response.

You and I might put that down to simple bad manners but the scientists say it actually means that people take it for granted they will co-operate with each other and, therefore, the words "thank you" are no longer needed. "Our findings indicate that saying 'thank you' is not necessary," said Professor Nick Enfield, from the University of Sydney, who led the research.

25   To my mind, though, there's no excuse for failing to say "thank you". I honestly believe we should not take other people for granted, no matter how closely related they might be.

Activity 1: Identifying ideas and intentions

1 Writers sometimes use opinions, supporting ideas or statistics from experts as evidence to support their points of view.

a) The writer of the article on page 116 presents supporting ideas by referring to a scientific study. What were the scientific study's findings?

b) How does the writer use this scientific study in his article? What effect does he intend it to have? Write one or two sentences explaining your ideas.

2 What is the reader intended to think and feel after reading the article? Write one or two sentences explaining your ideas.

Activity 2: Exploring sentences

1 Short sentences can be used to create emphasis. Look at the heading and first two paragraphs of the article on page 116.

a) In the first sentence, the writer introduces the subject of his article by placing it in a shorter sentence. Why is it important that this sentence is emphasised?

b) The writer then uses a long second sentence, a shorter third sentence and a very short fourth sentence. Read them aloud. What point seems to have most emphasis?

c) The second paragraph could have been structured in several shorter sentences:

> That lesson has lived with me from my early years. I tried to instil the same basic decency in my own children. I did my best. My wife helped. I think we did a reasonable job. Our children are generally well-mannered and polite. But it's their children I fear for. It's not because I think they will fail to teach them the same lessons. Society seems to expect it less and less.

How is the impact of this paragraph changed if all the sentences are shorter?

2 Positioning a key idea or word at the end of a sentence can give it greater emphasis. Look again at the following sentence from the article.

> To a parent of my age, it just seems rude.

The writer could have chosen to sequence the sentence's two clauses the other way around:

> It just seems rude to a parent of my age.

a) Which word or phrase is emphasised in the original version?

b) How does this help the writer to make his point?

Punctuation Boost: Dashes and semi-colons

Dashes and semi-colons can be used to add emphasis to key ideas.

Look at these two sentences from the article on page 116. The writer could have used a conjunction to link the two halves of each sentence instead of a semi-colon or a dash:

as

I think we did a reasonable job ; our children are generally well-mannered and polite.

So what if your mum has spent hours cooking your dinner or ironing your clothes – it's her job, isn't it?

because

1 Copy the sentences below. Cross out the conjunction in each one and replace it with a semi-colon.

   a) You shouldn't talk with your mouth full and you shouldn't eat with your elbows on the table.

   b) Do not interrupt people talking but wait patiently until it is your turn.

   c) Hold the door open for other people behind you and they'll be very grateful.

2 Copy the sentences in question 1 again. This time, replace the conjunction with a dash.

3 Which do you prefer: the sentences with the conjunction, the sentences with the semi-colon or the sentences with the dash?

Activity 3: Experimenting with sentences

Look at the following three sentences.

> Your friends or an adult are talking to you.

> Don't look at your phone.   It's disrespectful.

1 You are going to experiment with lots of different ways of structuring these sentences.

   a) Link the first two sentences with a conjunction and leave the third sentence as a single-clause sentence.

   b) Rewrite your answer to question 1a, swapping the two clauses in the first sentence around.

   c) Link the three sentences using conjunctions to create one, multi-clause sentence.

   d) Link all three sentences again but sequence them in a different order.

   e) Rewrite your answer again, replacing a conjunction with a dash or semi-colon.

   f) Look at all the different versions you have written. Which version has the greatest impact? Write one or two sentences explaining your choice.

Activity 4: Writing sentences

1 Choose **one** thing that you think adults should teach children in order to make the world a better place. You could choose from the options below or use your own ideas.

respect | kindness | honesty | generosity | sharing

2 You are going to write three single-clause sentences about your chosen topic.
   a) Think of a situation in which children should show this quality or skill. Write **one** single-clause sentence about it.
   b) Think of an example showing how children in this situation could demonstrate this quality or skill. Write one single-clause sentence about it.
   c) Think of a reason why children, in this situation, should demonstrate this quality or skill. Write **one** single-clause sentence about it.

3 Look at the three sentences you have written.

   a) Check that each one is a single-clause sentence.
   b) Try rewriting the sentences in **three** different ways. You could:
   • link all three sentences using conjunctions
   • link two of your sentences and leave one as a shorter, single-clause sentence
   • change the sequence of clauses or sentences
   • use a semi-colon or a dash.

Conjunction Bank

and	but	when
as	before	after
until	because	so that
unless	although	if
	as long as	even though

4 Write a paragraph on your chosen topic, arguing that it is an important quality that children should be taught.

In your paragraph, you should:
• make a key point ⟵————————————
• support your point with an example
• explain why your point and example show the importance of the quality or skill you are writing about.

You could identify a benefit of the skill or quality you are writing about, or a problem created when children do not have that skill or quality.

5 The best writers use a variety of sentence structures and conjunctions to give their writing clarity and impact. Look at the paragraph you have written. Make any adjustments needed so that you have:

   • used at least **one** multi-clause sentence
   • used at least **one** single-clause sentence
   • not used any conjunction more than **once**
   • structured your sentences in different ways to create impact.

Section 8
Using rhetorical devices

In this section, you will explore ways in which rhetorical devices can add impact to your ideas.

This extract is the introduction to a book that aims to help parents keep their homes tidy by buying less and making more of the things they already have.

▼ **Read the extract and then answer the questions that follow it.**

Nobody really believes possessions equal joy. In fact, if specifically asked the question, nobody in their right mind would ever say the secret to a joyful life is to own a lot of stuff. Deep down, nobody really thinks it's true. Yet almost all of us live like it is.

From the moment we are born, we are told to pursue
5 more. Advertisements from every television, radio, newspaper, magazine, billboard, and website scream to us on a daily basis that more is better. As a result, we spend countless hours comparing our things to the person next to us. We measure our family's
10 success by the wealth of our belongings. And we end up looking for jobs that pay enough money so we can spend our adult lives purchasing the biggest homes, fanciest cars, trendiest fashions, most popular toys, and coolest technologies. But we all know it's not
15 true. We all know happiness cannot be bought at a department store. More is not necessarily better. We've just been told the lie so many times we begin to believe it – without even noticing. We live in a world that loves accumulating possessions. And while
20 nobody would ever admit they are trying to purchase happiness, most people live like they are.

But what if there was a better way to live life? One that recognizes the empty promises of advertisements and consumerism. One that champions the pursuit
25 of living with only the most essential possessions needed for life. One that boldly declares there is more joy in owning less than can be found in pursuing more.

That truth would change everything about us. It would
30 change the way we spend our hours, our energy, and our money. It would change where we focus our attention and our minds. It would change the very foundation of our lives.

In short, it would free us to pursue the things in life of
35 lasting value. It would be a completely life-changing and life-giving realization. And it may just line up with everything your heart, deep down, has been telling you all along.

Activity 1: Understanding ideas

1 Complete the sentences below to summarise the writer's point of view in the extract.

a)

The writer thinks we should not

b)

The writer thinks we should

Activity 2: Exploring rhetorical devices

Rhetorical devices are language techniques that can add impact to a writer's ideas.

1 Match the name of each rhetorical device below to its correct definition.

Rhetorical device	Definition
a) rhetorical question	(i) sequence of connected items written one after another
b) triple structure	(ii) doing or saying something more than once
c) repetition	(iii) method of speaking directly to the reader or listener
d) list	(iv) persuasive pattern of three ideas
e) direct address	(v) question asked when an answer is not expected

2 Make a copy of the table below, leaving plenty of space on each row. Look carefully through the extract. Find and add one example of each rhetorical device to the 'Examples' column of the table.

Rhetorical device	Example	Effect
rhetorical question		
triple structure		
repetition		
list		
direct address		

How do I do that?

Scan the extract for a question mark to find a rhetorical question. Scan for commas to find a list or pattern of three. Scan for the words 'you' or 'we' to find direct address. Then read the extract aloud and listen out for repetition.

3 Different rhetorical devices have different effects. Look carefully at the examples you have chosen from the extract. What effect does each device have? Add your ideas to the 'Effect' column of the table. You could use the suggestions below or your own ideas.

It highlights the range or variety of supporting ideas.	It suggests the writer's ideas are relevant to me.	It adds emphasis to a key idea.	It encourages the reader to think about the writer's ideas.

Punctuation Boost: Using apostrophes

An apostrophe can signal a contraction:

You can test if an apostrophe is needed by expanding the contraction. Does the sentence have the same meaning?

An apostrophe can also signal possession:

You can test if an apostrophe is needed to signal possession by reorganising the phrase using 'belonging to'.

She's going to the cinema.

She is going to the cinema. ✓

We went to Ali's house.

We went to the house belonging to Ali. ✓

Remember

- The word 'its' is a possessive pronoun, like 'yours'. It does **not** need an apostrophe.

- The word 'it's' is a contraction of 'it is'. It **does** need an apostrophe. For example: 'It's a beautiful day.'

1 Copy and complete the sentences below by adding apostrophes in the correct places.
a) A pictures worth a thousand words, its said.
b) Its true that we should not judge a book by its cover.
c) Peoples possessions dont bring them happiness.
d) Everyones goal should be their familys happiness.

Activity 3: Using rhetorical devices

1 Rewrite the sentences below, using one or more rhetorical devices to add impact to your ideas.

Many people enjoy shopping.

When people buy something new, it can make them feel happy.

The feeling does not last long.

People soon feel bored with their new possessions.

People soon realise their house is filled with things they do not need or use.

You could rewrite one sentence as a rhetorical question: 'Do you…?'

You could replace the adjectives 'happy' or 'bored' with a triple structure of adjectives.

You could use direct address by replacing the word 'people' with a pronoun.

You could replace the word 'things' with a list giving examples of those things.

You could add a new sentence containing repetition of a word or phrase in a statement.

Activity 4: Adding impact to your ideas

You are going to write a paragraph arguing your point of view.

Choose your focus

1 What do you think people do too often or too much? You could choose from the ideas below or use your own ideas.

We create too much plastic waste.	We spend too long staring at computer screens.	We spend too much time on social media.
We watch television too often.	We worry about our appearance too much.	We spend too much money.

Gather your ideas

2 Think about the focus you have chosen for your argument.

   a) Note down **two** reasons why this is a poor use of people's time.

   b) Note down **two** things you think people should do instead.

Write

3 Think again about the focus you have chosen for your argument. Write **one** paragraph arguing that people should do this less. In your paragraph, you should:

- make a key point ◄─────── *You could mention one of the ideas you noted in question 2b as a solution to support your argument.*
- support your point with an example
- explain how your point and example show this is a poor use of people's time.

Review

4 Carefully reread the paragraph you have written, looking for opportunities to use one or more rhetorical devices to add impact to your ideas. You could:

- use direct address to make your ideas feel even more relevant to the reader
- use a rhetorical question to encourage the reader to think about your ideas
- use a triple structure or repetition to add emphasis to a key idea
- use a list to highlight the range or variety of a key idea.

Section 9
Introductions and conclusions

In this section, you will explore the contribution that introductions and conclusions make to effective argument texts.

Extract A is made up of two sections from the article you read in Section 7. Extract B is made up of two sections from the book introduction you read in Section 8.

For each extract, the first section is the text's first one or two paragraphs: its **introduction**. The second section is the text's last paragraph: its **conclusion**.

▼ **Reread the extracts and then answer the questions that follow them.**

Extract A

1 **Introduction**

I was brought up to always say "please" and "thank you".

That lesson has lived with me from my early years and I did my best, with my wife's help, to instil the same basic decency in my
5 own children. I think we did a reasonable job; our children are generally well-mannered and polite. But it's their children I fear for. Not because I think they will fail to teach them the same lessons but because society seems to expect it less and less.

Conclusion

10 To my mind, though, there's no excuse for failing to say "thank you". I honestly believe we should not take other people for granted, no matter how closely related they might be.

Extract B

Introduction

Nobody really believes possessions equal joy. In fact, if
15 specifically asked the question, nobody in their right mind would ever say the secret to a joyful life is to own a lot of stuff. Deep down, nobody really thinks it's true. Yet almost all of us live like it is.

Conclusion

20 In short, it would free us to pursue the things in life of lasting value. It would be a completely life-changing and life-giving realization. And it may just line up with everything your heart, deep down, has been telling you all along.

Activity 1: Exploring an introduction

An argument text should begin with an introduction. An effective introduction should:
- introduce the topic
- introduce the writer's point of view
- engage the reader.

1 Look again at the introduction in Extract A on page 124.
  a) What is the writer's topic? Which sentence or phrase introduces it?
  b) What is the writer's point of view? Which sentence or phrase introduces it?

2 Look again at the introduction in Extract B.
  a) What is the writer's topic? Which sentence or phrase introduces it?
  b) What is the writer's point of view? Which sentence or phrase introduces it?

Activity 2: Engaging the reader

An effective introduction must engage the reader, to ensure they read on. There are lots of ways in which writers can engage readers' interest in their arguments. They could use:

- a personal anecdote

  When I was around seven years old, my father took me to the

- a surprising fact or statistic

  It has been estimated that the world's population increases by one person every eleven seconds.

- a controversial statement

  The human race will destroy itself.

- a rhetorical question

  How will your life change in the next five years?

1 Look again at the introduction in Extract A on page 124.
  a) Which technique or techniques does the writer use to engage the reader?
  b) What does this introduction make you think and feel? Write one or two sentences explaining your response to the introduction.

2 Look again at the introduction in Extract B.
  a) Which technique or techniques does the writer use to engage the reader?
  b) What does this introduction make you think and feel?
    Write one or two sentences explaining your response to the introduction.

Activity 3: Exploring a conclusion

An argument text should finish with a conclusion. An effective conclusion should:
- summarise the writer's key ideas
- emphasise the writer's views
- leave the reader thinking about the writer's argument.

1 Look again at the conclusion in Extract A on page 124.
   a) Which sentence or phrase summarises the writer's key ideas?
   b) Which sentence or phrase emphasises the writer's views?
   c) What does the conclusion make you think and feel? Write one or two sentences explaining your response to the conclusion.

2 Look again at the conclusion in Extract B.
   a) Which sentence or phrase summarises the writer's key ideas?
   b) Which sentence or phrase emphasises the writer's views?
   c) What does the conclusion make you think and feel? Write one or two sentences explaining your response to the conclusion.

Skills Boost: Writing in a formal register

An argument text can be more persuasive when it is written in a formal register. This can make the writer's views seem to have more authority and the information seem more trustworthy. When you write in a formal register, you should:

avoid slang and contractions	~~don't~~	do not ✓
	~~won't~~	will not ✓
avoid double negatives	~~We will not never~~	We will never ✓
ensure you use correct subject–verb agreement	~~He do~~	He does ✓
avoid using first-person singular pronouns in very formal writing	~~It seems to me that~~	It seems that ✓

1 Rewrite the sentences below using a more formal register.
   a) We won't never save our planet if we doesn't change our ways.
   b) Our garbage will keep piling up and we'll disappear beneath it!!
   c) In my opinion, it'll be awesome if people stops throwing away their rubbish and starts recycling it.

Activity 4: Writing an introduction and conclusion

You are going to plan an article that argues your point of view. You are then going to write only the introduction and conclusion of your article.

Gather your ideas

Your topic is: Money cannot buy happiness.

1 Decide whether you are going to argue for or against this point of view.

2 Identify **three or four** key points you could use to build your argument. You could choose from the suggestions below or use your own ideas.

What people think they want	What people really want
• the latest technology	• good friends
• a good car and house	• a loving family
• fashionable clothes	• a sense of achievement

> According to psychologists, 90% of what makes us happy or unhappy has nothing to do with money or what it can buy.

Even very wealthy people can be unhappy.	People can lead unhappy lives in beautiful homes.	Having no money can make you miserable.	Everyone needs to buy things to survive.

Write your introduction

3 Now you are going to write the introduction of your article.
a) Write **one** sentence that introduces the topic.
b) Write **one** sentence that introduces your point of view.
c) Write one or two sentences that will engage the reader's interest. You could use an anecdote, a surprising fact or statistic, a controversial statement or a rhetorical question.
d) Sequence the sentences you have written for your introduction, considering how you could introduce your article and engage the reader most effectively.

Write your conclusion

4 Finally, you are going to write the conclusion of your article.
a) Write **one** sentence that summarises your key ideas on money and happiness.
b) Write **one** sentence that emphasises your views. You could do this by highlighting how your ideas will solve problems or improve lives.

This section links to pages 120–123 of the Workbook.

Section 10
Reviewing and revising

In this section, you will explore ways of correcting and developing a response to give it as much impact as possible.

The following extract is one student's article arguing for a change that would make the world a better place.

▼ **Read the extract and then answer the questions that follow it.**

We Need Less Concrete and More Flowers and Trees in our Towns and Cities

1   Lots and lots of people live in towns and cities. Cities are great becuase you can get whatever you need whenever you need it but they can also be dirty, smelly and crowded. That is why we need more flowers and trees in our cities to make them better places to live.

2   Trees can help the environment by cleaning the air, they help to get rid of harmful dust and pollution. Scientific research shows that one tree can remove more than ten kilograms of carbon dioxide out of our air every year. This helps stop carbon dioxide going into the Earths atmosphere and changing our climate.

3   If we can stop damaging the climate it would be good for animals and plants too because climate change is making them become extinct. We can build more cities but if we destroy our planet we cannot build another one.

4   If their are more parks and trees and flowers in our cities people will go out more. Being outdoors is good for our physical and mental health. One survey found that time spent enjoying nature can help people overcome stress and depression. If there is nowhere to go out, people spend their time their homes watching the television or staring at screens and this is bad for us.

5   The more we help nature, the more it helps us. We need to stop building up our cities and make some space for grass and trees and flowers because it would be good for the planet, and good for everyone on the planet.

Activity 1: Checking for key features

<u>Argument text checklist</u>
- The text begins with an introduction.
  - The introduction introduces the topic.
  - The introduction introduces the writer's point of view.
- The text builds its argument in the main body of the text.
  - Each paragraph in the main body includes a key point.
  - Each paragraph in the main body includes evidence.
  - Each paragraph in the main body features a comment that explains the importance of the point.
- The text ends with a conclusion.
  - The conclusion summarises the writer's key ideas.
  - The conclusion emphasises the writer's views.

1 Answer the following questions 'Yes' or 'No'.
   a) Does the extract on page 128 have an introduction?
   b) Does the introduction introduce the topic?
   c) Does the introduction introduce the writer's point of view?

2 Answer the following questions 'Yes' or 'No'. If you answer 'No', note down which paragraph or paragraphs are missing the feature.
   a) Does the extract have a main body in which the writer builds the argument?
   b) Does each paragraph in the main body make a key point?
   c) Does each paragraph in the main body include evidence or an example?
   d) Does each paragraph in the main body include a comment that explains the importance of the main point?

> **Remember**
>
> Evidence could be:
> - an expert's opinion
> - scientific research
> - statistics from surveys
> - an example from the writer's own experience.

3 Answer the following questions 'Yes' or 'No'.
   a) Does the extract have a conclusion?
   b) Does the conclusion summarise the writer's key ideas?
   c) Does the conclusion emphasise the writer's views?

4 Look again at your answers to questions 1–3. Each time you answered 'No', you identified a missing feature. For each missing feature, write one or two sentences that could be added to improve the extract.

Activity 2: Reviewing vocabulary and sentence structure

When you have finished writing a text, you should review your vocabulary choices to make sure every word is helping you to achieve your intention.

1 What is the writer's intention in the extract on page 128? Complete the following sentences.

A   The writer intends to present cities as

B   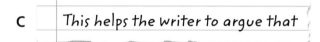The writer intends to present trees and flowers as

C   This helps the writer to argue that

2 Look at the vocabulary that the writer has used. Identify **three** words or phrases that add emphasis to the writer's ideas and help them to achieve their intention.

3 Identify **three** vocabulary choices in the extract that could be improved. For each one, suggest **two or three** options that would be more effective.

4 Think about the rhetorical devices the writer has used.
   a) Note down the name of any device you can spot in the extract. Add an example of each device you have identified.
   b) Choose a sentence from the extract that you feel could have more impact. Rewrite it using a rhetorical device.

Rhetorical devices

A writer could use:
- a rhetorical question
- a triple structure
- repetition
- a list
- direct address

5 Think about the sentence structures the writer has used.

Remember

Positioning a key idea or word at the end of a sentence can give it greater emphasis.

Look at each of the longer, multi-clause sentences in the extract. Choose **one** sentence and experiment with **two or three** different ways of restructuring it to add more emphasis. You could:
- break the multi-clause sentence down into two or more shorter sentences
- swap the clauses in the sentence around.

Skills Boost: Looking for careless errors

Some mistakes cannot be helped if you do not realise you have made them. You should, however, be able to find all of the mistakes in the extract on page 128. Use the table below to help you.

Missing or repeated words	Proofread slowly to spot missing words: when you are proofreading, you sometimes read what you think you have written, not what you have actually written.
Spelling errors in common words	You should aim to recognise when words that you see every day look incorrect or unfamiliar.
Comma splices	These are commas that should be full stops. Look at every comma you have used in your writing to be sure that it has been used correctly.
Missing apostrophes	Look out for contractions and any word that ends in 's'. Ask yourself: Is this word indicating possession?
Choosing homophones	Look out particularly for the following common homophones: their | there | they're | too | two to | no | know | hear | here

1 **a)** Read the extract carefully once, checking for mistakes. Note down each word or phrase in which you see an error and how you would correct it.

b) There is one error of each type in the extract. Read the extract again, looking for the errors you did not spot when you answered question 1a. Note them down in the order in which you find them. Note how you would correct each error.

2 Look again at your answers to question 1. They should tell you which common errors you can spot quickly and which errors require you to proofread more slowly and carefully. Use your answers to question 1b to create a proofreading checklist to help you revise all the errors in your writing.

Proofreading Checklist

1

2

3

This section links to pages 124–125 of the Workbook.

Section 11
Assessment

In this section, you will write an article arguing your point of view.

Activity 1: Planning

A magazine has asked you to write an article about something you think would make the world a better place. You will need to argue your point of view to convince readers to agree with you.

1 What will be your article's topic? You could refer to the suggestions below to help you choose or use your own ideas.

The environment

Wildlife

Recycling

Education

Technology

Money

2 Work out your point of view by answering each of the questions below:
- What is the problem?
- Why is it a problem?
- What should we do about it?

Note down two or three key points for each.

| Currently, it is clear that, | This will mean that |

3 **a)** Note down some evidence to support **two or three** of your key points. This could be:
  - an expert's opinion
  - scientific research
  - statistics from surveys
  - an example from your own experience.

b) Note down how the key point and evidence support your main argument.

Key point	Evidence	Comment
•	•	•
•	•	•
•	•	•

c) Decide on the order in which you will make each of your points. Number them.

4 Plan your conclusion using the following instructions.
  a) Note down **one** sentence summarising your key ideas.
  b) Note down **one** sentence summarising your point of view.

Activity 2: Writing

1 Write your article. Include all the key points you noted down, to ensure you have included all the features of argument texts you have studied during the unit.

As you write, use:
- a suitable language style
- precise, varied and interesting vocabulary
- a variety of sentence lengths, with a variety of conjunctions.

Activity 3: Reviewing and revising

1 Read through your article.

Check that:
- the register you have chosen suits your content
- you have made effective use of rhetorical devices
- you have made effective vocabulary choices
- you have used a variety of single- and multi-clause sentences
- you have consistently used the same tense and person throughout your writing
- your spelling, punctuation and grammar are accurate.

Unit 4
World of sport

This unit focuses on the topic of sport. Some of the sports covered in these texts are well-known around the world, such as cricket and volleyball, some are more familiar in certain countries, such as sepak takraw and sumo, and others are unusual in many countries, such as worm charming and gurning! Which sports do you think you might like to try?

In this unit, you will...

- develop your skills in reading, understanding and summarising an information text.

- explore how writers select information and add description to achieve their intention.

- develop your skills in selecting relevant, focused evidence to support your response to an information text.

- explore the writer's choice of vocabulary.

- develop your skills in responding to a text.

- answer questions on a short extract and write a critical response to assess your progress.

- explore ways of structuring information texts to guide the reader and convey information effectively.

- explore the writer's choice of different sentence structures and their impact on the reader.

- develop your skills in identifying significant choices the writer has made, so that you can comment on their effect.

- compare the information in two extracts, and the writers' different intentions.

- answer questions on two extracts to assess your progress in this unit.

By the end of this unit, you will be able to analyse an information text, exploring the writer's choices and their impact on the reader.

Section 1
Summarising

In this section, you will develop your skills in reading, understanding and summarising an information text.

▼ **Read the information text and then answer the questions that follow it.**

The history of cricket

1   Nobody really knows where or when cricket was first played. There are records of games played with a bat and ball as early as the eighth century in the Punjab region (in areas of eastern Pakistan and northern India), in the ninth century around the Mediterranean and in the twelfth century in Britain. However, the first mention of a game called 'creckett' was in 1597, in Britain.

5   In the late seventeenth and early eighteenth centuries, everyone from the wealthiest members of the nobility to the poorest farmworkers played cricket in Britain. The sport increased in popularity with the nobility as they became more competitive. People got more and more desperate to win: one story tells of a player in the early eighteenth
10 century trying to use a cricket bat that was even wider than the wicket, making it almost impossible for him to lose! Soon, rules were introduced, including setting the maximum width of the bat at 4 **inches**[1]. In 1744, an official "rulebook" was written and printed on a handkerchief. It gave the length of the pitch (22 **yards**[2]), the height and width of the
15 wicket (22 inches tall and 6 inches wide), and the weight of the ball (5–6 **ounces**[3]).

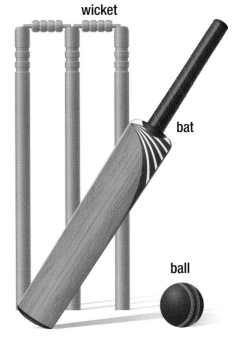

wicket

bat

ball

Cricket games in London soon began to attract attention, and huge crowds would gather. So, in 1787, Thomas Lord leased some land in London and created a private cricket ground where he and his
20 wealthy friends could play in peace and privacy. The ground became known as Lord's, and the cricket club that played there was named the Marylebone Cricket Club, or MCC. In 1788, the MCC published a collection of the game rules that they followed. Other cricket clubs quickly began to follow these rules. The MCC is still today responsible
25 for the official rules of cricket.

The most dramatic change to the rules came in 1864. Before then, only underarm bowling was allowed. With the introduction of overarm bowling, it became much harder to score runs and much easier for a player to be got out.

Over the next 50 years, cricket spread around the world to Australia, New Zealand, the Caribbean, Asia and South Africa. The first match between Australia and England was contested in 1877. Australia won, much to England's
30 surprise and horror. The following day, an English newspaper published an **obituary**[4] with the title 'The Death of English Cricket', saying that 'the body will be cremated and the ashes taken to Australia'. This is why the series of matches that has been played between
35 England and Australia approximately every two years ever since was dubbed 'The Ashes'.

Key vocabulary

inch[1]: a unit of length equivalent to 2.54 cm
yard[2]: a unit of length equivalent to 91.44 cm
ounce[3]: a unit of mass equivalent to 28.35 g
obituary[4]: a notice that someone has died, often found in a newspaper

Skills Boost: Word families

Thinking about word families can help you to understand and spell longer and unfamiliar words. All of the words below are part of the 'act' family: they are formed from the root word 'act' with the addition of a prefix, a suffix or both.

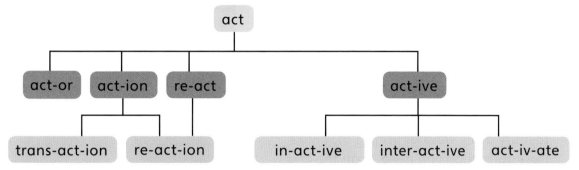

1 Note down all the prefixes and suffixes that have been added to the root word in the family tree above. Then list as many words as you can that begin or end with each of them.

Prefixes	re-: reread
Suffixes	-or: visitor

Activity 1: Working out unfamiliar words

Look again at the following sentences from the information text on page 136, focusing on the four highlighted words.

A In the late seventeenth and early eighteenth centuries, everyone from the wealthiest members of the nobility to the poorest farmworkers played cricket in Britain.

B So, in 1787, Thomas Lord leased some land in London and created a private cricket ground

C The first match between Australia and England was contested in 1877.

D This is why the series of matches that has been played between England and Australia approximately every two years ever since was dubbed 'The Ashes'.

1 Note down what you think or know each of the highlighted words means. For each one, write a sentence explaining the clues you used to work out its meaning.

How do I do that?

You may be able to work out the meaning of unfamiliar words by thinking about:
- their context: the rest of the sentence, which can give you some clues
- any similarities with a word you do know: if the unknown word is spelled in a similar way to a word you know, it may have a similar meaning.

Activity 2: Linking ideas

Sometimes you will need to find information and ideas that are linked or related in some way.

1 In the information text on page 136, there are a number of pieces of information about changes in the rules of cricket. Identify **three** of them.

How do I do that?

- Identify a key word or phrase that links the information you need. Scan the text to find a place where that word or phrase appears. In this case, you could scan the text for the word 'rules'.
- Every time you find the word or phrase you are scanning for, read around it to find the information you need.

2 Rewrite your answer to question 1 using full sentences to link the information you have found.

How do I do that?

There are different ways in which you can link the pieces of related information you have found.
- You could link them in a series of sentences, beginning each sentence with an adverbial, such as *Firstly*, *Secondly*, *Then* or *Finally*. See Example A below.

Example A

> The rules of cricket have changed several times over the years. Firstly, in the early eighteenth century, it was decided that

- You could use a colon to introduce a list. The list could be a part of the sentence or you could use bullet points. If items in a list are long, bullet points may be better. See Example B below.

Example B

> The rules of cricket have changed several times over the years:
> - In the early eighteenth century, it was decided that

Activity 3: Writing a summary

The information text on page 136 is over 400 words long. You are going to write a summary of the text in **75** words or fewer. As there are five paragraphs in the text, you will need to summarise each paragraph using an average of **15** words per paragraph. Consider the following two methods of summarising a paragraph of text.

Method 1: Select the most important sentence in the paragraph and rewrite it in your own words. For example, for the first paragraph:

> Nobody really knows   where or when cricket was first played.

> *No one is sure | who invented cricket.*

The sentence has been broken up and each part has been rewritten.

---

1 Use Method 1 to summarise the second paragraph of the text by completing these steps.
   a) Which sentence in the second paragraph gives you the most information about how and why cricket developed? Note down your chosen sentence.
   b) Break down your chosen sentence into **two or three** parts.
   c) Look at each part of the sentence. Cross out any that are not essential.
   d) Rewrite the information in each of the remaining parts using different words.
   e) Link what you have written to create your own sentence.

Method 2: Select all the important pieces of information in the paragraph and link them. For example, for the first paragraph:

- games played with a bat and ball
- eighth century in the Punjab region
- ninth century around the Mediterranean
- twelfth century in Britain

- first mention of a game called 'creckett' being played was in 1597, in Britain

> *People have played bat and ball games for centuries* ← The less important pieces of information have been summarised.

> *but cricket was first recorded in Britain in 1597.* ← The most important piece of information has been given separately.

---

2 Use Method 2 to summarise the third paragraph of the text by completing these steps.
   a) Identify **three or four** key pieces of information from the third paragraph.
   b) Select the **most important** piece of information and rewrite it in your own words.
   c) Add a comment that gives the general meaning of the other pieces of information you have noted.

3 Choose either method to summarise the fourth and fifth paragraphs of the information text.

Section 2
Informing and describing

In this section, you will explore how writers select information and add description to achieve their intention.

This is an extract from an article on a UK news website.

▼ **Read the extract and then answer the questions that follow it.**

The world's weirdest sports

1 There are some weird world-class events around – like the International Cherry Pit-Spitting Championship, where on Saturday new champ Brian Krause managed to spit his cherry stone an astonishing 80ft with the help of strong winds in Michigan, US. And pit-spitting – launched in 1974 to mark the local cherry harvest – sounds positively sensible compared with some of these other mad contests from around the globe…

5 **World gurning awards**
This ugly battle can be traced back to 1852. Competitors frame their nastiest expressions through a horse collar and compete for the world championship in Cumbria. Toothless people traditionally do it best. Last year's top gurner was 47-year-old Tommy Mattinson, a 15-time global champ unbeaten since 2000.

10 **Worm charming**
Enthusiasts descend on Willaston in Cheshire to bang, tap and stab the ground with pitchforks to entice worms to the surface. It began in 1980 when a farmer's son charmed 511 worms above ground. This year's winners managed 394.

15 **Extreme ironing**
Launched in Leicester in 1997, this risky activity requires contenders to iron clothes in locations such as mountainsides, on ice and under water. The Extreme Ironing Bureau says: "It is an outdoor activity that combines the danger and excitement of an extreme sport with the satisfaction of a
20 well-pressed shirt."

Baby crawling
First held in Colombia, this is now staged all over the world. Babies are enticed by their parents – some waving toys – to reach the finish line, crawling in a straight line for five metres. It took just eight seconds for 13-month-old Stanley Sim Ping Han to crawl 2.4 metres and win this year's contest in Singapore. Most entrants don't even finish
25 the course.

Indoor skydiving
Competitors leap through a giant wind tunnel and try to break records including the highest number of somersaults in a minute and the longest lasting free falls.

In 2012, Singapore's Ezriel Shah Rahmat broke the free-fall record with a marathon session lasting four hours, two
30 minutes and 12 seconds.

Activity 1: Understanding and responding

1 To answer each question below, identify a key word or phrase in the question and note it down. Then scan the extract on page 140 to find it, and read around the key word to find the answer to the question.

a) In what year was the International Cherry Pit-Spitting Championship launched?

b) In which event is Tommy Mattinson the champion?

c) In which event do competitors use a pitchfork?

d) Where can extreme ironing take place? Identify **three** locations.

e) Which event was won by Stanley Sim Ping Han?

> Key word: launched
>
> Answer: The Championship was launched in

2 a) Which of the sports mentioned in the extract do you find the weirdest?

b) Note down the **one** piece of information that most strongly influenced your answer, writing one or two sentences to explain your choice.

Activity 2: Types of information

Information texts about events, such as the sports events described in the extract on page 140, often given information about:

- **what** happens in the event
- **when** the event happens or first happened
- **where** the event happens
- **who** is involved in the event
- **how** the event is won.

1 Look at each of the events described in the extract. Has the writer given 'what', 'when', 'where', 'who' and 'how' information about each of the six sporting events described? Copy and complete a table like the one below, adding ticks to show whether the writer has included each type of information.

	What	When	Where	Who	How
1. Cherry pit-spitting					
2. World gurning awards					
3. Worm charming					

Activity 3: Informing and describing

In an information text, the writer's purpose is to convey facts to the reader. Adding some description to those facts can help to create a picture in the reader's mind. This picture can help the reader understand the facts, and make the text more interesting and engaging.

Look again at the sections on worm charming and indoor skydiving in the extract on page 140.

1 a) Identify **one** fact in the section on worm charming.
   b) Identify **one** word or phrase that the writer has used to add descriptive detail in the section on worm charming.
   c) Describe the picture this word or phrase creates in your mind.

2 a) Identify **one** fact in the section on indoor skydiving.
   b) Identify **one** word or phrase that the writer has used to add descriptive detail in the section on indoor skydiving.
   c) Describe the picture this word or phrase creates in your mind.

Skills Boost: Identifying intentions

A writer can intend to create certain responses in the reader. For example, the writer's intention could be to create a response of:

| humour | tension | fear | excitement | sympathy |

1 Look at each of the short extracts below. For each extract, note down what you think the writer's intention is and what elements of each extract helped you to identify this. You could consider:
 • the extract's content
 • the writer's vocabulary choice
 • whether the extract's register is formal or informal.

   a) When I had finished listing all his faults, I turned around – and there he was, standing right behind me!
   b) I stepped out onto the stage and looked out across the audience. I opened my mouth, but nothing came out. Silence.
   c) Holding my breath, I edged slowly forward into the darkness. The floorboards creaked with every step, and the pulsing of my blood thumped in my ears. I had to get out of there.

2 Look again at the extract on page 140. What do you think its writer's intention is?

Activity 4: Writing an information text

You are going to write an information text about an imaginary 'weird' sport.

Imagine

1 What sport will you create? For example, it could be:
- a kind of race, like baby crawling
- a distance event, like cherry-pit spitting
- an everyday activity carried out in an unusual place, like extreme ironing.

Plan

2 Note down some imaginary 'facts' about your imaginary sport. Include:
- **what** happens in the event
- **when** the event happens or first happened
- **where** the event happens
- **who** is involved in the event
- **how** the event is won.

3 Now think about the impression or picture you want to create in the reader's mind when they read about the event you have imagined.

a) Write one or two sentences describing the picture you want to create in the reader's mind.
b) Note down vocabulary that would help to create that picture in the reader's mind. You could think in particular about your choice of verbs. For example:

race | fly | hurtle | chase | dash | sprint | hurl | jump | dive | plunge | leap

4 Finally, think about your intention.

How do you want your reader to respond to the information and description you write? For example, you could create:

humour | fear | excitement | sympathy

5 Look at the choices you have made in your planning. Add **two or three** facts or descriptive details that would help you to achieve your intention.

Write

6 Write an information text about the sport you have imagined. Aim to:
- write **50–100** words
- use the information and descriptive vocabulary you have gathered in your planning
- think about your intention as you write.

Section 3
Selecting evidence

In this section, you will develop your skills in selecting relevant, focused evidence to support your response to an information text.

This extract is an information text about the southeast Asian sport of Sepak Takraw.

▼ Read the information text and then answer the questions that follow it.

1 It may be difficult to imagine a sport which combines elements of volleyball, badminton and football, but sepak takraw does all of this. It is a game which has become increasingly popular in Southeast Asia. The name is a combination of words from two
5 languages; 'sepak' is Malaysian for 'kick', and 'takraw' is the Thai word for 'ball'. The sport is similar to volleyball. However, whereas in volleyball the players keep the ball aloft with their hands, sepak takraw players must use the feet, chest, knees or head – a rule which requires amazing athleticism. Another
10 difference from volleyball is that sepak takraw is played with a ball woven from flexible woody vines called rattan.

The game originated in Malaysia in the fifteenth century and spread to Indonesia and Thailand. Originally, the attraction of the game was the opportunity for players to demonstrate their skills
15 by passing the ball while keeping it airborne. In 1933, a net was introduced, and in the following 20 years, the competitive version of the game spread rapidly across Southeast Asia, and formal rules were introduced.

Each game takes place on a court the size of a double badminton
20 court, with a net between 1.4 and 1.5 metres long, and three players per team. Points are scored by forcing the opposing team to commit a fault – these faults can include the ball failing to cross the net; landing outside the court boundaries; or touching the ground, ceiling, or another object. There are 21 points per
25 set, and to win the game, a team must have won two sets.

In Myanmar, there is a variation of the game called chinlone. Chinlone is considered to be a graceful, non-competitive sport, with a focus on the movements of the players and the art of the game. The beautiful movements are also one of the
30 main attractions in sepak takraw, with players demonstrating breathtaking agility and strength: leaping, twisting and kicking to get the ball past their opponents. As with volleyball, the most powerful point-scoring move is the spike, which involves standing near the net and striking the ball downwards with such force that it hits the ground before the opposition
35 can touch it. However, as the use of hands is forbidden in chinlone and sepak takraw, players are required to perform spectacular somersaults to get their feet above the net, turning their whole bodies elegantly in the air then quickly landing, or occasionally crashing, to the ground.

Activity 1: Identifying and inferring key ideas

Some of the ideas and information in the extract on page 144 are clearly stated, and some of them are implied. To answer the questions below, you will need to use your scanning skills and your inference skills.

1 What do the words 'sepak' and 'takraw' mean?

2 Where did the game originate?

3 The writer includes factual information about a sport very similar to sepak takraw, called chinlone, played in Myanmar. What impression does this information create of the difference between chinlone and sepak takraw?

4 When was a net first introduced to sepak takraw?

5 Look at the final paragraph of the text again. How does the writer suggest that players of Sepak Takraw are not always agile and elegant?

6 In what way is sepak takraw like:
   a) volleyball?
   b) football?

Activity 2: Exploring vocabulary choice

Look at these quotations from the extract on page 144.

A It is a game which is has become increasingly popular in Southeast Asia.

B However, whereas in volleyball the players keep the ball aloft with their hands, sepak takraw players must use the feet, chest, knees or head – a rule which requires amazing athleticism.

C As with volleyball, the most powerful point-scoring move is the spike, which involves standing near the net and striking the ball downwards with such force that it hits the ground before the opposition can touch it.

D The beautiful movements are also one of the main attractions in sepak takraw

1 Which word or phrase in which quotation most strongly suggests that:
   a) sepak takraw is liked by more and more people
   b) sepak takraw players are highly skilled
   c) sepak trakaw players are very agile and pleasant to watch
   d) the spike move in volleyball and sepak takraw requires strength.

Grammar Boost: Clauses

Clauses are the building blocks of sentences. Every clause is structured around a verb. Look at the sentence below. It is a **single-clause sentence** about hiding. Each word or phrase in the clause adds information to the verb 'hid'.

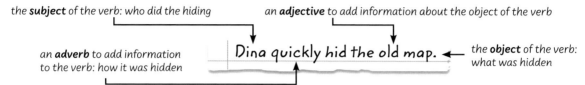

the **subject** of the verb: who did the hiding

an **adjective** to add information about the object of the verb

an **adverb** to add information to the verb: how it was hidden

Dina quickly hid the old map.

the **object** of the verb: what was hidden

1 How many clauses are there in each of these sentences from the text on page 146?

a) The game originated in Malaysia in the fifteenth century and spread to Indonesia and Thailand.

b) Each game takes place on a court the size of a double badminton court

c) There are 21 points per set, and to win the game, a team must have won two sets.

Activity 3: Focusing on evidence

When you write a response to a text, you need to support your ideas with evidence. The most effective quotations are short and focused on the point you are making.

1 Look at one student's choice of quotation to support their point below.

> The writer describes the sport to make it sound exciting: 'The beautiful movements are also one of the main attractions in sepak takraw, with players demonstrating breathtaking agility and strength: leaping, twisting and kicking to get the ball past their opponents.'

a) Divide this sentence into three parts or **clauses**. Which part of the sentence most clearly makes the sport sound exciting? Write it down.

b) Look at the part of the sentence you have written down. Identify one or two words or phrases that most clearly make the sport sound exciting.

c) Now, rewrite the student's point, replacing each **?** with your chosen words or phrases as evidence. For example,

> The writer describes the agility of the sport as **?** with players **?** to make it sound exciting.

2 You are going to make a point and support it with short, focused evidence.

a) Identify a sentence in the information text on page 144 in which the writer suggests the competitive version of sepak takraw became popular very quickly.

b) Which word or phrase in your chosen quotation most clearly emphasises or highlights how quickly the competitive version became popular?

c) Write a sentence in which you make the point that the writer suggests the competitive version became popular quickly, using your quotation to support it.

Activity 4: Writing a response

When you write a response to a text, you first need to identify the points you want to make and the evidence you will use to support those points. A good way to begin this is by focusing on the writer's intention: the response the writer wants to create in you, the reader.

> **Remember**
>
> Each paragraph of a response should include:
> * a **topic sentence** making a key point: what the writer has done
> * a short, relevant **quotation** as evidence to show where the writer has done this
> * a **comment** to explain the impression the writer has created in the quotation.

You are going to write **two paragraphs** in response to the following question: What impression of sepak takraw does the writer create?

Plan

1 What impressions do you get of the sport of sepak takraw from the extract on page 144? You could choose some of the ideas below or use your own.

2 Choose **two** of the ideas you have noted. These will be the focus of the two paragraphs you are going to write, so choose the two strongest. Circle them.

exciting　　popular　　skilful　　athletic　　dramatic

3 Now select a short, relevant quotation to support **each** of the ideas you have circled.

Write

4 Write a topic sentence about the first idea you have circled. You could include your quotation in your topic sentence or add it in a second sentence.

The writer creates the impression that

The word '____' suggests that the sport is

5 Finally, add a comment, explaining how the writer's choice of ideas or vocabulary in your quotation have helped to create the impression you noted.

This implies that the sport is

6 Repeat questions 4 and 5, using the second idea you have circled to write your second paragraph.

Section 4
Exploring vocabulary choice

In this section, you will explore the writer's choice of vocabulary.

▼ **Read the article and then answer the questions that follow it.**

Flying Frisians: The curious sport of Fierljeppen

1 As the whistle blows, Jacob de Groot sprints towards the canal. Just at the water's edge, he leaps up towards a vertical pole, grabs it and propels himself through the air above the muddy canal. As the pole lurches forward, de Groot frantically climbs up as momentum takes him to the other side of the water and dry land. This is the Netherlands oldest sport, Fierljeppen.

2 As de Groot reaches the very top of the pole, he leaps into the air using every ounce of his strength, jumps free and lands with a thud and an explosion of sand on the other side of the canal. The crowd roars its approval. De Groot is the men's world record holder and is looking to improve on his stunning record of over 22 metres.

3 Fierljeppen originated in the northern Friesland province of the Netherlands. Its name can be translated as 'far-leaping'. It is a bit like the pole vault, but instead of jumping over a bar you jump over a canal or river. A jump consists of a sprint to the pole (polsstok), jumping and grabbing it, climbing to the top of the pole over the water, and finishing by landing as far as possible onto a sand bed opposite to the starting point.

4 The sport has its own ruling body – the Polsstokbond Holland – with around 600 active Dutch fierljeppers, male and female, seniors and juniors. National championships are contested at events like the one where de Groot makes his jump. These are big events attended by thousands of passionate supporters. The crowd watching de Groot waved flags, wore colourful T-shirts depicting their favourite fierljepper, took selfies and tweeted. A traditional Dutch band provided a musical backdrop as beginners, young and old, enthusiastically tried the sport for themselves. Dutch television regularly covers the whole event and pulls in ever-bigger viewing figures each year.

5 Alongside these serious and competitive events, the sport is often practised for fun or to entertain tourists. Forms of Fierljeppen are now played around the Netherlands and in Germany, and versions of the sport have even appeared on American and Japanese television shows.

6 Although the sport originates from Friesland, where farmers used to vault the many canals that dotted their land, it has grown in popularity in other parts of the Netherlands because of the success of people like Jacob de Groot, who actually comes from Utrecht in South Holland.

7 His success has led to many more young people taking up the sport. Football and cycling are the most popular sports in this area but, with the growing media attention and now the world record-holder coming from the area, Fierljeppen is no longer seen as just a northern oddity.

Activity 1: Identifying key information

1 Look again at paragraphs 1–3 of the article on page 148, about the rules of the sport of Fierljeppen.
   a) What equipment is required to take part in Fierljeppen?
   b) Explain how contestants get across the water.

2 Look again at paragraphs 4 and 5 of the article, about the popularity of Fierljeppen.
   a) How many people practise the sport?
   b) Where can you try Fierljeppen yourself?
   c) In what other countries is Fierljeppen practised?

3 Look again at paragraphs 6 and 7 of the article, about the origin of the sport and its success.
   a) Why have people's attitudes to Fierljeppen changed in other parts of the Netherlands?
   b) How is the sport attracting young people away from more traditionally popular sports?

Activity 2: Exploring intention and vocabulary choice

1 Look again at the second paragraph of the article on page 148, which provides a description of the sport of Fierljeppen.
   a) In only **one** word or phrase, describe the impression that the writer has created of Fierljeppen. You could choose one of the suggestions below or use your own ideas.

   violent | exciting | glamorous | dramatic | physical
   loud | dangerous | spectacular | aggressive

   b) Note down **all** of the words or phrases in the second paragraph that help to create the impression you noted.

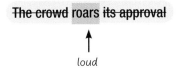

loud

2 Look again at the fourth paragraph of the article, about the popularity of the sport.
   a) In only **one** word or phrase, describe the impression that the writer has created of this event. You could choose one of the suggestions above or use your own ideas.
   b) Note down **all** of the words or phrases in the fourth paragraph that help to create the impression you noted.

Skills Boost: Exploring register

Every text, written or spoken, has a register: a level of formality created by choices of language and grammar.

- A formal register may be used in a professional speech, a class report or a polite letter. It suggests a text is authoritative and reliable.
- An informal register is used between friends in everyday life. It gives the text a friendly, conversational tone that can help to engage the reader.

Some texts contain some elements of formal language and some of informal language. This can make the information sound both reliable and engaging.

1 Look at the sentences in A, which are based on the article on page 148, then look at the re-written versions of those sentences in B and C.

A De Groot lands with a dull thud and an explosion of sand. The sizeable crowd roars its approval.

B Jacob hit the ground and sand went everywhere. The crowd went wild.

C Mr De Groot landed, sending sand into the air. The spectators enthusiastically expressed their delight.

Which version (A, B or C) is the most formal and which is the least formal? Write one or two sentences explaining your answers.

Activity 3: Selecting evidence

A response to a text should be supported with relevant evidence. Selecting evidence that features effective vocabulary choices helps you write the most effective response, because you can comment on the effect of those choices.

How do I do that?

To choose evidence featuring effective vocabulary choices, you need to look for words that create a powerful impression or have a strong effect on you, the reader.

1 Look at the following quotation from the article on page 148.

Just at the water's edge, he leaps up towards a vertical pole, grabs it and propels himself through the air above the muddy canal.

a) Which words give the reader **information** about the sport that the writer is describing?

b) Which words create a powerful **impression** of the sport or the competitor that the writer is describing?

2 Look again at paragraph 1 of the article on page 148. Select another quotation that creates a powerful impression of Fierljeppen and note down which words or phrases helped most to create this impression.

Activity 4: Responding to vocabulary choice

When commenting on effective vocabulary choice in a text, you could consider:
- the word's connotations : the ideas that a word suggests or creates in a reader's mind
- the word's implications: what you can infer from this word
- how the word contributes to the writer's intention.

1 Look again at the following quotation from the article on page 148.

> As the pole lurches forward, de Groot frantically climbs up as momentum takes him to the other side of the water and dry land.

a) What can you infer about the climb up the pole just from the word 'frantically'?

b) What are the connotations of the word 'frantically'?

hurried | uncontrolled | frenzied | desperate

c) What impression do these connotations create of a Fierljeppen jump?

Activity 5: Writing about vocabulary choice

You are going to answer the following question, focusing on vocabulary choice: What impression does the article give the reader of the sport of Fierljeppen? You could write about how the writer presents the Fierljeppen event, the popularity of the sport of Fierljeppen, or both.

1 To write your first paragraph, follow these three steps:

a) Write a sentence making a point about the writer's intention. Think about how the writer presents the sport of Fierljeppen and the impression they intend to create.

b) Identify a short, relevant quotation as evidence to support your point. Make sure your quotation contains effective vocabulary choices that you can comment on. Add your quotation to your paragraph.

c) Add one or two sentences commenting on the writer's vocabulary choices in your chosen quotation. Think about:
- the connotations of a powerful word or phrase
- the effect this has on the reader
- how this contributes to the writer's intention.

2 Write a second paragraph, making a new point about the writer's intention and repeating the steps in question 1.

This section links to pages 142–145 of the Workbook.

Section 5
Writing a response

In this section, you will develop your skills in responding to a text.

▼ **Read the newspaper article and then answer the questions that follow it.**

EXHILARATING WINTER OLYMPIC SPORTS

1 Bobsleigh
Fear factor 4/5

Short of tucking yourself into a washing machine and pressing the spin button, no sensation on Earth matches
5 a run in a four-man bobsleigh. Squeezed into a steel pod only 3.8 metres in length and weighing 600 kilograms, the driver has to negotiate up to 20 wickedly banked bends down a 1.5-kilometre course of glazed ice. You hit the biggest bends at more than 80 mph (miles per hour)
10 and 5G – that's five times the force of gravity.

The brakeman's job only begins at the end of the course when he releases steel spikes into the ice to stop the bob – braking during the run ruins the track and is absolutely forbidden. After the sprint start, the two guys
15 in the middle are just ballast.

It all began in St Moritz in 1928, on what is now the last remaining natural ice track and also one of the world's fastest.

Skeleton
20 **Fear factor: 5/5**

Face down on a tray and with your nose just 3 inches from the ice, you hurtle down a bobsleigh track at speeds of up to 90 mph. Of all the Olympic sports, this has to be the scariest. The main difference between this
25 and an Olympic bobsleigh run is that the tracks used for skeleton have more bends – and you have no brakes.

Luge
Fear factor 5/5

A close relative of the skeleton but you lie on your
30 back rather than front, on a sled that is 6 to 9 inches longer. Athletes will reach 90 mph on the icy chute, and it's considered to be even more dangerous than the skeleton. There are no brakes and you control the sled by flexing the runners with the calf of each leg.

Activity 1: Thinking about a first response

1 Answer the following questions to check your understanding of the article on page 152, and to help you begin thinking about your response to it.
   a) In which sport does the vehicle have brakes to stop it at the end of the course?
   b) In which sport do the participants travel face down, with their noses close to the ice?
   c) How many people form the crew of one bobsleigh?
   d) What does each member of the bobsleigh team do?
   e) What are the similarities and differences between the skeleton and the luge? Identify **one** similarity and **one** difference.

2 For each of your answers to the questions below, write a sentence explaining your choice.
   a) Which sport would you most like to try?
   b) Which sport would you least like to try?
   c) Which sport sounds the most frightening?
   d) Which sport sounds the most exciting?

Activity 2: Gathering evidence of intention

1 The writer of the article on page 152 is trying to give information about three different winter sports and describe the experience of taking part in them. Look at the following quotations from the article.

A tucking yourself into a washing machine and pressing the spin button

B the driver has to negotiate up to 20 wickedly banked bends down a 1.5-kilometre course of glazed ice.

C braking during the run ruins the track and is absolutely forbidden.

D with your nose just 3 inches from the ice, you hurtle down a bobsleigh track at speeds of up to 90 mph

   a) In which **one** of the quotations does the writer give the most detailed information about what the sport involves?
   b) Which **one** of these quotations do you feel describes the experience most vividly?
   c) Look again at the quotation you selected in answer to question 1b. Which word or phrase in this quotation describes the experience most vividly?

2 a) Identify **two** further quotations from the article that give detailed information about one of the featured winter sports.
   b) Identify **two** further quotations from the article that vividly describe the experience of taking part in a winter sport.

Grammar Boost: Sentence starts

Look at the following multi-clause sentence, which starts with a **main clause**.

> The idea of tucking yourself into a washing machine creates humour   ← *main clause*

> because   ← *subordinating conjunction*

> it is a strange and surprising image.   ← *subordinate clause*

The two clauses in the sentence can be swapped, so that the sentence begins with the subordinating conjunction:

> Because   ← *subordinating conjunction*

> it is a strange and surprising image,   ← *subordinate clause*

> the idea of tucking yourself into a washing machine creates humour.   ← *main clause*

1 Rewrite the following sentences so that they begin with the conjunction.
   a) The verb 'hurtled' creates an impression of terror because it has connotations of speed and being out of control.
   b) The writer adds the information that there are no brakes after he has highlighted the speed of the skeleton.
   c) The writer creates the impression that bobsleigh is exciting although it sounds terrifying.

Activity 3: Considering a paragraph

1 Look at the following sentences, taken from one student's response to the article on page 152.

> **A**   The writer compares bobsleigh to 'tucking yourself into a washing machine and pressing the spin button'.

> **B**   The writer uses a humorous comparison to describe the experience of bobsleighing.

> **C**   The comparison is used to suggest that the bobsleigh is very small and very fast.

   a) Which sentence contains a key point focusing on the writer's intention?
   b) In which sentence does the student support their point with a quotation?
   c) In which sentence does the student comment on the effect of the writer's choices?
   d) In what order would you sequence these sentences? Experiment with different sequences to build a fluent and clearly expressed paragraph.

Activity 4: Making points and commenting

You are going to write two paragraphs responding to the article on page 152. Each of your paragraphs should contain three basic elements:
- a key point focusing on the writer's intention
- a short, relevant quotation supporting your point
- an explanation of the effect of the writer's choices in your chosen quotation.

1 Look at the following quotation from the article, in which the writer gives the reader some information about the sport of bobsleigh.

> You hit the biggest bends at more than 80 mph and 5G – that's five times the force of gravity.

a) Write **one** sentence making a point about the writer's intention in giving the reader this information. You could choose from the words below or use your own ideas.

dangerous | exciting | fast-paced | exhilarating | terrifying

b) Look again at your answer to question 1a. Which **one** piece of information in the quotation creates that impression most strongly?
c) Write **one** sentence explaining the effect of that piece of information.

The phrase '____' highlights that

The phrase '____' emphasises how

2 Look at the following quotation from the article, in which the writer gives the reader some information about the sport of skeleton.

> with your nose just 3 inches from the ice, you hurtle down a bobsleigh track at speeds of up to 90 mph

a) Write **one** sentence making a point about the writer's intention in giving the reader this information.
b) Look again at your answer to question 2a. Which **one** piece of information in the quotation creates that impression most strongly?
c) Write **one** sentence explaining the effect of that piece of information.

The phrase '____' creates the impression that

The phrase '____' makes the sport of skeleton sound

3 Look again at your sentences. Experiment with sequencing the sentences in your paragraphs to make your response clearer and more fluently expressed.

This section links to pages 146–147 of the Workbook.

Section 6
Assessment

In this section, you will answer questions on a short extract and write a critical response to assess your progress.

▼ **Read the information text and then answer the questions that follow it.**

Dragon boat racing

1   The dragon has a symbolic meaning for the Chinese. A classic dragon has the head of an ox, a deer's antlers, the mane of a horse, the body and scales of a snake, the claws of an eagle and the tail of a fish. With its strength and power, the dragon rides the clouds in the sky and commands the wind, mist and rain.

5   The dragon boat is deeply embedded in China's dragon culture, with each boat having an ornately carved dragon's head at the **bow**[1] and a tail in the **stern**[2]. The **hull**[3] is painted with the dragon's scales. The paddles symbolically represent the claws.

10   Dragon boat racing has ancient Chinese origins and its history has been traced back more than 2,000 years. The first participants were superstitious Chinese villagers who celebrated the fifth day of the fifth lunar month of the Chinese calendar. Racing was held to avert misfortune and encourage the rains needed for prosperity – and the object of their
15   worship was the dragon. The dragon of Asia has traditionally been a symbol of water. It is said to rule the rivers and seas and dominate the clouds and rains.

Over the years, a second story was integrated to give the festival a dual meaning – the touching saga of Qu Yuan. Legend
20   has it that poet Qu Yuan was banished from the kingdom of Chu after the king fell under the influence of corrupt ministers. Qu Yuan spent many years wandering the countryside and composing great poetry until, on learning of his kingdom's defeat, he leapt into the Mi Lo River holding a great rock in a
25   display of his heartfelt sorrow. The people loved Qu Yuan very much and raced out in their fishing boats to the middle of the river in a vain attempt to save him. They beat on drums and splashed their oars in the water, trying to keep the fish away from his body.

30   Today dragon boat racing involves teams of up to 20 paddlers in a 40-foot boat with a drummer at the **helm**[4], paddling frantically to beat the other teams down the course. The drums, shouting and colourful boats all make it an impressive and exciting sport both to watch and to compete in.

Key vocabulary

bow[1]: front of a boat
stern[2]: back of a boat
hull[3]: main body of a boat
helm[4]: a boat's steering mechanism

Activity 1: Reading

1 How many different animals does the writer use to describe the appearance of a classic dragon?

2 Identify **three** pieces of information that the extract on page 156 gives about dragon boat racing.

3 Look again at the final sentence of the extract:

> The drums, shouting and colourful boats all make it an impressive and exciting sport both to watch and to compete in.

Identify the words in this sentence that create a vivid impression of the sport of dragon boat racing.

4 The writer implies that the reader would enjoy going to see, or taking part in, a dragon boat race. How does the writer suggest this?

5 Look again at the fourth paragraph of the extract, which tells the story of Qu Yuan. This paragraph is almost 130 words long. Write a summary of the paragraph in **35** words or fewer.

Activity 2: Writing

1 Write **two or three** paragraphs in response to the following question: What impression has the writer created of the sport of dragon boat racing in the extract on page 156?

Before you start writing
Plan your ideas. You could comment on:
- the writer's intention
- the ideas the writer has chosen to include
- the writer's vocabulary choices.

As you write
Ensure that you:
- express your ideas as clearly and fluently as you can
- use the three basic elements of a critical paragraph:
  - ○ a key point
  - ○ a supporting quotation
  - ○ an explanation of the quotation's effect.

This section links to pages 148–151 of the Workbook.

Section 7
Structuring an information text

In this section, you will explore ways of structuring information texts to guide the reader and convey information effectively.

▼ Read the information text and then answer the questions that follow it.

The history of ball games

1 Ball sports have been played for thousands of years, some believe as long ago as 2500 BCE according to ancient written and archaeological records from Greece, Egypt and China. There were, no doubt, other countries playing similar games, but those records have not survived.

2 The Romans played a game called **Harpastum**[1] in which two sides tried to keep possession of a small ball for as long as possible. The Greeks played a similar game known as **Episkyros**[2]. It is thought that these games were more like modern rugby than football. Perhaps the ancient game closest to football is the Chinese game of **Tsu'Chi**[3] or *Cuju*. The object of the game was to kick a small leather ball into a net stretched between two bamboo poles. Players could use their feet, torso and head to control the ball, but not their hands – which sounds very similar to football, until you learn that the goal net was several metres off the ground. Other similar ball games played around the ancient world included **Kemari**[4] in Japan, the Native Americans' *Pahsaherman*, indigenous Australians' *Marn Grook*, and the Maori's *Ki-o-rahi*.

3 Many other modern ball games may have much older origins than was once thought. The Chinese ball game of *Chuiwan* was played as long ago as the fifth century CE, the aim of the game being to knock a small wooden ball into a hole in the ground using a club. Some believe this to be the origin of the modern game of golf.

4 Football became popular in Europe during the medieval period, when entire towns or villages would divide into two teams and attempt to kick an inflated animal bladder from their own goal at one end of the town to the other team's goal on the other side of the town. There were no rules, and games often became violent, damaging both

Chuiwan

people and property. At several points in its early history, the game was banned and people were directed to practise their archery skills instead, which were thought to be much more useful in battle. Despite this, some towns still play this version of the sport today!

5 People continued to play the game of football according to their own rules, which developed over time. Then finally, in the nineteenth century, the rules of Association Football were agreed.

Key vocabulary

Harpastum[1]: comes from a term meaning 'snatch' or 'carry away'
Episkyros[2]: means 'shared ball'
Tsu'Chi[3]: means 'kick the ball'
Kemari[4]: means 'come here'

Activity 1: Reading and responding

1 Answer the following questions to check your understanding of the information text on page 158.

   a) For how many thousands of years have ball sports been played, according to the archaeological records mentioned in the text?

   b) What is the **one** key difference between modern football and the ancient Chinese game of Cuju?

   c) Identify **one** ancient sport that had similarities to the modern game of golf.

   d) According to the text, was archery or football more popular in medieval Europe?

   e) Which rules did games of football follow before the nineteenth century?

Cuju

2 Think about your response to the information text.

   a) Identify the **one** piece of information in the text that you find the most surprising or interesting. Write one or two sentences explaining your choice.

   b) Select **one** piece of information in the text that you find uninteresting and think could be omitted. Write one or two sentences explaining your choice.

Kemari

Activity 2: Exploring intention

1 What response do you think the writer of the information text on page 158 intended to create in the reader? Write one or two sentences to explain your answer. You could choose from the suggestions below or use your own ideas.

| **The writer's intention is...** | to provide the reader with factual information \| to create humour to describe the experience of playing different ball games |
| **to convey...** | enjoyment \| drama \| excitement \| action |

2 Look again at your answer to question 1. Which of the following features does the writer use to help achieve the information text's intended effect?

- dates
- examples from around the world
- humour

- vivid description
- informal language
- formal language

Activity 3: Exploring paragraph structure

Paragraphs in information texts usually contain:
- a key point or topic sentence
- examples or supporting information

1 Look again at the third paragraph of the information text on page 158.
- **a)** What is the key point in this paragraph? Summarise it in your own words.
- **b)** What example does the writer use to support this key point? Summarise it in your own words.

2 Look again at the fourth paragraph of the information text.
- **a)** What is the key point in this paragraph? Summarise it in your own words.
- **b)** What information does the writer use to support this key point? Summarise it in your own words.

Skills Boost: Using subheadings

Writers use subheadings to guide the reader through a text. An effective subheading gives a very short summary of the key point or focus of one or more paragraphs.

For example, in the article *Exhilarating Winter Olympic sports* on page 152, this subheading indicates the sport that the section will describe:

> **Skeleton**
> Fear factor: 5/5
> Face down on a tray and with your nose just 3 inches from the ice, you hurtle down a bobsleigh track at speeds of up to 90 mph.

1 Look again at the information text on page 158, and consider where you could add subheadings to help guide the reader through it.

Remember

Not every paragraph needs its own subheading.

- **a)** How many subheadings would you add?
- **b)** Where would you add the subheadings? Note down the number of the paragraph that would come directly after each subheading.
- **c)** Write the subheadings you would add to the extract. Make sure that they:
  - are very short
  - accurately indicate the content of the paragraph or paragraphs after them.

Activity 4: Writing an information text

You are going to invent an imaginary ball game and write an information text about it.

Imagine

1 Think about the aim of sports you know. For example:

- The aim of football is to kick or head the ball into the other team's goal.
- The aim of golf is to hit the ball over a long course and into a hole.
- The aim of cricket is to hit the ball a long way and run from one end of the pitch to the other as many times as you can.

a) What could be the aim of the ball game you will invent?

b) Will the game be played between two or more teams, like football or cricket, or will it be played by two or more individuals, like tennis or golf?

c) Note down your ideas for two or three new games.

d) Select just one of your ideas to write about: the ball game you would most like to play.

Plan

2 Think about the different sections you will include in your information text about your imaginary sport. For example, you could choose to focus on:

- its history
- the rules
- an important tournament or championship
- famous players.

a) Choose **two or three** key areas on which you will focus in your information text. Write a subheading for each one.

b) Note down the key point you will make under each of your subheadings.

c) Note down what examples or other information you will add to support or develop your key points.

d) Note down the order in which you will sequence the two or three sections of your information text.

Write

3 Use your subheadings, key points and supporting examples to write an information text about the sport you have imagined.

Section 8
Exploring vocabulary and sentence choices

In this section, you will explore the writer's choice of different sentence structures and their impact on the reader.

▼ Read the article and then answer the questions that follow it.

1 The main road through Hanuabada village on the outskirts of Port Moresby, Papua New Guinea is really the only open space among the thousands of wooden huts with their rusted iron roofs. Down by the water, the houses are built on stilts and reach a hundred metres out into the ocean, separated by planks of wood forming wobbly walkways. Once on shore, the village soon rises into the nearby hills, where homes are reached by narrow pathways.

2 So it stands to reason that cricket must be played right there in the middle of the main street. After all, with its rock-hard clay surface, it makes an ideal year-round pitch. The bounce is even and the **outfield**[1] is fast: very fast.

3 Former national captain Rarua Dikana still plays regularly in the village, always to a hero's welcome. "Cricket," he says, "is a way of life here. The kids  love it when me and some of the others from national teams go home and join in a game. We always play on the main road and just ignore the cars."

4 The cars, too, usually ignore the players, creeping to the edges of the wide expanse and cruising by without disturbing the game.

5 This random yet central location is where many of the Papua New Guinea's national team, the Barramundis, have honed their skills for decades. These new cricket stars are not the product of an English village green or a sunbaked sporting ground in Australia, but a single coastal village with a pitch on the main street.

6 Everyday scenes in the village would not be out of place in cricket-obsessed India. Some parents start walking their children to Hanuabada at 5.30 in the morning to join in an organised competition starting at 6.30 a.m. Many kids arrive by canoe. Before land transport improved, in the 1950s and 1960s, some groups travelled more than a day and a half from the village of Hula, 100 kilometres away. Hula, too, provides representatives in the national team, despite its small population. The tiny islands offshore, where cricket was introduced as an alternative to tribal fighting, provide teams as well.

7 As many as 50 teams line up to play in one of the three matches each day. Several matches are played at once in the tight confines of the main road. Well-struck **pull shots**[2] often have fielders plunging into the ocean to retrieve the ball. Some kids use plastic bats and stumps, but others still make do with planks of wood and soft-drink crates. Spectators sit on concrete blocks and wooden boxes at the edge of the road and chase the ball for the players when they belt it over or through the surrounding huts. National vice-captain and wicketkeeper Jack Vare says the umpires have a lot of discretion when calling the runs. If you hit a house and cause damage, it can be ruled out, but if you manage to clear it, then it's **a six**[3] without question.

Key vocabulary

outfield[1]: part of a cricket pitch furthest from the bowler and batsman
pull shot[2]: powerful hit of the ball made using a high swing of the bat
a six[3]: a score of six runs, awarded automatically when the ball crosses a boundary line

Activity 1: Reading and responding

1 Identifying some key points of information in the article on page 162 will help you develop your response to it. The following questions will ask you to look at each paragraph of the article in turn.

a) First paragraph: Using your own words, write **one** sentence describing the village of Hanuabada.

b) Second paragraph: Where in the village of Hanuabada do people play cricket?

c) Third paragraph: Note down everything you learn about Rarua Dikana – where he comes from, what he has done in his life and what the people of Hanuabada think of him.

d) Fourth paragraph: Using your own words, write **one** sentence describing what the writer implies people driving through Hanuabada must think about people playing cricket in the village.

e) Fifth paragraph: Using your own words, write one sentence explaining how playing cricket in Hanuabada may change people's lives.

f) Sixth paragraph: Identify **one** piece of information that the writer uses to imply that people in Hanuabada are obsessed with cricket.

g) Final paragraph: Identify **two** problems faced by people playing cricket in Hanuabada.

2 What impression does the article create of cricket in Papua New Guinea? Note down **two** adjectives from the suggestions below or use your own ideas.

fun | serious | successful | dedicated | popular | important

Activity 2: Exploring vocabulary choice and intention

The writer's vocabulary choices help to create an impression of cricket in Papua New Guinea.

1 Look at the highlighted number facts and figures in the following sentences. What impression of cricket in Papua New Guinea do these facts and figures create?

Some parents start walking their children to Hanuabada at 5.30 in the morning to join in an organised competition starting at 6.30 a.m. Many kids arrive by canoe. Before land transport improved, in the 1950s and 1960s, some groups travelled more than a day and a half from the village of Hula, 100 kilometres away.

2 Look at the highlighted noun phrases and verbs in the following sentences. Select **one** verb and **one** noun choice from these sentences. What impression of cricket in Papua New Guinea do these choices create? Write one or two sentences explaining your answer.

Well-struck pull shots often have fielders plunging into the ocean to retrieve the ball. Some kids use plastic bats and stumps, but others still make do with planks of wood and soft-drink crates. Spectators sit on concrete blocks and wooden boxes at the edge of the road and chase the ball for the players when they belt it over or through the surrounding huts.

Grammar Boost: Revising sentence types

There are some key terms you can use when writing about sentence structure:

- A clause is a group of more than one word, including a verb. In a single-clause sentence, there is just one clause.

The cricket match finished.

- In a multi-clause sentence, there are two or more clauses. The clauses in a multi-clause sentence are often linked with a conjunction.

They went home when the cricket match finished.

1 Look at the following sentences.

A   They play cricket in the main street.   B   There is not enough space anywhere else.

C   Players ignore cars when they drive through the cricket pitch.   D   Some players have a plastic bat but others have only a plank of wood.

E   Rarua Dikana comes to visit Hanuabada.   F   He is treated like a hero.

a) Which of the sentences above are single-clause sentences?

b) Which of the sentences above are multi-clause sentences?

c) Use **two** of the single-clause sentences to create **one** multi-clause sentence. Link the two clauses with a conjunction.

d) Rewrite **one** of the multi-clause sentences as **two** single-clause sentences.

Activity 3: Exploring sentence structures and intention

Writers can use different sentence structures to emphasise particular ideas or information in a text.

1 Look at the following sentences from the article on page 162.

> Some parents start walking their children to Hanuabada at 5.30 in the morning to join in an organised competition starting at 6.30 a.m. Many kids arrive by canoe.

Which idea is given more emphasis by its sentence structure: the information about parents walking their children, or the information that some children travel by canoe?

2 Look at the two clauses in the following multi-clause sentence.

> Before land transport improved, in the 1950s and 1960s, some groups travelled more than a day and a half from the village of Hula, 100 kilometres away.

a) Which idea is given more emphasis by the structure: the information about when transport improved, or the information about the distance people travelled?

b) Why do you think the writer chose to sequence the clauses as they did?

Activity 4: Writing a response

You are going to write two paragraphs in response to the following question:
What impression of cricket in Papua New Guinea does the writer create in the article on page 162?
Each of your paragraphs should contain three basic elements:

- a key point focusing on the writer's intention
- a short, relevant quotation supporting your point
- an explanation of the effect of the writer's choices in your chosen quotation.

Plan

1 Plan the topics of your two paragraphs. You could write about either of the topics below, or one paragraph about each of them.

- people's attitudes to cricket in Papua New Guinea
- the way people in Papua New Guinea play cricket

2 a) Consider the topic you chose for your first paragraph. Note down **one** point about the writer's intention in relation to it. Think about:

- how the writer presents the topic
- the impression of it that the writer wants to give the reader.

b) Note down **one** quotation from the article as evidence to support your point.

c) Note down ideas for an explanation of the effect of the language, structure or information in the quotation.

3 Repeat questions 1 and 2 to plan your second paragraph, noting a different point about the writer's intention.

Write

4 a) Look again at your notes for your first paragraph. Consider how you could sequence the ideas in your first paragraph to make your response clearer.

b) Write your first paragraph using full sentences. Consider your vocabulary choices and your choices of sentence length, to ensure your response is fluently expressed.

5 a) Look again at your notes for your second paragraph. Consider how you could sequence the ideas for it, perhaps in contrast to the sequence you chose for your first paragraph.

b) Write your second paragraph using full sentences. Consider your vocabulary choices and your choices of sentence length, to ensure your response is fluently expressed.

This section links to pages 156–159 of the Workbook.

Section 9
Planning a critical response

In this section, you will develop your skills in identifying significant choices the writer has made, so that you can comment on their effect.

This is an extract from an article about the rules and rituals of sumo, an ancient Japanese form of wrestling.

▼ Read the extract and then answer the questions that follow it.

1   Sumo is one of Japan's most revered traditional arts, and with a history dating back at least 1,500 years, it is believed to be the world's oldest organised sport. It was originally linked with **Shinto**[1], the national religion of Japan, and retains many elements of Shinto ritual, with wrestlers clapping, raising their hands, stamping, sipping sacred water, and
5   throwing handfuls of salt – gestures which are believed to banish evil spirits. It gained popularity as a professional sport in the seventeenth century in Japan, when it was used as a way of training Samurai warriors. Although sumo was introduced to America in 1854, it never really became popular. However, it is linked to the development of martial arts such as
10 judo, which have become immensely popular in the West, and it remains enormously popular in Japan. Every sumo tournament is broadcast live, and as the hour of the contest approaches, martial artists all over the country gather in front of their televisions. A supreme sumo champion, or **yokozuna**[2], is considered a national hero, and believes himself
15 superior to all other martial artists.

Sumo wrestlers, known as **rikishi**[3], are easily recognised by their traditional outfit – the **mawashi**[4], a loin cloth made of tightly wrapped fabric, and the hair tied in a top-knot, or **oicho**[5]. The contest takes place in a ring called a **dohyo**[6]. It is 4.6 metres in diameter, supported on a
20 platform of rice-straw bales, and has a surface of mixed sand and clay. The aim of the contest is for the wrestler to push his opponent out of the ring, or trip or throw him in such a way that his feet lose contact with the ground.

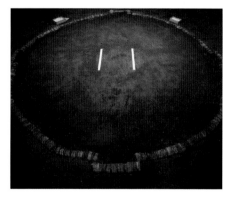

The fight is usually short. Most contests last little more than a few
25 minutes, but the moments before the fight commences create unbearable tension. Each wrestler circles, stamping, clapping, throwing salt, or taking a sip of sacred water, before he bows and settles into a crouch, glaring intently at his opponent, controlling his breathing, emptying his mind and gathering all
30 his power, ready to hurtle forward. At a sign from the referee, both men dash towards each other and meet with incredible force. The goal is to secure a grip on the opponent's loin cloth, in order to lift him off his feet, or to evade his rush so that he overbalances and falls out of the ring.

Key vocabulary

Shinto[1]: the traditional religion of Japan
yokozuna[2]: supreme champion
rikishi[3]: sumo wrestler
mawashi[4]: loin cloth
oicho[5]: top-knot
dohyo[6]: the ring in which the rikishi wrestle

Activity 1: Noting key points

When you are asked to write a critical response to a text, you need to make sure you understand it – and think about the ideas and information the writer has chosen to include.

1 Using no more than 15 words, write a sentence explaining what a dohyo is.

2 The writer describes a number of gestures that the wrestlers make which are 'elements of Shinto ritual'. Write down **five** of these symbolic movements.

3 The writer explains these symbolic movements in some detail. What does this suggest about the sport of sumo? Write a sentence or two explaining your ideas.

4 Once the rikishi have entered the dohyo, they crouch and glare at their opponent. Why do they do this? Write one or two sentences explaining your ideas.

5 Sumo was introduced into America but it never became popular. Write down one way in which it has influenced martial arts in the West.

Activity 2: Looking at structure

Once you have identified the key points in a text, look at how the writer has sequenced the ideas. Can you identify any significant structural choices that the writer has made and on which you could comment?

1 Note down in just a few words, the focus of each paragraph of the extract on page 166.

> In paragraph 1, the writer focuses on
> In paragraph 2,

How do I do that?

One way to think about summing up the content of a paragraph is to ask yourself: what would make a good subheading for this paragraph?

2 Why do you think the writer has structured these three areas of information in this order? You could choose one or more of the suggestions below, if you agree with them, or you could use your own ideas.

The order of the paragraphs makes the information clear and easy to understand.	It is organised in chronological order.	It makes the reader feel like they are watching the build-up to a sumo fight.	It begins with the most important information, so the reader is given the whole picture, and then the writer adds in more detail later.

Activity 3: Looking at vocabulary

When you are planning a critical response to a text, look out for parts of the text that make a significant impression on you – and then look for vocabulary choices that help to create that impression. Look out for parts of the text that :
- create a vivid picture in your mind's eye
- create a powerful response, for example a feeling of sadness, excitement or humour.

1 Identify a sentence in the extract on page 166 that created a vivid picture in your mind. Perhaps it created a vivid picture of a sumo wrestler, or of the battle between two sumo wrestlers.
  a) Write a sentence using your own words to describe the picture it created in your mind.
  b) Which word or phrase in the sentence that you identified really helped to create that picture?

2 Identify a sentence in the extract that is trying to create a powerful response in the reader. Perhaps it conveyed the feeling of tension in the build-up to a sumo fight, or the feeling of excitement once the fight begins.
  a) Write a sentence using your own words to describe the feeling it created.
  b) Which word or phrase in the sentence that you identified really helped to create that feeling?

Activity 4: Looking at sentence structure

When you are planning a critical response to a text, look out for sentence structures that the writer has chosen for effect. Reread the text, looking carefully at every sentence. Look out for the types of sentence outlined below:

- A shorter sentence that the writer has used to add drama or emphasis to a key idea. For example:

  Everyone fell silent.

- A longer sentence in which a key idea is positioned at the end to give it greater emphasis. For example:

  Finally, after several minutes, when we had almost given up, he opened his mouth and began to sing.

- A longer sentence in which the writer has used a series of clauses or phrases to highlight a rapid series of actions or events. For example:

  I turned, held my breath, clenched my teeth, and started running.

1 Can you identify any significant sentence structures that are chosen for effect in lines 24–32 of the extract on page 166? Copy out any significantly structured sentences, and then write a sentence or two commenting on their effect.

Skills Boost: Ways of gathering and organising your ideas

You are going to plan a response, in three paragraphs, to the following question:
What impressions has the writer created of the sport of sumo?

When you organise your ideas for a critical response, you could choose to use:

a list   **a spidergram**

Sumo
1
2
3

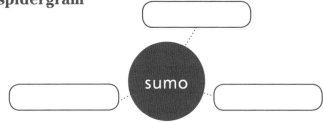

1. When you gather ideas for a critical response, you could choose to focus on different parts of the text, such as the ones below. Choose three of these suggestions for the extract on page 166 or use your own ideas, noting them as a list.

   mawashi | symbolic movements | the build-up to the fight | the fight

2. When you gather ideas for a critical response, you could focus on different impressions or responses to the extract, such as the ones below. Choose three of these suggestions or use your own ideas, noting them as a spidergram.

   complicated | exciting | tense | surprising | long |dramatic

3. Look at the list and the spidergram you have created.
   a) Which method do you prefer: using a list or a spidergram? Why?
   b) Which approach do you think is more effective: focusing on different parts of the extract or focusing on different impressions it creates? Why?

Activity 5: Putting a plan together

1. Note the points you will make in your response to the question at the top of this page, using either a list or a spidergram.

2. For each of the points you have noted, add a quotation showing the part of the extract on page 166 that created that impression.

3. Circle or underline any significant vocabulary or sentence structure choices in the quotations you have selected, and note their effect.

4. Can you add any comment on the structure of the extract to your planning? Looking at your response to Activity 2 on page 167 may help you.

5. Finally, number your points, showing the order in which you will write them.

Section 10
Comparing information texts

In this section, you will compare the information in two extracts, and the writers' different intentions.

▼ **Read Extract A and then answer the question that follows it.**

The history of volleyball

1 In 1895, William G. Morgan was the education director at the **YMCA** in Holyoke, Massachusetts, in the United States. Four years earlier, his colleague James Naismith had invented the game of basketball just
5 down the road, at the Springfield YMCA. Naismith's game was catching on quickly, but there was a drawback. Not everyone could keep up with the fast pace of basketball. Morgan decided to develop a game that could be enjoyed by middle-aged men.

10 Morgan conceived a court game that he originally called 'mintonette' because of its similarity to badminton. Mintonette was played on a court divided by a six-foot, six-inch net. Teams used their hands to hit a ball through the air (called 'volleying' the ball),
15 sending it back and forth across the net until one team missed. The first competitive game was played on 7th July 1896.

Quick change
Changes were made to Morgan's game
20 almost immediately.

- One of the first was the name. Alfred Halstead is credited with renaming the sport with the descriptive words 'volley ball'.
- The number of players on each team was limited.
25 Originally, a team was allowed to have as many players as could fit into its half of a 50- by 25-foot court. The number of players was first set at nine per side, and later reduced to six.
- The number of times a team could touch the
30 ball before it went over the net was eventually established at three. The first rules allowed an unlimited number of hits.

- The height of the net was raised to make play more challenging. Today, the net is just under 8 feet
35 (2.43 metres) for men's competitions, and just over 7 feet (2.24 metres) for women's.

Not just for middle-aged men
It quickly became apparent that volleyball had appeal far beyond the middle-aged men for whom it was
40 originally intended. Colleges and schools began to adopt the sport for both men and women. The first
45 US national volleyball championships for women were played in 1949, 54 years after women
50 began competing in the game. The first international championships for women were played
55 in 1952, in Moscow.

Key vocabulary

YMCA (Young Men's Christian Association): charity set up in the nineteenth century to provide low-cost, clean housing for young men, and now young women, moving into towns and cities

Activity 1: Identifying key information

1 There is a lot of information in Extract A on page 170 about volleyball. Note down all the words that could replace the **?** in the sentence below.

*Extract A gives the reader information about the **?** of/for volleyball.*

▼ **Read Extract B and then answer the questions that follow it.**

Volleyball

1 Two teams of six players battle for supremacy on the 18 m × 9 m volleyball court, separated by a high net (2.24 m for women, 2.43 m for men). The aim of the game is to land the ball in your opponent's half of the
5 court.

Each match consists of five sets. The first four sets are won with a score of 25
10 points, while the fifth is the first to 15 points. However, play in each set continues until the winning
15 team is at least two points ahead of the other.

Three players are positioned at the back of the court while the other three are at the net. One player –

the libero – specialises in defence and can replace any one of the three back players at any time in the
20 match. The libero is easily identified: they wear a different-coloured top from the rest of the team.

The teams volley the ball back and forth over the net until it either bounces on or leaves the court. Players will pass, or 'set', the ball for a teammate to hit it, or
25 'spike' it, over the net, hoping to drive the ball past the waiting opposition and to the ground.

Mighty jump serves begin each point, the server firing the ball over the net while blockers leap to stop the attack or throw themselves into flying dives to
30 recover the ball before it hits the ground.

Volleyball was invented as a slower, quieter version of basketball, for older players – but that's all changed now. Few sports can match the modern game's pace, energy and heart-stopping action.

Activity 2: Comparing key information

1 Look again at your answers to Activity 1.

a) Consider the similarities between the two extracts. Note down all the words that could replace the **?** in the sentence below.

*The extracts give similar information about the **?** of/for volleyball.*

b) Consider the differences between the two extracts. Note down all the words that could replace the **?** in each sentence below.

*Unlike Extract B, Extract A gives the reader information about **?***

*Unlike Extract A, Extract B gives the reader information about **?***

How do I do that?

Reread each extract. When you find some significant information, check to see if it appears in the other extract. If it doesn't, note it down.

Grammar Boost: Adverbials for comparison

Look at the two images.

Image 1   **Image 2**

Adverbials of comparison

whereas | however | on the other hand

both | similarly | also | as well | too

1 Identify **five** points of comparison
between the subjects of these two images, including at least **one** similarity and
one difference. In each case, use an adverbial of comparison to signal whether
you are identifying a similarity or a difference.

Activity 3: Comparing intentions and viewpoints

1 Look again at the two extracts on pages 170 and 171. Both aim to give the reader
information. What other intentions might the writers of both extracts have had?
a) Copy and complete the sentences below in as many different ways as you can.

> The writer of Extract A has tried to

> The writer of Extract B has tried to

You could choose from the ideas below or use your own.

| convey the excitement and drama of volleyball |

| persuade the reader to watch or even play volleyball |

| help the reader understand the rules of volleyball so they enjoy watching it more |

| create humour to entertain the reader |

| explain why volleyball has become so popular |

| advise the reader how to improve their volleyball skills |

b) Choose a quotation to support each of your answers to question 1a.
c) Identify what element of each quotation most helps the writer to achieve their
intention. You could comment on an idea, word, phrase or sentence structure.
d) What is the effect of the element you have identified in each quotation?

> In Extract A, the writer has tried to convey

> For example, the writer describes how 'the

Activity 4: Writing a comparison

You are going to write a short comparison of the two extracts on pages 170 and 171, referring to the ideas you have gathered in Activities 2 and 3.

You are going to write:
• one paragraph comparing the information in the two extracts
• one paragraph comparing the writers' intentions in the two extracts.

Use the instructions below to help you write your comparison.

1 When you compare the information in the two extracts, you can organise your ideas by identifying information that appears in both, and information that appears in only one.

a) Write an introductory sentence explaining what the two extracts are about.

> Both Extract A and Extract B are about

b) Identify two or three similarities in the information that both writers have included.

> In both extracts, the writer

c) Explain each similarity, using examples or quotations from the extract.

> For example, in Extract A the writer
> Similarly, in Extract B

d) Use an adverbial of comparison to signal that you are introducing a difference.

> However   On the other hand

e) Identify one or two differences in the information given in the two extracts.

> Extract A is the only one that
> and only Extract B

2 When you compare the writers' intentions in the two extracts, you can use a similar structure to organise your ideas: identifying a key point, supporting it with evidence and adding an explanation.

a) Write a key point explaining a similarity and a difference in the writers' intentions.

> Although both extracts are informative, the writer of Extract B also tries to

b) Select evidence from one or both of the extracts to support this key point.

> For example, the writer

c) Write an explanation of how the writers' choices of vocabulary or sentence structure have helped to achieve the intentions you identified.

> The fact that the sentence is
> suggests that volleyball is

3 Look again at the two paragraphs you have written, making sure you have expressed your ideas as clearly and as accurately as possible.

This section links to pages 164–165 of the Workbook.

Section 11
Assessment

In this section, you will answer questions on two extracts to assess your progress in this unit.

Extract A is a fictional account in which a professional women's footballer recalls her struggle to be taken seriously as a footballer when she was younger, and her determination to succeed.

▼ **Read Extract A and then answer the questions that follow it.**

1 Compared with some of my teammates, I was fortunate. Most of them came from deprived backgrounds and spent their time playing in the street. I was lucky because my Mum encouraged me to pursue my ambition. For my seventh birthday, she bought me a proper kit. From that
5 moment, I played whenever I could, even if it was only a kick-about on a patch of waste ground with stones for goalposts.

Opportunities to play for real were rare. My schoolteachers said football was too rough for girls, and made me play hockey. It makes no sense; hockey is just as rough as football, and the risks of injury equally great.

10 Luckily, there was a club near my home. They let me join in with the boys, and when I started scoring, they realised they couldn't afford to leave me out of the team. I became a regular at weekend matches. The pitches were small and muddy, and the refereeing was poor, but I was proud to take part. However, I dreamed of playing as a professional, and I
15 knew that there was no future for a woman in the men's game, no matter how good she might be.

Then I heard about an opportunity to sign for a professional women's team at one of the major clubs. I went along and played in a series of trials, and was thrilled when I was selected. Now I'm playing on full-size
20 pitches, with floodlights and proper refereeing. My mum is so proud.

Activity 1: Responding to Extract A

1 Note down **five** things you learn about the writer's childhood.

2 Write two paragraphs in response to the following question: What impressions does the writer create of her childhood?
You could comment on:
- the writer's family
- her struggle to be taken seriously as a female footballer.

Remember

You should support your ideas with evidence from the extract and comment on the writer's choices.

In Extract B, a journalist writes about a football match he watched on a visit to South Sudan.

▼ **Read Extract B and then answer the questions that follow it.**

1 Almost every evening, dozens of young South Sudanese churn up the dust at Buluuk Grounds, in a suburb of Juba, as they play one of their favourite sports: soccer.

On this particular evening, 11-year-old John William
5 watches from the sidelines as the older boys play a hotly contested game. As he watches, William daydreams about a day in the future when he will run onto a perfectly manicured pitch at an international match, wearing a South Sudan jersey. William's teacher at
10 Buluuk A primary school, Peter Odwa, says many kids in South Sudan have the athletic ability to excel at sports, including football. What they lack is good equipment and training facilities.

But William and other youngsters have already decided
15 they will play football, in spite of the hardships they face – including not having a ball to play with.

To overcome that handicap, the boys pooled their pocket money and came up with enough to buy a soccer ball. It cost the boys 100 South Sudanese pounds, or around
20 30 dollars.

"We get that ball with all our money; we collected two pounds, two pounds, that's how we can buy a ball," 14-year-old Luke Yokwe says.

Yokwe says his mother
25 encouraged him to start playing football. Her reasoning, he says, is that she thinks one day he might be able to make
30 a living as a football player. But Yokwe wants to go one better than just make a living at his favourite sport: he wants to be South Sudan's answer to
35 Côte d'Ivoire and Chelsea striker, Didier Drogba.

But this evening, Yokwe and William have to wait their turn to get a touch of the only ball they have for around 50 football-crazy kids. When the older boys kick the ball out of bounds, the younger kids take it and run with it.

40 As they dribble that old, ordinary football between the legs of their rivals and take a shot at an imaginary goal, they daydream about that manicured pitch they might run out onto one day, the crowd cheering, a FIFA-approved football at their feet, and a South Sudan
45 jersey on their backs.

Yokwe's mother will be proud as punch of her son when that happens.

Activity 2: Responding to Extract B

1 Note down **three** facts you learn about Buluuk Grounds.

2 **a)** What impressions does the writer create of the children in Buluuk? Write **three or four** sentences explaining your ideas.

b) What impressions does the writer create of attitudes to football in Buluuk? Write **three or four** sentences explaining your ideas.

Activity 3: Writing

1 Write at least **two** paragraphs of a comparison of the content and intentions in Extracts A and B. You may wish to consider:
- your answers to Activities 1 and 2
- the main subjects of the extracts
- the key ideas in each extract
- the viewpoint of the narrator in each.

Remember

You should support your ideas with evidence from the extract, and explain the effects of the writers' choices of structure, sentence structure or vocabulary.

Unit 5
A moment in time

In this unit, you will explore fiction and non-fiction texts written to capture a moment in a person's life. Some of these experiences are awe-inspiring, such as swimming with hammerhead sharks, or life-changing, such as becoming paralysed in an accident. These texts use varied vocabularies and dramatic story structures to engage your emotions.

In this unit, you will...

- explore some of the key features that help writers to explain and describe a moment in time.

- explore how writers structure a text to control the reader's response.

- explore ways in which you can engage readers by structuring your text like a story.

- explore the importance of careful vocabulary choice when you are writing to explain and to describe.

- answer questions on a short article and write your own article to assess your progress.

- explore different ways in which writers convey thoughts and feelings.

- explore the structure of paragraphs when writing to explain and describe.

- explore different ways in which sentences can be structured to add clarity and impact to a writer's ideas.

- explore ways to engage your reader with an effective opening.

- experiment with creating a satisfying ending for your writing.

- write an article explaining and describing a memorable experience.

By the end of this unit, you will be able to write an article, evocatively describing and explaining a personal memorable event.

This section links to pages 166–169 of the Workbook.

Section 1
Writing autobiographically

In this section, you will explore some of the key features that help writers to explain and describe a moment in time.

In the following extract, a teenage boy remembers an accident which caused him to become paralysed. He recalls the time before and after the accident.

▼ **Read the extract and then answer the questions that follow it.**

1 I remember waking in a strange room. I don't know where I am. There is a machine next to my head beeping softly. A dark-haired lady in a white coat is at the foot of my bed, reading a chart. She looks up,
5 smiles briefly, and hurries away. I remember asking, "Why can't I feel my body?" I feel like crying.

I remember a beach…the first time we came there… bright sun, the smell of salt wind, the cries of seagulls, the sensation of warm sand under my feet. Mum was
10 gazing at the sea, her golden hair tied back in a loose ponytail. In my memory, she turns, looking into my eyes, a happy smile on her face. "Happy birthday," she says. Dad is beside me, holding a cake with a number 5 written in red icing. I'm perfectly happy.

15 I remember another beach party. I am thirteen. Jason and Mari are with me. We are perched on the rocks, laughing and screaming in our wetsuits. Jason looks at me, his eyes full of excitement and challenge. "Go on…I dare you!" he yells.

20 I jump, high, wrapping my arms around my knees, and plummet, closing my eyes, waiting for the shock and splash. I feel a sharp heavy impact at the base of my spine. There is no pain – I am only suddenly very cold. Terror seizes me. I can't feel my body.

25 I remember weeks of exhausting exercise. Janet, in her white uniform, smiling encouragingly as I drag myself forward on handrails, searching for feeling and control, trying to remember how to move. My hands won't work, my legs are a dead weight. I want to give
30 up, but I know that Mum and Dad are in the room outside, talking in low voices, worrying and hoping. I can't let them down. I have to remember.

I remember sitting at home, looking out of a window at a little garden. A black cat is crouched on the lawn.
35 It's been a year since the accident. I look down at the computer in my lap – the screen with its lines of neat sentences. It is an effort, awkwardly punching out the words letter by letter as the pictures and stories rise and flood my mind. But at least I can do it. A door
40 opens behind me, and the delicious smell of freshly baked cake wafts in. I turn the lever of my chair and see Mum, Dad, Jason and Mari standing in front of me, smiling. Mum has her hair tied back in a loose ponytail and is carrying a tray with a large chocolate
45 cake on it, with the message 'Happy 14th Birthday'. We eat, talk and laugh about good times. I turn back to the window and think; I am happy to be alive.

Activity 1: Identifying key ideas

Answer these questions to check your understanding of the extract and help you identify the key information the writer gives the reader.

1 How old is the writer when he writes about his first memory in the extract on page 178?

2 Look at the description of the 'strange room' in the opening paragraph.
   a) What do you think the room was?
   b) What clues did you use to infer this?
   c) What does this suggest about what has happened to the writer?

3 Look at the writer's final memory of the extract, described in the last paragraph.
   a) How old is he?
   b) Write down **two** significant things that have changed by the time of this memory.

Activity 2: Pulling ideas together

When you are trying to make sense of a text, you often need to gather all the ideas you are given and pull them together to create a clearer picture.

1 Look at some of the key ideas you can find in the first paragraph of the extract on page 178.

   | I remember waking in a strange room. | I don't know where I am. |

   | I remember thinking, 'Why can't I feel my body?' | I feel like crying. |

   a) How is the writer feeling in this first memory?
   b) What does the writer suggest has made him feel this?
   c) Write a sentence or two explaining the clues that helped you to work this out.
   d) Write a summary of first paragraph pulling together all the information you were given and all the ideas you have been able to infer from them.

Skills Boost: Key points for summarising

The first step in writing an effective summary of a text is to identify the key ideas or information in each paragraph.

1 Throughout the extract on page 178 you are given information about:
- the writer's age
- things that happened in his life
- how he felt.

Note down what you learn about each of these three information areas in the final paragraph of the extract.

2 Write **one** sentence summarising the final paragraph. You could replace the **?** marks below or use your own ideas.

> When he was **?** years old, the writer remembers that he **?** and felt **?**.

Activity 3: Responding to ideas

1 In the extract on page 178, the writer focuses on five memories of his life. None of them tell a story and the writer does not clearly link them.

a) How easy did you find it to understand what was happening in the writer's early life? You could choose one of the suggestions below or use your own ideas.

easy | clear | unclear | impossible | confusing | puzzling | strange

b) Why do you think the writer wrote his memories in this way? Write one or two sentences explaining your ideas.

2 Think about the kinds of information the writer gives you in the extract.

a) Copy the table below, adding two more examples from the extract to each column.

Facts	Senses: sight, etc.	Emotions	Dialogue
'I am thirteen'	'I hear a machine beeping softly'	'I feel like crying'	'"Go on...I dare you!" he yells.'

b) Which of these different kinds of information do you find most effective and engaging in the story of the writer's early life: facts, senses, emotions or dialogue? Choose one or two answers and explain why you chose them.

Activity 4: Writing about a moment or two

You are going to plan and write a text in which you use **information** and **description** to create three 'pictures' of your early life.

Plan

1 Copy the table below, leaving plenty of space on each row to add your ideas.
   a) What memories do you have from the first five or six years of your life? Note down some **facts** in the first column of your table.
   b) For each memory, think about everything you can remember:
   • **senses**: what you remember seeing or hearing or smelling or feeling
   • **emotions**: whether you laughed or cried or felt frightened or something else
   • **dialogue**: things you said or that were said to you.
   Add these ideas to the table.

You do not need to write something in every cell of every row – but every row should have at least two or three different ideas in it.

	Facts	Senses: sight, etc.	Emotions	Dialogue
Memory 1				
Memory 2				

Write

2 The extract on page 178 is written in the first person and in the present tense.
   a) Write the first sentence of your text, focusing on your first memory.
   Write it in the **first person** and the **present tense**.

> I am six. It is my first day at school

   b) Rewrite that first sentence in the **third person** and the **simple past tense**.

> She was six. It was her first day at school.

   c) Which version do you prefer? Which version will be more engaging for the reader do you think?

3 Now you have chosen the **tense** and **person** in which you will write, complete your text – and remember to stick to the same tense and person throughout!

This section links to pages 170–173 of the Workbook.

Section 2
Exploring structure and intention

In this section, you will explore how writers structure a text to control the reader's response.

▼ Read the newspaper article and then answer the questions that follow it.

DIVING WITH SHARKS

1 The morning of the shark dive, we were on the boat. It was a beautiful day and I wondered if I wouldn't be happier sunning myself on deck. Captain 'Snoopy' Cooper, our dreadlocked captain, turned the boat in
5 circles, the engines revving furiously as a sign for the sharks to roll up for dinner. The noise and smoke added to the tension, and the **adrenaline**[1] was pumping quickly.

On deck was a stinking, bloody dustbin full of frozen
10 fish carcasses, known as a 'chumsicle'. It started to melt in the sun; blood was oozing out on the deck. It was hard to believe that sharks would rather eat this muck than a pound or two of fresh, living human. Peering anxiously over the side of the boat, we saw grey-black shadows
15 circling in the blue. It was our first view of the sharks, their anticipation obviously matching ours. Gary briefed us: get in the water, descend and kneel on the seabed in a circle; don't touch the food, don't ride the sharks. "You can touch them," he said, "but it's better not to touch
20 their sides as they're very sensitive there."

The chumsicle was lowered into the water and sharks gathered, worrying at it, jerking and twisting as they ripped away chunks of flesh. Others milled around the fringes, weaving in and out of the pack. The water
25 was thick with them – at least 100, mainly Caribbean reef sharks and blacktips. Gliding past, silver-grey skin, blank eyes, jaws open wide, their movement in the water graceful and smooth, they were awe-inspiring. I peered deep into their mouths at the most terrifying aspect
30 of these creatures – the massed rows of jagged, overlapping teeth.

Meanwhile, the divemaster signalled to us to mingle with them. I was surprised at this. I thought we would just be onlookers, but now we joined the circus. I dared
35 myself to reach up and touch one, gingerly reaching out, worrying that it would turn and snap at my fingers. Its white underbelly was soft and silky, its **nonchalance**[2] proof that we were about as interesting to them as the rocks on the seabed. From time to time they bumped
40 into me, like a powerful underwater battering ram, knocking the breath from my body.

Back on the boat, we were all exhilarated and excited. Far from being the terrifying experience we were expecting, we unanimously agreed that it had been
45 surprisingly calming – the slow, deliberate circling motions of the sharks had actually made us feel relaxed.

Key vocabulary

adrenaline[1]: chemical related to danger and excitement
nonchalance[2]: state of being unconcerned

Activity 1: Gathering impressions and inferring ideas

1 Look again at the following quotations from the article on page 182. For each one, note down either the writer's thoughts and feelings at the time, or the impression the writer creates of the sharks.

a) It was a beautiful day and I wondered if I wouldn't be happier sunning myself on deck.

b) the adrenaline was pumping quickly

c) On deck was a stinking, bloody dustbin full of frozen fish carcasses, known as a 'chumsicle' ...
It was hard to believe that sharks would rather eat this muck than a pound or two of fresh, living human.

d) The chumsicle was lowered into the water and sharks gathered, worrying at it, jerking and twisting as they ripped away chunks of flesh.

e) From time to time they bumped into me, like a powerful underwater battering ram, knocking the breath from my body.

f) it had been surprisingly calming – the slow, deliberate circling motions of the sharks had actually made us feel relaxed

> **Remember**
>
> When you are reading about a writer's experiences, think how their thoughts and feelings change, and how yours change as you read the text.

> In this quotation, I think the writer is feeling

> In this quotation, the writer creates the impression that sharks are

Activity 2: Tracking your response

The writer intends to influence a reader's response throughout a text, using the ideas and vocabulary they choose.

1 Look again at the article on page 182, and at the quotations in Activity 1 above. Track how your response to the text changes as you read, using a flow chart like the one below. You could add some of the following ideas or use your own.

tension | excitement | fear | relief | disgust | humour

| Paragraph 1 | → | Paragraph 2 | → | Paragraph 3 | → |

Grammar Boost: First, second and third person

Most texts are written in the **third person** using the pronouns 'he', 'she' and 'it'. They are written as though the narrator is observing the events.

When writing about a personal experience, writers often choose to write in the **first person**. They refer to themselves and others using the pronouns 'I' and 'we'. Writing in the first person can make the reader feel they are experiencing the same things as the writer.

Texts can also be written in the **second person**, using the pronoun 'you'. Texts written in the second person create the effect that the writer is speaking directly to the reader.

Pronouns		
	Singular	**Plural**
1st person	I / me	we / us
2nd person	you	you
3rd person	he / him she / her it	they / them

1 Rewrite the following third-person sentences using the first person.
   a) When they first met the sharks, they did not dare touch them.
   b) She thought the sharks would be frightening, but she soon saw they had no interest in her.

2 Rewrite the following third-person sentences using the second person.
   a) If he ever gets the opportunity, he should consider facing his fears.
   b) He will find the experience strangely calming.

Activity 3: Creating a response

Look again at the following two sections of the article on page 182.

> On deck was a stinking, bloody dustbin full of frozen fish carcasses, known as a 'chumsicle'. It started to melt in the sun; blood was oozing out on the deck. It was hard to believe that sharks would rather eat this muck than a pound or two of fresh, living human.

> Gliding past, silver-grey skin, blank eyes, jaws open wide, their movement in the water graceful and smooth, they were awe-inspiring. I peered deep into their mouths at the most terrifying aspect of these creatures – the massed rows of jagged, overlapping teeth.

1 **a)** Which section of the article is intended to create a feeling of disgust in the reader?
   b) Which words or phrases help to create that response?

2 **a)** Which section of the article is intended to create a feeling of tension in the reader?
   b) Which words or phrases help to create that response?

Activity 4: Structuring your writing

You are going to plan and write a short text in which you explain and describe a frightening encounter with an animal.

Imagine

1 Ask yourself some questions to gather and note ideas.

> Will I describe a real experience or will I make one up?

> What animal will I write about?

> Where, how and why will I say our encounter has taken place?

Plan

You are going to plan **two or three** paragraphs.

2 Note down the different responses you want to create in the reader in each paragraph. You could use your response to Activity 2 on page 183 to help you.

3 Think about the ideas and vocabulary you will use to create those responses. For each paragraph, note down:
- what you will write about
- vocabulary you could use to describe it.

Paragraph 1
<u>Response</u>: fear
<u>Ideas/vocabulary</u>: I open a cupboard and see the mouse.
- beady, staring black eyes
- huge, sharp white teeth
- I give a piercing, deafening scream

Write

4 Using all the ideas you have gathered, write a short article explaining and describing your encounter. As you write each paragraph, think about:
- the response you are aiming to create in the reader
- the ideas and vocabulary you are using to create that response.

This section links to pages 174–177 of the Workbook.

Section 3
Using narrative structure

In this section, you will explore ways in which you can engage readers by structuring your text like a story.

▼ **Read the extract and then answer the questions that follow it.**

1 Yang Zhifa leapt back as he emptied his bucket of soil onto the ground. A lump, almost a sphere rolled briefly along the dry, stony ground. A head – a human head! Even as Zhifa gasped in shock, he realised there was
5 something strange about it. He kneeled and slowly reached out to brush its face with his fingers. Two stern eyes, a cracked nose, an impression of hair. It was a life-size man's head made from some sort of pottery, and brightly painted. Zhifa had found broken
10 pots and jugs before, but never anything like this.

For four days, Zhifa and his brothers had been searching for water. It was 1974, in China, and the farmers were facing a serious drought. The brothers were all poor farmers. They lived near a small village
15 and needed a good harvest this year just to survive. They talked to their neighbours and everyone agreed: they must dig a well.

On 23rd March they began to dig a hole. It was hard work because they only had hand tools. By
20 28th March, they had dug over 50 foot straight down but still not found water. Zhifa had been at the surface, hauling up heavy buckets of earth while his brothers burrowed deeper into the dark. It was while carrying out this back-breaking work that Zhifa had
25 discovered the head.

Looking more closely at the heap of earth beside the hole, Zhifa found other pieces of broken pottery: fingers, a foot, and other fragments. His brothers and neighbour discussed the objects but decided they
30 must carry on searching for water, so they got back to work.

The next day, as the well got deeper, the men found more puzzling pieces of statue and weaponry. An even bigger surprise was finding a neatly laid brick floor.

35 The brothers decided they must report their discovery. They hadn't found water but perhaps they could sell some of their finds for money to buy food for their families.

Remarkably, what Zhifa and his family had discovered
40 was a vast model army that was over 2,200 years old: the **Terracotta**[1] Army. Qin She Huang, First Emperor of what we now call China, was buried near the well in 210 BCE. To protect him in his **afterlife**[2], a life-size model of his army was made from terracotta
45 and buried in his tomb. Many foot soldiers, generals and chariots have been dug up, but there are probably many more thousands to be discovered in the future.

Key vocabulary

terracotta[1]: brownish-red clay that is shaped and then hardened by fire
afterlife[2]: spiritual life after death

Activity 1: Organising key points

1 On what date did Zhifa and his brothers start digging a hole?

2 On what date did Zhifa find the head of a terracotta statue?

Remember

Chronological order is the order in which events happen or happened.

3 Make a chronological list of all the events described in the article on page 186.

Activity 2: Exploring narrative structure

The article on page 186 is a non-fiction text: it is about real events. The events are still told as a story, however, and the article includes all the key elements of narrative structure.

Exposition	This 'exposes' the situation at the start of the story, introducing characters and setting.
Conflict	In a conflict, one or more of the characters has a problem. Conflicts could be disagreements, difficulties or challenges, for example. There could be more than one conflict in a story.
Climax	The climax of a story is often its most exciting moment. Characters attempt to solve their conflicts once and for all – for example, in a battle – and their challenges seem huge.
Resolution	At the end of the story, the conflict is resolved: it is settled and explained. Sometimes it is resolved successfully, giving the story a happy ending – but not always!

Answer the questions below to identify these elements. You could use your answers to Activity 1 for support.

1 Think about the exposition of the story. What is the situation that makes Yang Zhifa, his brothers and his neighbours start digging a hole?

2 Think about the conflict in the story. What problem do Zhifa, his brothers and his neighbours encounter while digging the hole?

3 Think about the climax of the story. How do Zhifa, his brothers and his neighbours eventually deal with the problem?

4 Think about the resolution to the story. How does the story of Zhifa, his brothers and his neighbours end? In what way has the conflict been settled?

Activity 3: Exploring the writer's intention

1 The story of Yang Zhifa is not told in chronological order. Instead, the writer has chosen to begin it with a mysterious event.

   a) What is this mystery?

   b) How much of the article on page 186 do you need to read in order to discover the explanation of this mystery?

   c) Why do you think the writer chose to structure the article in this way? You may wish to choose from the vocabulary suggestions below or use your own ideas.

engage | discover | mystery | reveal | tension | surprise | withhold

2 Look again at the third paragraph of the article.

   a) How long did Zhifa and his brothers spend digging a hole?

   b) How deep was the hole they dug?

   c) Why do you think the writer chose to include so much detail about them digging a hole? Write one or two sentences explaining your ideas.

Skills Boost: Chronological and non-chronological structure

Stories are often told in chronological order. However, some are non-chronological: the writer takes an exciting event from the middle of the story to engage the reader's interest at the start. The events below all come from one story, but they are not ordered chronologically.

The Pied Piper of Hamelin

A   The mayor agrees to the piper's deal.

B   A city called Hamelin is overrun by a plague of rats.

C   Neither the piper nor the children are ever seen again.

D   The piper offers to rid the town of its rats, if the mayor pays him.

E   The piper takes revenge: his music lures children from the town into the mountains.

F   A mysterious man with a musical pipe hears about the rats and goes to Hamelin.

G   The mayor refuses to pay the piper.

H   The piper's music lures the rats into the river.

1 Structure the story chronologically, noting down the letters of the sentences in the correct order.

2 Which event do you think would make the most engaging, exciting opening for the story? Why is that? Write **two or three** sentences explaining your choice.

Activity 4: Planning to tell a tale

You are going to plan your own article about a surprising discovery. You could write about a real discovery, or an imagined one.

Gather ideas

1 Think about the basic facts you will include in your article.
   a) Note down who made the discovery.
   b) Note down what the discovery was. You could choose from the suggestions below or use your own ideas.

   treasure | an ancient object | a great painting | an important book

   c) Note down where the discovery happened. You could choose from the suggestions below or use your own ideas.

   at home | deep in the jungle | in the middle of a desert | underground

   d) Write **one** sentence summarising what was found, where it was found and who found it.

2 Think about the events that happened before and after the discovery.
   a) Note down what the finder was doing when they made the discovery, and why they were doing it.
   b) Note down how the finder felt when they made the discovery, and what they did next.

Plan

3 **a)** Make a list of all the key events you will include in your article. Write them in chronological order.
   b) Copy the planning table shown. Add each of the key events in your story to a row in the left-hand column, thinking carefully about what pieces of information should make up each part of the story.
   c) Think about how you want the reader to respond to each part of your story. Add your ideas to the right-hand column of the table.
   d) Select which event in the story would make the most engaging, exciting start for the article.
   e) Write **one** sentence that could begin your article. Ensure that it will engage the reader's attention immediately.

1. Exposition	Response
2. Conflict	Response
3. Climax	Response
4. Resolution	Response

This section links to pages 178–181 of the Workbook.

Section 4
Choosing precise vocabulary

In this section, you will explore the importance of careful vocabulary choice when you are writing to explain and to describe.

▼ Read the newspaper article and then answer the questions that follow it.

WHY I LOVE SCUBA DIVING

1 **The blue sapphire sea in front of me suddenly darkened. Nearly 30 metres down in the depths of the Indian Ocean, I knew we were about to come across something big. I just didn't know what.**

2 As my four fellow divers and I swam closer, the grey mass slowly began to take shape and come into focus.

3 It was the cold glint of a steely eye that gave it away, an eye in such a strange position and on such an oddly-shaped body, it could only be one creature.

4 Then suddenly, they were upon us: hundreds and hundreds of hammerhead sharks. Above me. Below me. To the side of me. Silhouetted against the sky and as far as the eye could see.

5 I stopped breathing, not through fear, but from sheer awe and wonder. I may have only been diving a couple of years but I knew this was something special, something few had ever seen.

6 We hung in the water, motionless, letting the hammerheads swim around us. Naturally shy, although potentially ferocious creatures, they gave us a good few metres of space and carried on their journey.

7 And then, just as suddenly, they were gone.

8 Eight years, and more than 150 dives later, I still remember those precious few minutes like they were yesterday. It's for moments like that that I dive.

9 Because, no matter how many times you dip beneath the waves, you never know what you're going to see. Or when you'll see it. When we came across that school of hammerheads, we'd been down for 40 minutes, seen nothing and were getting bored. Then they magically appeared.

10 Dive the same site 10 times, and you'll have 10 very different experiences. One day, you'll look in a little cave to see the huge eyes of an octopus, the next a cuttlefish will scoot past you or a moray eel will waft out and give you the evil eye.

11 The sheer amount of wildlife under our waters is incredible.

12 I've choked back tears as a turtle allowed me to swim alongside her in Borneo, stroked the tail of an angel shark lying buried deep in the sand in Lanzarote and chased after stingrays all over the world.

13 It's the serenity of the ocean that appeals to me. The moment you leap off the boat, you're submerged into a different world, an utterly silent world, with no idea what you're going to find.

Activity 1: Identifying explanations

The article on page 190 is an explanation text: it explains why the writer loves scuba diving. The writer also uses a lot of description to help explain why this is.

1 Look again at the following section of the article, and then at paragraphs 1–8. In under 20 words, summarise what happened in the 'precious few minutes' mentioned below.

> Eight years, and more than 150 dives later, I still remember those precious few minutes like they were yesterday. It's for moments like that that I dive.

2 Identify **one** reason that those minutes were special, according to paragraphs 1–8.

3 Look again at paragraphs 9–13. Identify **two** further reasons the writer loves scuba diving, according to these paragraphs.

Activity 2: Responding to vocabulary choice

Writers choose every word of a text very carefully. The right vocabulary choice can add a great deal of impact to the writer's ideas.

1 Look again at the first paragraph of the article on page 190.
   a) Identify the **one** phrase that the writer uses to describe how the ocean looked.
   b) What impression does this vocabulary choice create of the ocean? Write one or two sentences explaining your ideas.

2 In the second and third paragraphs, the writer creates an impression of the hammerhead sharks.
   a) Identify **two** words or phrases that you feel create the most powerful impression of the sharks.
   b) Write one or two sentences explaining the impression that each of your chosen words or phrases creates.

3 In the last paragraph of the article, the writer creates a powerful impression of diving under the ocean.
   a) Choose **two** words or phrases that you feel create the most powerful impression.
   b) Write one or two sentences explaining the impression that each of your chosen words or phrases creates.

4 **a)** Would you like to go scuba diving? Write one or two sentences explaining your answer.
   b) Identify the **two** words or phrases from the article that have the greatest influence on your attitude to scuba diving.

Skills Boost: Using a thesaurus

You can use a thesaurus to help you make more effective vocabulary choices. However, when you find a synonym in a thesaurus, you should make sure you know the word and understand its meaning and connotations before you use it.

1 Look at the sentence below and follow the steps (**a–d**) to find a replacement for the word 'worried'.

> As I opened the envelope with shaking fingers, I felt worried about what would be inside.

> worried
> anxious, discombobulated, frightened, insecure, nervous, upset

a) Note down the synonyms for 'worried' that you recognise and understand.

b) Use a dictionary to check the meanings of any words you don't know.

c) Note down the words you might consider using to replace 'worried'.

d) Look at the words you might consider. Select **one** word to replace 'worried' and rewrite the sentence to include it.

Activity 3: Exploring vocabulary choices

Look again below at the opening of the article on page 190. Look at the possible synonyms for each underlined word.

> The blue sapphire sea in front of me <u>suddenly</u> darkened. Nearly 30 metres down in the depths of the Indian Ocean, I knew we were about to come across something <u>big</u>. I just didn't know what.

abruptly, quickly, unanticipatedly

enormous, large, sizeable, substantial

> As my four fellow divers and I swam closer, the grey <u>mass</u> slowly began to take shape and come into focus.

crowd, density, lump, multitude

> It was the cold <u>glint</u> of a steely eye that gave it away, an eye in such a strange position and on such an oddly-shaped body, it could only be one creature.

glimmer, sparkle, twinkle

1 Rewrite the paragraphs above, replacing some or all of the underlined words with your own vocabulary choices.

2 Write one or two sentences explaining your reasons for each choice.

Activity 4: Explaining and describing

You are going to write a short article about an activity or experience that you have enjoyed.

Plan

1 Which activity or experience will you explain and describe? It could be, for example:
- a hobby you enjoy
- a sport you play regularly
- a place you love to visit
- a film or book you have enjoyed.

Note down two ideas and then choose one of them.

Remember

When you are planning a piece of writing, aim to think of more ideas than you need – then you can choose the best one.

---

2 Note down **two** reasons that you love your chosen activity or experience. Try to think of two very different reasons in order to give the reader the fullest possible explanation.

> I love the excitement of skateboarding.
>
> I love meeting new people and learning new moves from them.

3 Note down at least **three** things about your chosen activity or experience you could describe. These could be:
- details about something that happened, including when and where it happened
- descriptions of what you saw, heard, smelt, touched or tasted
- a description of how the experience made you feel.

4 In the article on page 190, the first part focuses on description of one particular scuba-diving experience, while the second part of the article focuses on reasons why the writer loves scuba diving. In what order will you structure your text?

> Part 1: My first visit to a theme park.
>
> Part 2: The reasons I love theme parks.

Write and review

5 Using the ideas and structure you have planned, write your article.

6 Read through your writing, thinking about every word you have used. Can any of your vocabulary choices be improved? If so, alter them.

Section 5
Assessment

In this section, you will answer questions on a short article and write your own article to assess your progress.

▼ **Read the newspaper article and then answer the questions that follow it.**

MY FAMILY WAS ATTACKED BY LIONS

1 I was five when we arranged to go to Longleat **safari park**. As it was a special occasion, we had borrowed my Uncle Meirion's car. It was shiny and new and, more importantly, big, so that we could fit everybody in it. This was in the days before seatbelts and it was the norm to ram as many people into the car as possible.

2 We set off with Mum and Dad in the front, and layers of aunts, uncles and cousins in the back. There were nine of us in total. My mum was particularly concerned that we take care of Uncle Meirion's car, so we were instructed not to eat our sandwiches, and to sit nicely.

3 On arrival, it was decided that we could not possibly drive through the monkey enclosure, in case the monkeys did any damage to the car. For us children, this was a great disappointment.

4 So, with a car full of grumbling children, we missed the monkeys and drove to the lion enclosure. We parked up and there, right by the driver's side window, was a beautiful lion. While everyone was chatting away, I wound down the window to pat the lion on the head. My dad, with his hand over mine, frantically tried to get the window back up again, but before he could, the lion stuck its head up to the open window and roared.

5 While the many other occupants of the car began screaming, I sat smiling, with my hair blowing slightly in the breeze of the lion's roar. Dad got the window up but, for whatever reason, the lions then went into a frenzy. They started to climb over Uncle Meirion's car, leaving the imprints of their feet on the roof. One sat on the bonnet with its feet on the windscreen and I sat matching my little hands up to its great big paws, while the rest of the family flung themselves from side to side, trying to shake off the lions.

6 Looking back, I can see that there was just a sheet of glass separating us from them, and we were their dinner. But I was five, and these lions were my friends.

7 The lions then began to eat the tyres. My brother remembers a hissing sound when a lion punctured one of them, making the car tilt to one side. Dad leant on the horn to try to summon help. The park rangers eventually arrived (they had been taking their lunch break) and they shot the lions. I now know that they would have just shot them with tranquillisers, but to five-year-old me, they had killed them. I was devastated.

8 My family's hysteria, meanwhile, started to abate as they realised that this day was not to be their last. We were ushered into the rangers' truck and Uncle Meirion's car was hooked up to the back, limping sadly along behind as we left the park.

> ### Key vocabulary
> **safari park**: zoo with large, mainly open-air enclosures in which wild animals roam freely, and through which visitors drive

Activity 1: Reading

1 Look again at the first two paragraphs of the article on page 194. How does the writer use language in these paragraphs to suggest that the car was crowded?

2 Look again at paragraphs 4–8.
a) Identify **two** words or phrases that show the danger of the narrator's situation.
b) For each word or phrase you have chosen, write one or two sentences explaining how the writer's vocabulary choice creates this impression.

3 Consider the narrative structure of the article.
a) Which paragraphs include the exposition of the story?
b) Which paragraphs include the conflict of the story?
c) Which paragraphs include the climax of the story?
d) Which paragraphs include the resolution of the story?

4 In one word, summarise your response to the article.
You could choose one of the responses below or use your own ideas, then write one or two sentences explaining your response. Use evidence from the article to support your ideas.

humour | anxiety | tension | fear | disbelief

Activity 2: Writing

1 Write an article describing a time in your life when you made a mistake or something went wrong.

Before you write
Plan your ideas. Think about:
• how to organise your writing to engage your reader and hold their attention
• how you want the reader to respond at each point in your writing. You could use a table like the one shown to organise your ideas and track your intended responses.

Exposition	
Conflict	
Climax	
Resolution	

As you write
• Choose your vocabulary carefully to make your story vivid and exciting.

When you have finished writing
• Check to see if any of your vocabulary choices could be improved.
• Check that your spelling and punctuation are accurate.

Section 6
Expressing feelings

In this section, you will explore different ways in which writers convey thoughts and feelings.

▼ Read the extract and then answer the questions that follow it.

1 On 24 July 1908, the final day of athletics at the Olympics, 100,000 people crammed into the stadium at White City in London to witness the conclusion to the marathon.

2 Every five minutes, after each mile of the route, the name of the current marathon leader was read out: first Thomas Jack then Jack Price, both Englishmen, then for most of the second half of the race, Charles Hefferon. But Hefferon was fading, and with two miles to go he was passed by the Italian Dorando Pietri. Inside the stadium, the crowd turned towards the gate and waited for the first sight of the leader.

3 Pietri was 5ft 2in, a pastry chef, and looked younger than his 22 years. "As I entered the stadium, the pain in my legs and in my lungs became impossible to bear," he wrote seven years later. "It felt like a giant hand was gripping my throat, tighter and tighter. Willpower was irrelevant now. If it hadn't been so bad I would not have fallen the first time. I got up automatically and launched myself a few more paces forwards. They tell me that I fell another five or six times. I don't remember anything else."

4 When he first fell, Jack Andrew, the clerk of the course, and Dr Michael Bulger, the chief medical officer, went to his aid. In doing so they destroyed his chances of success. Nearly 50 years later, Andrew's daughter discovered his account of the race.

5 "As Dorando reached the track he staggered and after a few yards fell. Dr Bulger went to his assistance. Each time Dorando fell I had to hold his legs while the doctor massaged him to keep his heart beating. Each time he arose we kept our arms in position behind (not touching him) to prevent him falling on his head."

6 It is at this point that a second athlete enters the stadium. The American, Johnny Hayes, completed his circuit of the track without drama and lodged an appeal. Pietri was disqualified.

7 Queen Alexandra insisted that the Italian should get some reward for his efforts, and during the closing ceremony presented him with a small silver cup. "When I was called to see Her Majesty, I was trembling all over," he said. "I felt as if I should fall as I did in the race. Then she spoke to me very kindly. 'Bravo' was the only word I could understand, but I knew what she meant by her smile."

Activity 1: Inferring information

Writers sometimes use description to give the reader key information and ideas.

1 Look again at the first paragraph of the extract on page 196.
   a) Identify **one** piece of factual information about the race that is clearly stated, not implied.
   b) Identify **one** word or phrase the writer uses to imply that the marathon race in the 1908 Olympics attracted a lot of interest and attention.

2 Look again at the third paragraph of the extract. Identify **two** words or phrases the writer uses to imply that Dorando Pietri was exhausted as he attempted to complete the marathon.

3 Look again at the final paragraph of the extract. Identify **one** word or phrase the writer uses to imply that Dorando Pietri was nervous about meeting Queen Alexandra.

Activity 2: Responding to people and events

When writers describe people, places and events, they may intend to control the reader's response: how the reader feels.

1 Look again at paragraph 6 of the extract on page 196.
   a) Note down all the details that the writer gives about the athlete Johnny Hayes.
   b) Do you feel that the writer intends the reader to respond strongly to the presentation of Johnny Hayes? Write one or two sentences to explain your answer.
   c) What is your response to the writer's presentation of Johnny Hayes? You could choose from the suggestions below or use your own ideas.

   humour | disgust | annoyance | admiration | sympathy

   d) Write one or two sentences explaining your response.

2 Look again at the whole extract.
   a) Note down all the details that the writer gives about Dorando Pietri.
   b) Do you feel that the writer intends the reader to respond strongly to the presentation of Dorando Pietri? Write one or two sentences to explain your answer.
   c) What is your response to the writer's presentation of Dorando Pietri?
   d) Write one or two sentences explaining your response.

Activity 3: Describing feelings

Readers often respond to the feelings of the people that they are reading about. When you are writing about people's feelings, you can choose from these methods:

- name them. For example: *I felt very happy.*
- describe them. For example: *I smiled and felt warm inside.*

1 Which of the above methods do you think is more effective?

2 Note down at least **three** details or vocabulary choices you could use to describe each of the following feelings.
  a) exhaustion   b) anger   c) fear   d) excitement

How do I do that?

- Think about facial expressions: for example, someone who is angry may narrow their eyes and clench their teeth.
- Think about physical feelings: for example, if you are angry, you might feel like you have a fire burning in your stomach.

Skills Boost: Direct and reported speech

Direct speech	In **direct speech**, a person's words are written exactly as they were spoken. For example,'*I am determined to win the race,*' he declared.
Reported speech	In **reported speech**, the writer or narrator describes a person's words. For example, *He declared that he was determined to win the race.*

1 Identifiers are the phrases used to identify who is speaking in direct speech. Note down at least **five** verbs that could complete the identifier in the sentence shown.

'*I cannot run any faster!*' she **?**.

2 Rewrite the following examples of reported speech using direct speech.
  a) He explained that he had injured his leg.
  b) She said she did not expect to win the race.
  c) Eric's mother loudly encouraged him to do his best.

3 Rewrite the following examples of direct speech using reported speech.
  a) 'That's not fair!' cried Marjani.
  b) 'I think he's a cheat,' she whispered angrily.
  c) 'You are a great athlete, Matias,' said Waahid.

Activity 4: Writing an account

You are going to plan an account of a moment in your life at which you had a great success or a great disappointment. It could be, for example:
- a sporting event
- a test or exam
- a musical or drama performance.

1 Note down the key points during this event.

| feeling nervous before going on stage | starting to speak |
| going on stage | forgetting the words |

2 Copy and complete a table like the one below, answering the questions to develop and organise your ideas.

Exposition	Set the scene. Where were you? Who was there? What details could you use to describe the scene?
Conflict	Note down the task you faced or the problem you experienced. How did it make you feel?
Climax	Note down how the task or problem progressed, and its most heightened moment. How did it make you feel? How did it make other people feel?
Resolution	Conclude the account. How did the experience end – in success or in disappointment? How did your feelings change?

3 a) Look again at the exposition you have planned. Write a sentence to describe the scene for your reader. Aim to give the reader details from which they can infer information about your experience.

b) Look again at your notes for describing the conflict in your account. Write a sentence to describe your feelings in response to it.

c) Look again at your notes for describing the climax of your account. Write a sentence using direct speech or reported speech to show your reader what happened, or how you or other people were feeling.

d) Look again at the resolution you have planned. Write a sentence to describe your feelings in response to it.

This section links to pages 188–191 of the Workbook.

Section 7
Structuring paragraphs

In this section, you will explore the structure of paragraphs when writing to explain and describe.

In this extract, the writer describes a mysterious and dramatic event that took place at the beginning of the twentieth century in Siberia, a vast frozen region of Russia.

▼ **Read the extract and then answer the questions that follow it.**

The Tunguska event

1 On a summer morning in 1908, reindeer herders and **home-steaders**[1] in central Siberia were startled to see a brilliant blue-white fireball brighter than the Sun streak across the sky. Still descending, it exploded with a blinding flash and an intense pulse of heat. One eyewitness account states:

> *The whole northern part of the sky appeared to be covered with fire … I felt great heat as if my shirt had caught fire … there was a … mighty crash … I was thrown on the ground about [7 metres] from the porch. A hot wind, as from a cannon, blew past the huts from the north*

2 The blast was heard up to 1,000 km (600 miles) away, and the resulting pulse of air pressure circled Earth twice. For a number of nights following the blast, European astronomers, who knew nothing of the explosion, observed a glowing reddish haze high in the atmosphere.

3 When members of a scientific expedition arrived at the site in 1927, they found that the blast had occurred above the stony Tunguska River valley and had flattened trees in an irregular pattern extending to a radius of about 30 km (20 miles). The trees were knocked down pointing away from the centre of the blast, and limbs and leaves had been stripped away. The trunks of trees at the very centre of the area were still standing, although they had lost all their limbs. No crater has been found, so it seems that the explosion, estimated to have equalled 12 megatons (12 million tons) of TNT, occurred at least a few kilometres above the ground.

4 In 1993, astronomers produced computer models of objects entering Earth's atmosphere at various speeds and concluded that the most likely candidate for the Tunguska object seems to be a stony asteroid about 30 m in diameter. The models indicate that an object of this size would have exploded at just about the right height to produce the observed blast. This conclusion is consistent with modern studies of the Tunguska area showing that thousands of tons of powdered material with a composition resembling **carbonaceous chondrites**[2] are scattered in the soil.

Key vocabulary

home-steaders[1]: farming families that grow their own food
carbonaceous chondrites[2]: a type of meteorite

Activity 1: Responding to the text

1 Look again at paragraphs 1, 2 and 3 of the extract on page 200. For each paragraph, note down **one** effective detail, word or phrase that the writer has used to show the dramatic impact of the Tunguska event.

> In paragraph 1, the writer uses the word

> In paragraph 2,

Activity 2: Exploring structure

1 The extract on page 200 refers to three different years.
   a) How many years after the Tunguska event did members of the scientific expedition discover the flattened trees? Write a sentence explaining how you worked out your answer.
   b) How many years after the Tunguska event did astronomers explain what had happened using computer models?
   c) How would you describe the structure of this extract? Choose one of the suggestions below and then write one or two sentences explaining your choice.

logical | chronological | non-chronological | narrative

2 The paragraphs used in information and explanation texts often include both key information and supporting detail.
   - The first one or two sentences give the most important information. These are sometimes called topic sentences.
   - The other sentences in the paragraph add description or factual detail.

Look at each of the paragraphs in the extract. Which **two** of them follow this structure?

Remember

logical: clear and reasonable
chronological: following the order in which events occurred
non-chronological: not following the order in which events occurred
narrative: a story

Skills Boost: Paragraphing

There are four reasons to start a new paragraph:
- a change of topic   • a change of time   • a change of setting   • a change of speaker.

1 Which of these four reasons do you think is likely to be the most common in an explanation or description text? Write one or two sentences explaining your answer.

2 Look at the passage below. Note down where the passage should be split into different paragraphs by giving the first three words of each new paragraph.

Krakatoa is a volcano in the Pacific Ocean. It is located between the islands of Java and Sumatra. Its most dramatic eruption occurred in August 1883. The 1883 eruption created the loudest sound ever recorded. The eruption was heard 3,000 miles away. The force of the eruption fired hot ash 15 miles into the air. The ash filled the sky so that it was as dark as night for 72 hours after the eruption. The shock wave of the eruption circled the Earth seven times. Huge tsunamis followed the eruption. It is thought that more than 36,000 people died as a result of the eruption, shockwaves and tsunamis.

How do I do that?

All the pieces of information in each paragraph should be on the same topic. If a piece of information is not on the same topic as the others in the paragraph, it belongs in a different paragraph.

Activity 3: Building paragraphs

Look at these notes about the 1906 earthquake that shook San Francisco, USA.

began at 5.12 a.m. on 18th April 1906	destroyed San Francisco city hall
felt along 850 miles of Californian coast	destroyed 28,000 buildings
said to sound like 'the roar of 10,000 lions'	was followed by a fire
shook the entire city of San Francisco	fire burned for four days
lasted just a minute	took nine years to rebuild the city

1 **a)** Choose **one** fact that could form the key information in a paragraph. Write the first sentence of that paragraph.
    b) Now choose **two or three** further facts that could be used to add more detail to the key information you have chosen.

2 Write the paragraph you have planned.

Activity 4: Writing a paragraph

You are going to write the first paragraph of an article that explains and describes a time when a large city was hit by a dramatic and destructive storm.

Plan

1 Note down all the facts and details you could include in your article. Aim to gather 15–20 different ideas. You could think about:

when and where the storm took place	signs a storm was approaching	what the storm itself was like	the damage caused by the storm	how people's lives were affected

2 Note down what will be the main focus of your first paragraph. You could choose from the ideas above or use one of your own.

3 Write **one** sentence that explains the key piece of information that will begin your paragraph and introduce your topic.

4 Note down **two or three** supporting details you can add to your key piece of information. You could choose from the ideas below or use your own.

darkness | clouds | thunder | wind | rain | lightning | flooding

shuddering | rattling | lifting

roads | cars | trees | shops | roofs | buildings | windows

adults | children | animals

Write

5 Now you have gathered your ideas and planned your writing, write the first paragraph of your article.

Remember

Your first sentence should focus on the key information you have planned. The rest of your paragraph should give the reader two or three pieces of supporting information or detail.

This section links to pages 192–195 of the Workbook.

Section 8
Experimenting with sentences

In this section, you will explore different ways in which sentences can be structured to add clarity and impact to a writer's ideas.

▼ **Read the article and then answer the questions that follow it.**

A lightbulb moment?

1 Imagine the moment when a great scientific discovery is made. What do you imagine?

The scientist sits in her laboratory, surrounded by bubbling test tubes and beakers of coloured liquid.
5 She is deep in thought. Suddenly, her eyes light up and she begins to laugh. She grabs two test tubes and tips the liquid from one into the other. Smoke billows from the test tube. '**Eureka!**[1]' cries the scientist. 'It works! It works!' – and her discovery goes on to
10 change the course of human history forever.

Most great scientific discoveries are, however, not made in a single moment. Most are not the result of what is sometimes called 'a lightbulb moment': a moment of sudden inspiration. Most are the result
15 of months or even years of slow progress, gradual improvement and teamwork.

Take, for example, the invention of the lightbulb. It is widely believed that Thomas Edison invented the lightbulb in 1879. However, scientists had been
20 experimenting with electric light since the early 1800s. The problem was that their bulbs were too expensive or burned out too quickly.

Thomas Edison had a bright idea. He and his team of scientists invented a more efficient vacuum pump
25 that would remove all the air from the bulb. Their lightbulbs burnt longer – but not long enough.

Edison and his team started experimenting with different **filaments**[2]. They experimented with thin strips of **carbonised**[3] paper, but the bulbs
30 burned out in minutes. They tried filaments made of carbonised cotton. The bulbs burned out after just a few hours.

Edison and his team spent months testing more than 6,000 plants to find the best material for their
35 filaments. Eventually, they discovered that a filament made from bamboo would burn for more than a thousand hours.

Finally, the lightbulb was cheap enough and efficient enough to be used in homes, shops and
40 factories – but it was the work of many scientists over many years. It was most certainly not the result of a lightbulb moment!

Key vocabulary

Eureka![1]: exclamation of success, literally meaning 'I have found it!'
filaments[2]: thin strands that glow inside lightbulbs when electricity is passed through them
carbonised[3]: heated until it turns to carbon (the black substance that makes up charcoal, amongst other things)

Activity 1: Reading and responding

Use this activity to check your understanding of the article on page 204, and think about the writer's intention.

1 Thomas Edison and his team of scientists experimented with lots of different improvements to make lightbulbs cheap and efficient.
   a) List the things they did in order to perfect their invention, according to the extract.
   b) Why do you think the writer gives details of the different experiments? You could choose some of the ideas below or use your own.

> The writer wants to present inventors as

hard-working. | dedicated. | determined.

> The writer wants to present the life of the inventor as

frustrating. | exciting. | satisfying.

2 The article gives the reader information about:
   - the life of Thomas Edison
   - the invention of the lightbulb
   - the time and hard work that goes into great inventions.
   Which of these topics was the writer's main focus? Explain your answer.

Activity 2: Structuring sentences for impact

Short sentences can add impact to key ideas. Look again at lines 28–32 of the extract on page 204. Compare this section of the extract with the version below.

> They experimented with thin strips of carbonised paper, but the bulbs burned out in minutes so they tried filaments made of carbonised cotton, but the bulbs burned out after just a few hours.

1 What similarities and differences can you identify in these two paragraphs?

2 In the first version, the writer has used short sentences. Look again at the writer's key topics that you explored in Activity 1, question 2. Which of these topics is given added emphasis by the short sentences in lines 28–32 of the extract?

3 Which version do you prefer? Why is that? Write one or two sentences explaining your answer.

Grammar Boost: Restructuring sentences

Sequences of events can be linked using subordinating conjunctions that indicate time. For example:

> Edison experimented with many filaments
> <u>before</u> he found the best one.

The two clauses highlighted in this sentence can be swapped without changing their meaning:

> Before he found the best one,
> Edison experimented with many filaments.

1 Use conjunctions that indicate time to link each of the following groups of sentences into a multi-clause sentence.

a) I walked to school. I whistled a happy tune.   As I walked to

b) I whistled a happy tune. I arrived at school.

c) I worked hard in every lesson. It was time to go home.

d) I left school. I walked through the town. I met my friends.

2 Look at each of the sentences you have written. Restructure each one by swapping the clauses around, without changing the meaning.

Temporal conjunctions		
after	when	before
while	until	as

Activity 3: Structuring sentences for clarity

Look again at lines 3–8 of the extract on page 204. In these sentences, the writer has used a mixture of multi-clause sentences, which contain two or more points of information, and single-clause sentences, which contain just one. This adds variety to the text and helps the writer to make their meaning clear.

1 In the first sentence (on lines 3–4), there are **two** points of information:

A scientist sits in her laboratory.   She is surround by scientific equipment.

How many points of information are there in each of the other five sentences in lines 3–8?

2 Look at each of the following points of information about Isaac Newton's theory of gravity.

- It was the year 1666.
- Isaac Newton was in his mother's garden.
- He was sitting under an apple tree.
- An apple fell to the ground.
- He wondered why the apple dropped straight down.
- He realised a force was pulling it.

Write **three to five** sentences using all of these six points. Consider which you will combine in multi-clause sentences and which will remain as single-clause sentences.

3 Look again at each of the multi-clause sentences you have written. Restructure each one by swapping the clauses around, without changing the meaning.

Activity 4: Reviewing sentence structure

You are going to write a first-person description of someone trying to complete an extremely difficult homework problem.

Plan

1 Note down **six or seven** key points of information that you will include in your description. You could consider:

- where you are and what you are doing as you think. You could use the suggestions below or your own ideas.

  sitting | pacing up and down | staring out of the window | scratching your head
  sighing in frustration | grinding your teeth

- what happens when you suddenly realise how to complete the problem. You could use the suggestions below or your own ideas.

  smile | cheer | punch the air | run around in circles

Write and review

2 Using the key points you have noted, write **three to five** sentences of description. Consider which you will combine in multi-clause sentences and which will form single-clause sentences.

3 Use the same key points of information to write your description again. Aim to make your sentence structures as different as you can from those in your first version. For example, you could rewrite multi-clause sentences as single-clause sentences or use conjunctions to link clauses together.

4 Compare the two descriptions you have written. Which version do you prefer?

5 Rewrite your description a third time, combining the best parts of both versions to produce the clearest possible descriptive writing.

Section 9
Experimenting with openings

In this section, you will explore ways to engage your reader with an effective opening.

This is an extract from an article in which the writer describes trying the sport of skeleton: sliding down an ice track as fast as you can while lying face down on a small sled. The Cresta Run is an ice track in St Moritz, Switzerland.

▼ **Read the extract and then answer the questions that follow it.**

Death or glory: Simon Usborne rides the Cresta Run

1 You wonder if it's not too late to back out when the day starts with the Death Talk.

2 As David Payne, the man in charge, prepares our group for the world's oldest and most terrifying toboggan run, X-rays hang against a window. 'As you can see,' Payne says, 'it is possible for you to break every part of your body riding the Cresta Run.' Four men have lost their lives here. Would I soon join them?

3 The knee, elbow and gladiator-style knuckle guards strapped on, the crash helmet cranked tight and the steel-spiked shoes laced up, I lie on a 40-kg tea tray, my chin inches from the ground. Every muscle is tense. A man's boot planted in front of my sled is the only thing stopping me from hurtling, headlong and with limited control, down a steep, winding chute of ice at 50 mph. Shivering with cold and fear, I grip my toboggan as if my life depends on it – which it does. And then the man removes his foot.

4 My sled immediately starts accelerating at an alarming rate. I have been instructed to use the steel spikes attached to my boots to control my speed. Pinballing back and forth against the rock-hard ice banks, I get round the first two bends OK. But then comes Shuttlecock, the most notorious and feared part of the course. Approach it too fast, and you're guaranteed to be spat out of the run.

5 Sure enough, I haven't raked with my feet enough and barely have time to anticipate what is about to happen when my toboggan starts rising up the bank. And then I am airborne – briefly – before I cartwheel and finish in a heap. Winded, shocked but in one piece, I stagger to my feet.

6 The course record stands at 50.09 seconds. Beginners are told to aim for 70 seconds. But to do that, they must get to the bottom.

7 Determined not to bail out again on my second run, I dig my toes in hard and crawl round Shuttlecock. Entering the long straight after the danger zone, I drag my body forwards, lift my toes, and let rip. It feels like suicide – most of my body is hanging over the front of the sled – but it works and the next few seconds are a terrifying yet utterly exhilarating blur of diamond-hard ice, gritted teeth and bruising body slams. I cross the line in 73.39 seconds, having topped 50 mph. Not fast enough.

Activity 1: Responding to ideas

1 Look again at paragraphs 1 and 2 of the extract on page 208.
   a) What do you learn about the sport of skeleton from the paragraphs? Note down:
   - all the clues you can find
   - what they suggest about skeleton.
   b) Why might the writer have chosen to begin the extract in this way? Write one or two sentences explaining your answer.

2 Look again at paragraph 3 of the extract.
   a) Note **two** items of clothing the writer had to wear.
   b) What do these details suggest about the sport of skeleton?

3 Look again at paragraphs 4 to 7 of the extract.
   What do you learn about the writer's experience of skeleton in these four paragraphs? Note down:
   - all the clues you can find
   - what they tell you about his experience.

Activity 2: Exploring openings

1 The extract on page 208 contains the following four key topics.

| the Death Talk | getting dressed and ready for the skeleton | a first terrifying attempt at the skeleton | a second, more successful attempt at the skeleton |

   a) Which **one** of the key topics above do you think would make the most gripping first paragraph for the extract?
   b) What effect would your chosen opening have on the reader? You could choose from the suggestions below or use your own ideas.

   Opening the extract with '_____' would help to...

   ...create tension. | ...make the text sound exciting. | ...make the sport sound terrifying.

   ...make the reader want to find out what happens next. | ...highlight the dangers of the sport.

2 The extract is the beginning of a longer article. Later in the article, the writer describes completing the skeleton in less than 70 seconds, on his fifth attempt.
   In your opinion, would that section of the article have made an effective opening?
   Write one or two sentences explaining your answer.

Grammar Boost: Guiding the reader with adverbials of time

When they are positioned at the beginnings of paragraphs, adverbials of time can help to guide the reader through texts. Look at the short paragraphs below. The adverbials of time are highlighted.

> At first, I hated it. The task was huge, and I was certain I wasn't prepared for it.

> Eventually, I came to appreciate the experience. The scenery around me was beautiful.

1 Are the two paragraphs in the correct order? How can you tell?

2 Look at the sentences below. They summarise paragraphs, or groups of paragraphs, in the extract on page 208.

A   He makes his first attempt at skeleton.

B   He makes a second attempt with more success.

C   He puts on his safety clothing.

D   The writer is warned about the dangers of skeleton.

Adverbials of time	
Yesterday,	At first,
Tomorrow,	Then,
Eventually,	Next,
Soon,	After this,
Later,	In the end,

a) Put the sentences into the correct order.
b) Rewrite the sentences using adverbials of time to guide the reader.

Activity 3: Selecting an opening

Look at the following summary of eight topics covered in an article about learning to parachute.

A	training and learning to parachute for six long hours	**B**	getting into the plane and taking off
C	waiting in the doorway of the plane	**D**	jumping out from a height of 1 km
E	feeling relief when the parachute opens	**F**	floating down to the ground for five minutes
G	looking out over miles and miles of landscape	**H**	landing safely back on the ground

1 In your opinion, which topic would make the most effective opening? Write one or two sentences explaining your choice.

Activity 4: Planning an opening

You are going to write the opening to an article in which you describe doing something new that made you feel nervous. It could be, for example:

- trying a new sport
- starting a new school
- trying an unfamiliar kind of food.

It could be a real or imagined experience.

Imagine

1 a) What new experience will you describe? Note down **two or three** possible ideas before selecting **one**.

b) Why did you decide to undertake this daunting experience? Did you want to do it or did someone else encourage you? Write one or two sentences explaining your reasons.

c) Why did this experience make you feel nervous? Write one or two sentences explaining your ideas.

Plan

2 Each of the following questions focuses on a different topic you could include in your article. Note at least **three** ideas in each answer.

a) Note down what you had to do before this new experience. Did you have to train or prepare? Did you have to buy special clothing or equipment?

b) How did you feel just beforehand? Consider thoughts, emotions and physical sensations.

c) How did your feel during the new experience?

d) How did you feel afterwards or when you experienced the new thing again? Did you feel better or worse about it?

3 Look again at the different ideas you have gathered for each topic. Which **one** topic will you use as the opening of your article? Write one or two sentences explaining your ideas.

Write

4 Write **one** paragraph as the opening of your article, using the **one** topic you have chosen.

Section 10
Experimenting with endings

In this section, you will experiment with creating a satisfying ending for your writing.

This extract is an account of the writer's visit to the Himalayas.

▼ **Read the extract and then answer the questions that follow it.**

Why a tiny plane is the best way to climb Mount Everest

1 Our flight is delayed for an hour because of a leopard on the runway. As we walk to our plane, we see a family of monkeys sauntering across the tarmac.

2 We climb aboard. This is certainly the smallest plane I have ever been on, and our cabin crew of one welcomes us aboard. Every passenger is allocated a window seat, and we sit silently waiting to depart.

3 Some passengers applaud as we complete take-off. We fly over Kathmandu, and head out towards the Himalayas.

4 Our crew member acts as mountain guide, pointing out the different peaks – Gaurishankar and Chugimago, Numbur and Gyachung Kang. She tells us stories about the first climbers, the oldest and the youngest, those who did it fastest and those who did it best. She points out the peak that must never be climbed out of respect for the gods, and invites us, one by one, to the front to see the view.

5 She stands back and stretches out one arm as we fly over Everest. And it is magical. The height of the summit, she says, is the same as the cruising altitude of a jumbo jet. Nothing prepares you for quite how, well, big it is.

6 The top of the mountain pokes through the cloud and the sun bounces off the snow, creating dazzling bursts of light. There is silence among the passengers now, except for the relentless click of cameras and then repeated sighs of amazement as we set our cameras down and stare.

7 We fly over the entire mountain range, then circle back and fly over it again, so that each side of the plane can get a good view, though none of the passengers has remained in their seats. Strangers, we have climbed over each other and around each other to see the view.

8 As mountains give way to plains again, we find our seats and our voices, and the journey back to Kathmandu is considerably noisier than before. The plane lands with only a slight bump, and the applause breaks out again. I applaud, too.

Remember

Effective writers choose the structure of their text, the structure of each sentence and every word in those sentences. Nothing is left to chance!

Activity 1: Responding to ideas

1 Look again at paragraphs 1 and 2 of the article on page 212. Identify **three** details that suggest the plane is not taking off from a large city airport.

2 Look again at paragraphs 5 and 6 of the article.
a) What impression does the writer create of the Himalayas in these paragraphs? Write one or two sentences to explain your answer.
b) Identify **one** detail or **one** vocabulary choice that the writer has chosen to create this impression.

3 How have the mood and behaviour of the passengers on the plane changed by the end of the trip? Explain your answer with reference to the article.

4 a) What overall impression does the writer create of her journey in the tiny plane? Write one or two sentences to explain your answer. You could choose from the suggestions below or use your own ideas.

strange | frightening | boring | enjoyable | exciting | inspiring | astonishing

b) Identify **one** detail or **one** vocabulary choice that the writer has used to create this impression.

Activity 2: Exploring endings

1 The article on page 212 contains the following five key topics.

A	B	C	D	E
the airport and plane	the views of the Himalayas	the view of Everest specifically	the flight back	the landing

The climax of the article is topic C. The writer could have chosen to end the article with this topic, omitting the flight back and the landing.
a) Which **one** of the key topics C or E do you think would make the most effective ending to the article?
b) What effect would your chosen ending have on the reader?

2 After the flight to see the Himalayas, the writer may have:

A	B	C	D	E
returned to her hotel	had something to eat	talked with other travellers	gone to bed	dreamed about the mountains

Which **one** of the key topics A–E do you think would make the most effective ending to the article? Write a sentence or two explaining your choice.

Skills Boost: Polishing your proofreading skills

When you have finished writing a text, it is important to check your spelling. In particular, look out for words that feature easily confused letters such as those in the table below.

'k'	's'	'sh'	'f'
The 'k' sound can be spelled 'c', 'k' or 'ck'.	The 's' sound can be spelled 's' or 'c'.	The 'sh' sound can be spelled 'ti', 'si', 'ci', or 'sh'.	The 'f' sound can be spelled 'f' or 'ph'.

1 Using the table to help you, choose the correct spelling for each word.
   a) 'k' sound:
      i) kitchen / citchen   ii) cricket / kricet   iii) cuckumber / cucumber
   b) 's' sound:
      i) circle / sircle   ii) selebrate / celebrate   iii) pensil / pencil
   c) 'sh' sound:
      i) decision / decition   ii) station / stacion   iii) musitian / musician
   d) 'f' sound:
      i) telephone / telefone   ii) fotograf / photograph   iii) alphabet / alfabet

Activity 3: Selecting an ending

Like a good story, an effective description should have a satisfying ending. It could describe the dramatic resolution of a significant problem, the lasting effects of an experience or the satisfying end to an enjoyable journey.

1 The table below contains ideas that could be used in a description of a disastrous journey into the Sahara desert. Working from top to bottom, choose one option (A, B, C or D) from each row to create an effective description. Focus particularly on what ending would be most satisfying.

Early that morning, we got on a plane and flew out across the desert. Far below, we saw...			
A miles and miles of nothing but hot sand.	B a train of camels and a Bedouin camp.	C the greenery of an oasis on the horizon.	

Then, all of a sudden, ...			
A the pilot fell ill and passed out.	B the engines began to fail.	C we flew into a storm.	

We crash-landed and were stranded for hours. As evening approached, ...			
A a camel and rider appeared in the distance.	B we set out, determined to find the oasis before dark fell.	C the skies above us began to clear.	D the endless sand dunes started to become deathly cold.
A The pilot recovered, and found tents and a radio phone.	B Hungry and thirsty, we shivered as night fell.	C A stranger led us to his camp.	D Just as we were starting to give up, we saw the glint of water.

Activity 4: Planning an ending

You are going to plan an article in which you describe visiting a place you have always wanted to go to.

Imagine

1 Where in the world would you most like to visit? It could be, for example:
- an area of natural beauty, such as the Himalayas
- a city, such as New York
- a building, such as the Taj Mahal.

Note down **two or three** possible ideas before choosing **one** you will describe.

Plan

2 Answer each question below to help you develop your ideas. Note at least **three** ideas in each answer.

You may wish to organise your ideas in a table like the one in Activity 3 on page 214, with a row for each question. Then, when you have finished gathering ideas, you can select one from each row.

a) How did you get to your destination? Was it a simple journey or did you face challenges along the way?

b) When you reached your destination, what could you see, hear, touch or smell?

c) Did you encounter any problems? Try to think of both small and large problems.

d) Were your problems resolved? How?

e) What were the highlights of your visit?

f) What happened at the end of your trip? Did you return to a hotel room, to your home or somewhere else?

3 Look again at the ideas you have noted.

a) Tick the ones that you will use in your article.

b) Add a cross by the ones that you will **not** use.

c) Use your selected ideas to write a summary of the experience.

This section links to pages 204–205 of the Workbook.

Section 11
Assessment

In this section, you will write an article explaining and describing a memorable experience.

Activity 1: Planning

The school magazine has invited you to write an article explaining and describing the most memorable moment of your life so far. You could choose to describe a happy or painful memory. It could be a real or an imagined experience.

1 What will be the topic of your article? You could refer to the suggestions below to help you choose or use your own ideas.

You could write about:
- a place you have visited
- a person you met
- a family celebration.

It could be a time when you:
- hurt yourself
- enjoyed yourself
- felt frightened
- saw something amazing.

I will never forget the time when I

When I was four years old, I

I will remember this moment for the rest of my life

Whenever I think of this moment, I feel

2 Identify **four** key topics for your writing: the four key ideas that you will use to explain your most memorable moment. You could use the following narrative structure:

	Put the title of your story here
Exposition	
Conflict	
Climax	
Resolution	

3 For each of the four topics you have identified, note down **one** key piece of information.

4 Note down **two or three** pieces of supporting detail to add to each key piece of information.

5 Think about the opening and the ending of your article.
   a) Select the topic that will most engage the reader's attention. Plan your opening sentence.
   b) Select the topic that will form the most satisfying ending to your article. Plan your closing sentence.

Activity 2: Writing

1 Write your article.
As you write, remember to:
   - think about your intention: the response you want to create in the reader
   - organise your paragraphs in a way that suits your intention
   - begin each new paragraph with key information
   - add supporting detail to each piece of key information.

Activity 3: Reviewing and revising

1 Read through your article.
Check that:
   - you have made effective vocabulary choices
   - you have used a variety of single-clause and multi-clause sentences
   - your spelling, punctuation and grammar are accurate.

Unit 6
Dramatic!

This unit focuses on plays and the way in which they are written and performed, from everyday classroom scenarios to extraordinary murders. You will find out how playwrights build their characters using the words that they say and how you can perform the same text in very different ways. These texts will help you explore drama and its ability to capture our imaginations, from curtain up to the final bows.

In this unit, you will...

- explore ways in which a play can engage its audience.
- explore how a writer can introduce setting, mood and character in just a few lines at the very beginning of a playscript.
- explore ways in which a script can be created from a story written in prose.
- explore how playwrights can use conflict to shape stories.
- explore how playwrights use dialogue to create character.
- answer questions on a short extract and write a critical response to assess your progress.
- explore Shakespeare's language, and how he uses dialogue to develop characters and relationships.
- explore how performing a scene in different ways can change your response to characters and events.
- explore how Shakespeare explores the theme of power in the play *Macbeth*.
- develop your critical writing skills, exploring ways of introducing and concluding your responses.
- answer questions on a text to assess your progress in this unit.

By the end of this unit, you will be able to analyse a play extract, exploring the writer's choices and their intended impact on an audience.

Section 1
Curtain up

In this section, you will explore ways in which a play can engage its audience.

This is an extract from the opening of a play called *The Terrible Fate of Humpty Dumpty*.

▼ **Read the extract and then answer the questions that follow it.**

1 *(On waste ground. Stubbs, with the members of his gang – Jimmy, Pete, Kathy, Kay, Janet and Tracey – are surrounding Terry Dumpton. Sammy stands to one side.)*

5 Pete   *(To Terry.)* See my frisbee, Humpty? My best frisbee, this is. I've had this frisbee for ages. I love it. I'd hate to lose it. I'd go mad if I lost this frisbee. Want to see how it works?

(Pete throws the frisbee into the air. Then he says:)

10   Oh, dear. It's got stuck in the pylon. What am I going to do now?

Stubbs   You'll have to get it back, Pete.

Pete   I know. Only trouble is, I'm scared of heights. Can't stand them. I get a nosebleed
15   just going to the top of the stairs.

Stubbs   You'll have to get somebody to fetch it down for you, then.

Pete   That's right. Who, though?

(Stubbs points at Terry.)

20 Stubbs   Him!

(There is a pause. Then Stubbs says:)

        All right, Humpty? Up you go. Get Pete's frisbee back for him.

(There is tension. Then Stubbs continues:)

25   Go on. Climb the pylon. Get it back.

(Terry stares up at the pylon. Stubbs goes on:)

        Perhaps you ain't our mate, then. Perhaps you don't like us at all. That means you're the kind of person who'd sneak on us.

30 *(He walks towards Terry.)*

Terry   All right, I'll get it.

Sammy   Don't, Terry.

Stubbs   Shurrup, Sammy.

Sammy   It's dangerous.

35 Kathy   You wanna go up there instead?

(There is a pause.)

Stubbs   Go on.

(Terry starts to climb the pylon. Egged on by Pete, the members of the gang start to chant 'Humpty Dumpty!'
40 *over and over again, and then shout comments up at Terry. Sammy runs forward.)*

Sammy   Don't, Terry. Come down.

Activity 1: Reading between the lines

When you read a script, try to imagine the play being performed. Look carefully at the **stage directions** as well as the **lines** the characters are given to speak.

1 Look at the first stage direction in the extract on page 220.
  a) Draw a diagram showing where each character is standing at the very start of the play.
  b) What can you infer from this stage direction about the relationship between Terry and the members of Stubbs's gang?
  c) What can you infer from this stage direction about the relationship between Sammy and the members of Stubbs's gang?

2 Identify **one** line spoken by each of the characters below. What can you infer about the character from the one line you have chosen?
  a) Stubbs   b) Terry   c) Sammy

3 Humpty Dumpty is a children's nursery rhyme. It tells the story of an egg that falls from a wall, smashes and cannot be mended.

Humpty Dumpty sat on a wall
Humpty Dumpty had a great fall
All the king's horses and all the king's men
Couldn't put Humpty together again.

  a) What does the nickname 'Humpty' suggest about Terry's appearance?
  b) What does the nickname 'Humpty' suggest about what happens to Terry during the play?

Activity 2: Responding to characters and action

1 Look again at your answers to Activity 1. How do you respond to each of the characters below? Write one or two sentences about each of them, explaining your ideas.
  a) Terry   b) Stubbs   c) Sammy

You could choose from the following suggestions to help you or use your own ideas.

humour | fear | sympathy | disgust | anger | admiration

Activity 3: Deciding where to begin

Look at the following short synopsis of the play from which the extract on page 220 is taken: *The Terrible Fate of Humpty Dumpty.*

A   Terry starts a new school.

B   Terry is bullied.

C   Terry's only friend, Sammy, will not stand up for him.

D   Terry stops going to school.

E   Terry is bullied into climbing an electricity pylon.

F   Terry is electrocuted and dies.

G   Sammy tells the police what happened.

1 As much of the story is told through **flashbacks**, the playwright could have begun the play at any point. Why do you think the writer decided to start the play as Terry is about to climb the electricity pylon? Write one or two sentences to explain your answer.

2 Identify **one** other point in the story that could have made an effective first scene. Write **two or three** sentences explaining your choice.

Skills Boost: Setting out a script

There are conventions that a writer should follow when writing a **script**.

1 Look again at the extract on page 220. Use it to help you write a set of instructions, under the title 'How to Write a Script'.

a) Make sure your instructions answer all the questions below.
- How do you show which character is speaking?
- How do you show what each character says and does?
- How do you show the difference between dialogue and the stage directions?

b) Check that your instructions include all of these words: left | right | margin

You could also make use of these words: brackets | italics | paragraph | lined up

2 Use your rules to rewrite the text below as a script.

"You're late!" said Guang.

"Sorry," mumbled Mei, looking away. "I got lost."

"Lost?" cried Guang, laughing. "How?"

Activity 4: Writing an opening scene

You are going to plan and write the first part of the first **scene** of a play set at school.

Plan

Consider ideas for your engaging opening scene. You could choose from the suggestions with each instruction below or use your own ideas.

1 For your scene, you will need to select main characters and a setting.

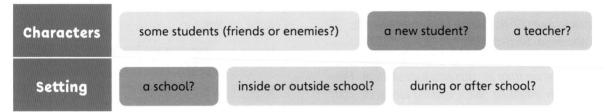

| **Characters** | some students (friends or enemies?) | a new student? | a teacher? |
| **Setting** | a school? | inside or outside school? | during or after school? |

a) Note your choices of **two or three** main characters, a setting and a time.
b) Give each of your chosen characters a name.

2 You will also need some action: something for the characters to do and talk about, and that engages the audience's interest.

| having an argument? | telling a secret? | making a plan? | playing a game? |

Write **two or three** sentences summarising what will happen during the opening scene of your play.

3 Look again at the two or three main characters you have chosen to include in your scene. What impression do you want each of them to give the audience? For example, they could be friendly, funny or mean. Write **two or three** sentences describing their personalities and their relationships with each other.

Write

4 Think about your setting and the relationships between your characters. Write a stage direction to tell the actors where and how they should stand when the play begins.

5 Decide who will be the first character to speak, and what you want the audience to infer about the character from that first line. Write the first line.

6 Complete the first page or so of your script, thinking about what each character will say, and what this will show about them.

Section 2
Setting the scene

In this section, you will explore how a writer can introduce setting, mood and character in just a few lines at the very beginning of a playscript.

This scene from a play is set in a British school at the beginning of a school day.

▼ Read the extract and then answer the questions that follow it.

1 *(Desks in rows fill the stage, facing out towards the audience. Students in uniform are sitting on their desks or standing around, talking. There is sudden silence from all students except Liam. They*
5 *slide slowly into their seats, looking forwards. They respond as though a teacher in front of them is calling out their names to check attendance. Liam remains sitting on Darren's desk, chatting.)*

Laura B Yes, Mr Lewis.

10 Ben Yes, sir.

Darren Sir.

Liam *(Excitedly, to Darren)* You haven't? I can't believe it! You haven't played it yet?

Sara *(As though bored)* It's Sara, sir... Not Sarah.
15 *(Pause)* Yes, sir.

Dan Rhymes with 'tiara', sir. *(Pause)* Wasn't meant to be funny, sir. *(Sulking playfully)* Just trying to be helpful, sir.

Liam *(Miming actions as he speaks)* So you're
20 climbing down, yeah, and they're shooting at you, yeah? And you jump – weeeeeee ...

Daisy Yes, Mr Lewis.

Laura E Yes, sir.

Liam And, then, like, kabbooooooom!

25 Neil Here, sir.

Liam And he goes *(robotic, monotone voice)* 'Stop or we must eliminate you, intruder.'

Stuart Yes, Mr Lewis.

Liam And you're running and running, right, and
30 they're shooting and you're running ...

Craig Yes, sir.

Liam And you're like: Bang! Bang! Bang! Bang-bang-bang-BANG!

35 Katie Yes, sir.

Liam ... big grenade things that just blow them to PIECES!

Nigel Yes, Mr Lewis.

Liam ... and they're like *(imitating machine-gun*
40 *fire)* huh-huh-huh huh-huh-huh ...

Gemma Yes, sir.

(There is a long pause. Everyone turns to Liam. Liam realises he's in trouble.)

45 Liam *(As though finishing his conversation with Darren)* ... and that's how you get the square root of a prime number.

(There is a pause. Then Liam turns to the front, as though surprised to be interrupted.)

(As though shocked) Me, sir? I wasn't talking, sir.

Activity 1: Building a picture

Look again at the extract on page 224. Imagine this script being performed on stage.

> **Remember**
>
> Think about what members of the audience would see and hear at a performance of this play.

1 Note down the first thing in the performance that would reveal each of the following ideas to the audience.
a) The characters are students.
b) The scene is set in a classroom.
c) It is the start of the day.
d) A teacher has entered the room.

2 Look again at your answers to question 1. Against each answer, note down whether the information is given to the audience through:
A Dialogue: what the characters say
B Stage directions: what the characters do
C Costumes: what the characters are wearing
D Setting: any scenery or furniture on the stage.
You may wish to note more than one letter by some answers.

Activity 2: Creating mood and character

1 Fourteen characters speak in the extract on page 224:

Laura B | Ben | Darren | Liam | Sara | Dan | Daisy
Laura E | Neil | Stuart | Craig | Katie | Nigel | Gemma

a) About which characters does the extract give no real information?
b) What do you learn about the other characters? Write a sentence for each of them, explaining what you learn and how the writer has given you this impression.

2 a) How would you describe the mood or atmosphere of the classroom depicted in the extract? You could choose from the suggestions below or use your own ideas.

serious | solemn | tense | purposeful | chaotic | friendly | happy

b) How has the writer tried to create that mood or atmosphere?

Spelling Boost: Drama terminology

Some key words related to drama and scripts can be difficult to spell. For example:

audience | character | dialogue | playwright | rehearse

rehearsal | scene | scenery | stage directions | theatre

1 **a)** Some of the words above contain 'silent' letters: letters that are not sounded independently when a word is spoken aloud. For example, the words *knee*, *knock* and *know* all have a silent 'k'.'Note down each word, circling the 'silent' letters.

b) Some of the words above contain pairs of vowels that form one sound. Note down each word, circling the pairs of vowels.

Remember

There are five vowels in the alphabet:

A | E | I | O | U

Activity 3: Exploring the writer's intentions

Playwrights have a very clear idea of the response they want to create in their audience. They choose their characters, settings and language to achieve that intention. Answer the following questions to help you understand the writer's choices.

1 In your opinion, how realistic is the school depicted in the extract on page 224?

A realistic   **B** quite unrealistic   **C** fantastical

Write one or two sentences to explain your answer.

2 What audience do you think the writer had in mind when writing this script?

A very young children   **B** children your age
C adults   **D** elderly people
Write one or two sentences to explain your answer.

3 How has the writer tried to engage the audience in this opening scene?

A with humour   **B** with mystery
C with tension   **D** with adventure

4 Look again at your answers to question 3.

a) Which characters help to create the writer's intended response?
b) How do those characters help to create the writer's intended response? Write one or two sentences explaining your ideas, using evidence from the script to support them.

Activity 4: Writing a scene

You are going to write a short script for a scene set in a school playground. In the scene, a group of two or three characters stand on stage looking out at the audience, giving the impression that they are looking across a school playground at break time.

1 What response do you want this scene to create in your audience? You could choose from the suggestions below or use your own ideas.

    humour | mystery | tension | excitement

2 Think about the characters you will create.
 a) How many characters will you include in the scene?
 b) What are their names?
 c) How old are they?
 d) What are these characters like? Note down one or two words to describe each of them. You could choose from the suggestions below or use your own ideas.

    funny | miserable | neat | naughty | sensible | worried | confident | shy

3 Think about the dialogue you will write.
 a) Note down ideas for what the characters could say to give the audience clues that:
 - the characters are students
 - the setting is a playground
 - the scene is set during break time.
 b) Note down ideas for what the characters could say to suggest what they can see, hear, smell, or feel.
 c) Look again at your answers to question 2d. Note down ideas for what the characters could say to reveal their personalities.

> **Remember**
>
> The audience cannot see, hear, smell or feel the playground – it is the characters' job to set the scene for them.

Write

4 Write your script, using as few stage directions as possible. Make sure you set out your script correctly.

> **Remember**
>
> When you write your script:
> - Write the name of the character in the margin on the left to show who says each line.
> - Write the words the character has to speak next to their name.
> - Put stage directions in brackets.
> Look again at the extract on page 224 to help you.

Section 3
From page to stage

In this section, you will explore ways in which a script can be created from a story written in prose.

Extract A is a dramatised version of the opening of *Great Expectations*, written by Charles Dickens in 1860.

▼ **Read Extract A and then answer the questions that follow it.**

1   *(A graveyard)*

    Pip   *(Reading the names on a grave)* Philip Pirrip … Georgiana, his wife … and their five sons, Alexander, Bartholomew, Abraham, Tobias,
5   and Roger …

    (A man in wet, muddy clothes jumps out. He has a chain around his leg. He grabs Pip by the chin.)

    Man   Keep still or I'll cut your throat.

    Pip   Please don't cut my throat, sir. Please!

10 Man   Tell me your name! Quick!

    Pip   It's Pip, sir.

    Man   Louder!

    Pip   Pip, sir.

    Man   Show me where you live. Point out the place!

15 *(Pip points. The man turns Pip upside down. A piece of bread falls out of his pocket. The man eats it greedily.)*

    Man   What fat cheeks you've got. I feel like I could eat them, and I might!

    Pip   Please! No!

20 Man   Where's your mother?

    Pip   There, sir! *(Points at the grave.)* Georgiana. That's my mother.

    Man   Oh, and is that your father too, buried there?

    Pip   Yes sir. My father too – also dead.

Activity 1: Working out information

1 Where does this scene take place?

2 Look at what is stated, not implied, about the two characters.
    a) What information does the script state about Pip? Note down all of the information you can identify.
    b) What information does the script state about the Man? Note down all of the information you can identify.

3 Look at what is implied, not stated, about the two characters.
    a) What information does the script imply about Pip? Note down all of the ideas you can identify, and the words or phrases that implied them.
    b) What information does the script imply about the Man? Note down all of the ideas you can identify, and the words or phrases that implied them.

Extract B is from the novel *Great Expectations*. It details the same events as the script that formed Extract A on page 228.

▼ **Read Extract B and then answer the questions that follow it.**

1 My first most vivid impression seems to me to have been gained on a memorable raw afternoon towards evening. At such a time I found out for certain that this bleak place overgrown with nettles was the
5 churchyard; and that Philip Pirrip, late of this parish, and also Georgiana wife of the above, were dead and buried; and that Alexander, Bartholomew, Abraham, Tobias, and Roger, infant children of the aforesaid, were also dead and buried.

10 "Hold your noise!" cried a terrible voice, as a man started up from among the graves at the side of the church porch. "Keep still, you little devil, or I'll cut your throat!"

A fearful man, all in coarse grey, with a great iron on
15 his leg. A man with no hat, and with broken shoes, and with an old rag tied round his head. A man who had been soaked in water, and smothered in mud, and lamed by stones, and stung by nettles; who limped, and shivered, and glared, and growled; and
20 whose teeth chattered in his head as he seized me by the chin.

"Oh! Don't cut my throat, sir," I pleaded in terror. "Pray don't do it, sir."

"Tell us your name!" said the man. "Quick!"

25 "Pip, sir."

"Once more," said the man, staring at me. "Give it mouth!"

"Pip. Pip, sir."

"Show us where you live," said the man. "Point out
30 the place!"

I pointed to where our village lay, on the flat in-shore among the alder-trees and pollards, a mile or more from the church.

The man, after looking at me for a moment, turned
35 me upside down, and emptied my pockets. There was nothing in them but a piece of bread. When the church came to itself – for he was so sudden and strong that he made it go head over heels before me – I was seated on a high tombstone, trembling while
40 he ate the bread ravenously.

"You young dog," said the man, licking his lips, "what fat cheeks you ha' got. "Darn me if I couldn't eat em," said the man, with a threatening shake of his head, "and if I han't half a mind to't!"

45 I earnestly expressed my hope that he wouldn't, and held tighter to the tombstone on which he had put me; partly, to keep myself upon it; partly, to keep myself from crying.

"Now lookee here!"
50 said the man. "Where's your mother?"

"There, sir!" said I. "Also Georgiana.
55 That's my mother."

"Oh!" said he. "And is that your father alonger your mother?"

60 "Yes, sir," said I; "him too."

Activity 2: Comparing stories

Sometimes, when a writer turns a novel into a play, film or television programme, they change some elements of the story.

1 **a)** Look again at your answers to Activity 1. Is all the information you noted and inferred from the script also included in the novel extract above? Note down any that isn't.

b) How closely does the story in the script follow the story in the original novel? Write one or two sentences to explain your ideas.

Activity 3: Comparing the script and the novel

1 Look at these sentences from the script and the novel of *Great Expectations*. Compare the words spoken in the script with the words spoken in the novel.

Extract A: Script	Extract B: Novel
Man: Keep still or I'll cut your throat.	"Hold your noise!" cried a terrible voice, as a man started up from among the graves at the side of the church porch. "Keep still, you little devil, or I'll cut your throat!"

a) How are the words spoken by the Man the same in both versions? How are they different? Write **two or three** sentences to explain your ideas.

b) What details is the reader given in the novel that do not appear in the script?

c) How could an audience watching the play be given that information? Think about:
- performance: what the actors do, and how they speak
- costume: what the actors are wearing
- sound effects: recorded sounds played in time with events onstage
- scenery: painted backdrops and objects onstage.

2 Look again at your answers to Activity 1, and consider the whole of both extracts.

a) List at least **three** things from the novel extract that are not in the script.

b) How could an audience watching a performance of the playscript be given that information? Again, consider performance, costume, sound effects and scenery.

Activity 4: Responding to the script and the novel

1 Write one or two sentences explaining your response to each of these questions.

a) Imagine you are watching a performance of the script. How would you respond to the character of Pip? Choose from the suggestions below or use your own ideas.

sympathy | humour | fear | excitement | anxiety | tension

b) Which part or parts of the script made you respond in that way?

c) Was your response to Pip in the novel different? If so, how?

d) Which part or parts of the novel extract made you respond in that way?

2 Write one or two sentences explaining your response to each of these questions.

a) Imagine you are watching a performance of the script. How would you respond to the character of the Man? Choose from the suggestions above or use your own ideas.

b) Which part or parts of the script made you respond in that way?

c) Was your response to the Man different in the novel? If so, how?

d) Which part or parts of the novel extract made you respond in that way?

Activity 5: Putting it on stage

Extract C is another section from the novel *Great Expectations*. You are going to write a script for a performance based on this extract.

1 "Who d'ye live with, – supposin' you're kindly let to live, which I han't made up my mind about?"

"My sister, sir, – Mrs. Joe Gargery, – wife of Joe Gargery, the **blacksmith**[1], sir."

"Blacksmith, eh?" said he. And looked down at his leg.

After darkly looking at his leg and me several times, he came closer to my tombstone, took me by both arms,
5 and tilted me back as far as he could hold me; so that his eyes looked most powerfully down into mine, and mine looked most helplessly up into his.

"Now lookee here," he said, "the question being whether you're to be let to live. You know what a **file**[2] is?"

"Yes, sir."

"And you know what **wittles**[3] is?"

10 "Yes, sir."

After each question he tilted me over a little more, so as to give me a greater sense of helplessness and danger.

"You get me a file." He tilted me again. "And you get me wittles." He tilted me again. "You bring 'em both to me." He tilted me again. "Or I'll have your heart and liver out." He tilted me again.

I was dreadfully frightened, and so giddy that I clung to him with both hands, and said, "If you would kindly
15 please to let me keep upright, sir, perhaps I shouldn't be sick, and perhaps I could attend more."

He gave me a most tremendous dip and roll. Then, he held me by the arms, in an upright position on the top of the stone, and went on in these fearful terms:–

"You bring me, to-morrow morning early, that file and them wittles. You bring the lot to me, at that old **battery over yonder**[4]. You do it, and you never dare to say a word or dare to make a sign concerning your
20 having seen such a person as me, or any person sumever, and you shall be let to live. You fail, or you go from my words in any partickler, no matter how small it is, and your heart and your liver shall be tore out, roasted, and ate."

Key vocabulary

blacksmith[1]: someone who creates objects in metal
file[2]: tool for cutting through metal
wittles[3]: food
battery over yonder[4]: building over there

1 Write a short summary of everything that happens in Extract C.

2 Write a short script based on Extract C. You could:
- change the words that the characters speak – but make sure they tell the same story
- use brief stage directions to tell the actors how they should speak or what they should do, based on the descriptions in the extract.

Section 4
Creating conflict

In this section, you will explore how playwrights can use conflict to shape stories.

This extract is from the beginning of a play called *The Girl and the Snake*.

▼ Read the extract and then answer the questions that follow it.

1	Father	My children, I am dying. Come closer, my son.
	Brother	I'm here, father.
5	Father	When I am gone, tell me which you would rather have – my possessions or my blessing? I cannot give you both.
10	Brother	Dear father, if I must choose, then I would have to ask for your possessions.
	Father	Come closer, my daughter.
	Sister	I'm here, father.
15	Father	Tell me which you would have, when I am gone, my possessions or my blessing?
	Sister	Dear father, I ask for your blessing.
	Father	In that case your brother will have what he wants and you, my daughter, will have my blessing.
20	*(The Father dies.)*	
	Singer/Narrator	The mother's heart, it broke with sorrow
		She cried, O husband, let me follow.
	(The Mother dies.)	
25		And so both parents died as one,
		Leaving their daughter and their only son
		All alone.
30	*(The Father and Mother are carried away, leaving the Sister grieving and the Brother hard-hearted.)*	
	Brother	Everything that belonged to our father and mother now belongs to me.

35		Help me gather it up – every bit of furniture, all the clothes, the blankets, the pots, the pans – they're all mine.
	(The Sister starts to help her Brother gather all his possessions. Neighbours approach to watch and are shocked by what is happening.)	
40		I'm taking the whole lot to my new house on the other side of the village.
	Neighbour 1	But you must leave your sister something.
45	Brother	She has what she asked for – my father's blessing. Everything else is mine.
	Neighbour 2	How can a brother do this to his sister?
	Neighbour 3	What will she sleep on?
	Neighbour 4	What will she wear?
50	Neighbour 5	How will she eat?
55	Brother	All right then, to show you I'm not completely heartless, to prove that I'm a fair-minded man and to shut up the lot of you – I allow my sister to keep this fine cooking pot. There! She's entitled to nothing and I've given her the pot. Now leave me alone!

Activity 1: Responding to ideas

1 In the extract on page 232, the father gives his children a choice.
a) What choice does he give them?
b) Why does he say he must give them a choice?
c) Why does the writer include the need for a choice?

2 Think about how the sister is presented in the extract. Choose **one or two** words to describe your impression of her, giving evidence from the text to support your answer.

> **Remember**
>
> A character's actions, and what other characters say about them, may reveal more about them than their own words.

3 Think about how the brother is presented in the extract.
a) Choose **one or two** words to describe your impression of him.
b) The most effective quotations are short and focused. Look at the very long quotation below.

Brother	Everything that belonged to our father and mother now belongs to me. Help me gather it up – every bit of furniture, all the clothes, the blankets, the pots, the pans – they're all mine.

Choose **three** words or phrases from this quotation that reveal most about the character of the brother.

4 Look at what the five neighbours say in the extract. Why do you think the writer included these characters in this scene?

Activity 2: Creating conflict

In any story, there is likely to be conflict. Sometimes the conflict in a story or a play is caused by the actions of the characters. There are lots of different types of conflict. For example:

two characters disagreeing | one character treating another badly
losing someone or something

1 What conflict is created in the extract on page 232?

2 Who or what causes this conflict?

3 Could the characters have avoided this conflict? If so, how?

Activity 3: Building a story

In most stories, the reader expects justice: the good characters being rewarded for their goodness and the bad characters being punished for their badness.

1 What do you think will have happened by the end of *The Girl and the Snake*?

2 Imagine a different story in which two characters have a disagreement. Select and sequence **two or more** of the following elements to form an engaging story in which the conflict is overcome and justice is done. You can choose any of the elements and put them in any order.

A Both characters declare they will never speak to each other again.	**B** The characters come to an agreement and make peace.	**C** Both characters suffer as a result of their argument.
D The two characters discuss the problem.	**E** The disagreement turns into an argument.	**F** Neither character will change their mind.

Grammar Boost: Word classes

Remember

- A **noun** names a person, place, object or idea. For example: *The elderly <u>father</u> suddenly died.*
- A **noun phrase** is a group of words (containing a noun) that names a single person, place, object or idea. For example: *<u>The elderly father</u> suddenly died.*
- An **adjective** adds information to a noun. For example: *The <u>elderly</u> father suddenly died.*
- A **verb** names an action or state of being. For example: *The elderly father suddenly <u>died</u>.*
- An **adverb** adds information to a verb or adjective, and can indicate time, place or how something happened. For example: *The elderly father <u>suddenly</u> died.*
- A **pronoun** replaces or stands in for a noun or noun phrase. For example: *<u>He</u> suddenly died.*

Look again at the following lines from the extract on page 232.

Brother	All right then, to show you I'm not completely heartless, to prove that I'm a fair-minded man and to shut up the lot of you – I allow my sister to keep this fine cooking pot. There! She's entitled to nothing and I've given her the pot. Now leave me alone!

1 Identify **one** example of each of the following word classes in the brother's speech.
   a) verb   **b)** adjective   **c)** adverb
   d) noun   **e)** noun phrase   **f)** pronoun

Remember

Adverbs often end '–ly', but not always.

2 Do any of the words you have identified reveal anything significant about the brother's character? Write a sentence or two explaining your ideas.

Activity 4: Planning conflict

You are going to plan the plot for a play in which conflict is created between two characters, and write a script for its opening.

Plan

1 **a)** Choose **two or three** of the following characteristics to plan **two** main characters.

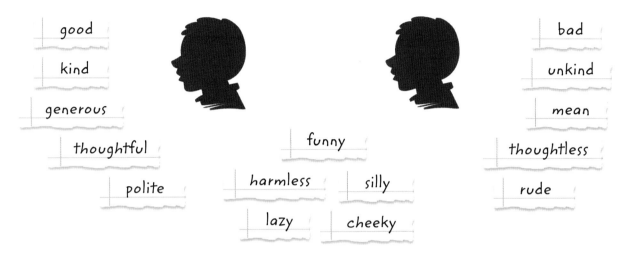

good

kind

generous

thoughtful

polite

funny

harmless   silly

lazy   cheeky

bad

unkind

mean

thoughtless

rude

b) Decide on the relationship between the main characters. You could choose from the suggestions below or use your own ideas.

a brother and sister | two friends | a parent and child

c) Note down names for your characters.

d) In the extract on page 232, the neighbours highlight the difficult situation that the brother has created for the sister. What other characters could you use to highlight the result of the conflict? Note down your ideas.

2 Think about what will happen in the play. Write notes to answer each of the questions below.

a) Plan the conflict between your two characters. Does one treat the other badly? Do they argue about something?

b) Plan the result of the conflict. How are the lives of these two characters affected?

c) Plan the resolution of the conflict. How does the situation come to an end? Is justice done?

d) Look again at your answers to the other parts of question 2. Summarise the story of your play in **two or three** sentences.

Write

3 Write the opening scene of your play. Use your notes to ensure that:
- your two main characters show the characteristics you have selected for them
- a conflict develops between them
- other characters highlight the conflict.

This section links to pages 218–221 of the Workbook.

Section 5
Crafting characters

In this section, you will explore how playwrights use dialogue to create character.

This extract is the ending of a short play called *Windfalls*. Max Sails has come to see Flora Bramley. He is trying to persuade her to sell him part of her garden so he can build a care home for the elderly. She is collecting up the windfall apples that have fallen from her apple tree.

▼ Read the extract and then answer the questions that follow it.

1 **Max**   It's big. Must be a full-time job looking after all this. It's more than I could manage. Hard work.

Flora   You get used to it.

Max   Can't be getting any easier for you.

5 **Flora**   Put the windfalls in the other basket while you're standing there. It's getting dark.

(Max is encumbered by his clipboard and throws the apples with one hand.)

   Don't throw them! — they've got enough
10 bruises already.

Max   Sorry. *(He tries to deal with the clipboard and continues to pick apples.)* I know the old-style nursing homes often had a bad press. But 'Resthaven' means no need to
15 worry about laundry or cooking or cleaning. Splendid gardens to sit and enjoy without any of the effort of digging and weeding. Every room has its own en-suite toilet and TV point. You can have a telephone installed
20 and everyone can bring three items of their own furniture with them. *(He pauses but gets no response.)* It's just like being on holiday. Permanently. *(Pleased with this flourish, he bites into an apple.)* Urghh!

25 **Flora**   They're cookers.

Max   You won't be able to cope for much longer. Taking thirty feet off the end of this garden makes a lot of sense. Acorn Developments will pay you instead of you having to pay for a
30 gardener. It's the last piece of the jigsaw. We get access into Chestnut Lane, the community gets a fabulous facility and you're sitting on a small fortune. What do you think?

Flora   You've missed some. You'll have to speed up
35 a bit. It's getting darker.

(He obeys her for a while, then ...)

Max   Look. Never mind the apples. We're talking a two million pound project here with £80,000 for you and first pick of a room. *(No
40 response.)* £100,000 maybe. You're an old woman. You can't read the letters I send you. You can't hear the doorbell. I know all the changes in the last twenty years must be confusing, but you seem to have totally lost
45 touch with the modern world. *(A phone rings. Max reaches for his mobile.)* Max Sails here.

(But the phone continues to ring. Flora extracts one from her clothing.)

Flora   Hello, love. Yes, I'm just finishing. Yes. You
50 bring the **video**, I'll get something out of the freezer. OK. *(She comes down and stuffs apples in Max's pockets.)* Thank you. At the end of the day a bit of help can make all the difference.

55 *(She walks off towards the house leaving Max to find his clipboard and the way out in the*
60 *rapidly gathering gloom.)*

Key vocabulary

video: a recording of a movie or programme

Activity 1: Exploring character

1 There are only two characters in the play *Windfalls*. They are very different to each other.
  a) Imagine the characters on stage. Write one or two sentences describing the people you have imagined.
  b) Note down **three differences** between the two characters. You might think about their age, what they are wearing, how they speak, how they stand or how they move.

2 In the extract on page 236, Max tries to persuade Flora to sell him part of her garden.
  a) At the end of the extract, Max offers her 'first pick of a room'. What does he mean?
  b) Identify **two** other ways in which Max tries to persuade Flora to sell him part of her garden.

3 At the end of the extract, Max tells Flora that she seems 'to have totally lost touch with the modern world'. How has the writer shown that this is not true? Support your answer with evidence from the extract.

4 Do Max and Flora talk and act in the way that you would expect them to? Write two or three sentences explaining your ideas.

Activity 2: Exploring language choices

1 Look again at Flora's six lines in the extract on page 236.
  a) How would you describe the length of the sentences that make up these lines?
  b) How might this help to show the way that Flora is feeling?

2 In two of her lines, Flora uses imperative verbs.
  a) Identify the imperative verbs she uses.
  b) How do you think an actor should say these lines?

3 Look again at Flora's final line. How might an actor's tone of voice change when speaking it?

> **Remember**
>
> An imperative verb gives an order. For example:
>
> Wake up!

4 Max uses persuasive language when trying to convince Flora to give up her garden. Identify **three** examples of words or phrases he uses to influence Flora's decision.

> **How do I do that?**
>
> Look for vocabulary choices that make Flora's garden sound negative and the care home sound positive.

5 Sometimes, a character's silence reveals a great deal about them. Why do you think Max doesn't speak at the very end of the extract?

Skills Boost: Referring back

One way to link your ideas and make your meaning clear is by using pronouns to refer back to an earlier sentence, for example:

> Max has come to see Mrs Bramley. ~~Max~~ He tries to be persuasive. ✓
> ~~Max~~ He offers ~~Mrs Bramley~~ her a free place in the care home. ~~The free place in the care home~~ This does not persuade ~~Mrs Bramley~~ her. ✓

1 Re-write the sentences below using pronouns to replace repeated nouns and noun phrases.

Pronouns

he	she	it	this
him	her	they	that
	his	them	

a) Max thinks Mrs Bramley's garden is a lot of work for Mrs Bramley. Max thinks Mrs Bramley should give up Mrs Bramley's garden.

b) Max says Mrs Bramley should move into the care home that Max wants to build.

c) Mrs Bramley thanks Max for helping Mrs Bramley. Thanking Max is the last thing Mrs Bramley says to Max.

Activity 3: Writing a response to characters

1 A stereotype is an idea about a type of person or thing that is widely believed but often inaccurate.

a) Note down **three or four** stereotypical ideas about elderly people. They could be about appearance, attitudes, abilities or any other attributes.

b) Think about the writer's presentation of Flora. Is she a stereotypical elderly lady? Write one or two sentences, making reference to the extract on page 236.

2 You are going to write **one** paragraph responding to the writer's presentation of Flora in the extract. You could consider the way Flora speaks to Max or what her words and actions reveal about her.

a) Write one or two sentences that make a key point, stating an impression of Flora that the writer intended to create.

b) Write another one or two sentences that include a short, focused quotation giving evidence for your point.

c) Write one or two more sentences to explain how your evidence proves your point, and how the writer's choices help to achieve their intention.

Activity 4: Building character

You are going to create two characters who are not stereotypical.

Plan

1 Think about stereotypes of people: the way in which someone may expect a type of person to look, think or behave.

a) Note down **five** words describing a stereotypical school student. They could be words describing appearance, attitudes, abilities or any other attributes.

b) Note down **five** words describing a stereotypical teacher. Again, they could be words describing appearance, attitudes, abilities or any other attributes.

2 Think about how you could create two characters that contradict the stereotypes you have described.

a) Note down **three** words to describe a school student who is nothing like the stereotype you detailed in question 1a.

b) Note down ideas about what a student like this could say or do to reveal these attributes.

c) Note down **three** words to describe a teacher who is nothing like the stereotype you detailed in question 1b.

d) Note down ideas about what a teacher like this could say or do to reveal these attributes.

3 Choose a subject for a conversation that your non-stereotypical student and teacher could have. You could choose from the suggestions below or use your own ideas.

a lesson | homework | another student | another teacher

Write

4 Write a short script for a conversation between your non-stereotypical student and teacher.

As you write, remember to:
- use the correct layout for a script
- reveal details about the relationship between the characters
- reveal the ways in which the characters are not stereotypical.

This section links to pages 226–227 of the Workbook.

Section 6
Assessment

In this section, you will answer questions on a short extract and write a critical response to assess your progress.

In this extract, a young boy called Conrad has just been told a bedtime story about a boy called Lucien and a tiger.

▼ Read the extract and then answer the questions that follow it.

1 Conrad   Can I have a tiger, Mother?

Mother   Perhaps. When you're older.

Conrad   Can't I have a tiger now?

Mother   The apartment's too small. Where would a
5   tiger live?

Conrad   On top of the wardrobe. He could make sure nobody was hiding inside.

Mother   I don't think you're being very sensible. What would your father say? If he came home to
10   find a tiger living in your bedroom?

Conrad   He'd be cross.

Mother   He'd be very cross.

Conrad   Yes. (*Pause.*) Maybe if it was just a small tiger?

15 Mother   You know we can't keep animals in the apartment.

Conrad   I'd take the tiger for walks.

Mother   It's a very dangerous place outside, Conrad. There are dangerous things and dangerous
20   people. And we worry, Conrad, me and your father.

Conrad   I'd be very careful.

Mother   (*Nervously.*) We wouldn't want anything to happen to our precious little angel. Because
25   dangerous people do dangerous things ... dangerously. Do you understand me, Conrad?

Conrad   No.

Mother   I don't feel very well.

30 (*Conrad passes Mother a paper bag from the drawer*

of his bedside table. Mother takes two deep breaths of air.)

Conrad   I want to have a very special friend ... like Lucien did.

35 Mother   Aren't you happy here?

Conrad   I just want to go outside.

Mother   But we have to protect you, darling.

(*She kisses him goodnight.*)

Conrad   But who's going to protect *you*, Mother? If I
40   had a tiger you'd always feel safe.

(*Mother laughs, anxiously.*)

Mother   Goodnight.

Conrad   Goodnight, Mother.

Activity 1: Reading

1 **a)** Why does Conrad think it would be a good idea to have a tiger? Identify **two** reasons.

   b) Why does Conrad's mother think it would **not** be a good idea to have a tiger? Identify **two** reasons.

2 What can you infer from the extract on page 240 about Conrad's father? Write one or two sentences explaining your ideas. Support your ideas with evidence from the extract.

3 Conrad's mother is nervous of the world outside their apartment. How does the writer use vocabulary choice to emphasise this idea?

4 Conrad reveals he wants three things: a tiger, a special friend and to go outside. What does this suggest about Conrad's life? Write one or two sentences explaining your ideas.

5 Identify **two** things you learn about Conrad's mother from the extract. Think about:
   • her attitude to Conrad
   • her thoughts and feelings.
   Support your ideas with evidence from the extract.

Activity 2: Writing

1 Write **two or three** paragraphs in response to the following question: What impressions has the writer created of Conrad and Mother in the extract on page 240?

Before you start writing

You could consider:
• the setting and situation that are implied
• what each character says
• what you can infer about each character's thoughts, and what they do not say.

As you write

You should:
• include a key point, evidence and an explanation in each paragraph
• express your ideas as clearly and fluently as you can.

This section links to pages 228–231 of the Workbook.

Section 7
Shakespearean speech

In this section, you will explore Shakespeare's language, and how he uses dialogue to develop characters and relationships.

The two parts of this extract are from the beginning of Shakespeare's play *King Lear*. Lear is a king of the Britons who is deciding how to divide his kingdom between his three daughters: Goneril, Regan and Cordelia.

▼ **Read the extract and then answer the questions that follow them.**

1	King Lear	Which of you shall we say doth love us most?
		That we our largest **bounty**[1] may **extend**[2]
		Where nature doth with merit
		challenge[3]. Goneril, Our eldest-born, speak first.
5	Goneril	Sir, I love you more than words can wield the matter;
		Dearer than eye-sight, space, and liberty;
		Beyond what can be valued, rich or rare;
		No less than life, with **grace**[4], health, beauty, honour;
		As much as child e'er loved, or father found;
10		A love that makes breath poor, and speech unable;
		Beyond all manner of so much I love you.
	Cordelia	*(Aside)* What shall Cordelia do? Love, and be silent.

> **Key vocabulary**
>
> **bounty**[1]: gift
> **extend**[2]: give
> **where nature ... challenge**[3]: to the daughter that deserves it most
> **grace**[4]: status, respect

Regan, too, tells her father that she loves him more than anything else in the world. Then it is Cordelia's turn.

1	King Lear	Now, our joy,
		Although the last, not least; **to whose young love**
		The vines of France and milk of Burgundy
		Strive to be interess'd[1]; what can you say to draw
5		**A third more opulent**[2] than your sisters? Speak.
	Cordelia	Nothing, my lord.
	King Lear	Nothing!
10	Cordelia	Nothing.
	King Lear	Nothing will come of nothing: speak again.
	Cordelia	Unhappy that I am, I cannot heave
		My heart into my mouth: I love your majesty
		According to my **bond**[3]; nor more nor less.

> **Key vocabulary**
>
> **to whose young love ... interess'd**[1]: whom the King of France and the Duke of Burgundy would like to marry
> **a third more opulent**[2]: an even richer part of the kingdom
> **bond**[3]: duty, relationship

Activity 1: Checking understanding

Answer the following questions to check your understanding of the extract on page 242.

1 Look again at King Lear's first speech, in the first part of the extract.
   a) How does he plan to judge which of his daughters should be given the richest part of his kingdom?
   b) Do you think that this is a good way for him to make his decision? Why?

2 Lear's daughter Goneril claims to love her father more than, or as much as, many different things. Name **three** of them.

3 When the term 'aside' appears in a script, it indicates that the other characters will not hear what this character is saying. Look again at Cordelia's first speech, in the first part of the extract. It tells the audience Cordelia's thoughts.
   a) What do Cordelia's thoughts suggest she is feeling at this point?
   b) What decision does Cordelia make in this speech?

4 Look again at the second part of the extract. King Lear calls Cordelia 'our joy'. What does this suggest about his relationship with Cordelia and with his two other daughters?

5 Cordelia says that she loves her father according to her bond.
   a) How much does this suggest Cordelia loves her father?
   b) How would you describe King Lear's thoughts and feelings when he hears this?

Activity 2: Responding to dialogue

1 Consider what you have learned about the characters of King Lear, Goneril and Cordelia.
   a) How honest do you think each character is? Give each of them a score from 0 (entirely dishonest) to 10 (entirely honest).
   b) How wise do you think each character is? Give each of them a score from 0 (entirely foolish) to 10 (entirely wise).
   c) How selfish do you think each character is? Give each of them a score from 0 (entirely unselfish) to 10 (entirely selfish).

2 Write one or two sentences describing each of the three characters, explaining your choices with reference to the extract on page 242.

I think King Lear is very foolish because

Spelling Boost: Word families

A word family is a group of words that are all formed from the same root word. They could be any part of speech: a verb, a noun, an adjective or an adverb. Understanding this can help you to spell difficult words correctly.

Verb	flatter	exaggerate	–	astonish	believe	disbelieve
Noun	flattery	exaggeration	honesty	astonishment	belief	disbelief
Adjective	flattering	exaggerated	honest	astonishing	believable	unbelievable
Adverb	flatteringly	exaggeratedly	honestly	astonishingly	believably	unbelievably

1 Write six sentences describing what happens in the extract on page 242. In each sentence, use at least **one** word from the table above.

Activity 3: Exploring dialogue

Look again at what Goneril and Cordelia say to their father in the extract on page 242:

Goneril	Sir, I love you more than words can wield the matter;
	Dearer than eye-sight, space, and liberty;
	Beyond what can be valued, rich or rare;
	No less than life, with grace, health, beauty, honour;
	As much as child e'er loved, or father found;
	A love that makes breath poor, and speech unable;
	Beyond all manner of so much I love you.

Cordelia	Nothing, my lord.
Cordelia	Nothing.

1 **a)** How many sentences does each character speak in these lines?
b) How many words does each character use?
c) Which character's lines did you find easier to understand?
d) How would you describe the kind of language used by each of these two characters? Write **one** sentence about each of them. You could choose from the suggestions below or use your own ideas.

simple | complicated | straightforward | insincere | shocking | dishonest
excessive | blunt | deceptive | honest | misleading | sincere

2 How does the way in which Shakespeare has written each character's lines add to your impression of her? Write one or two sentences about each character, explaining your ideas.

Activity 4: Writing a script

You are going to write a script in which:
- two characters have done something they should not have done
- each must explain themselves to a third character, who has authority
- one character is very deceptive and dishonest
- the other character is very straightforward and honest.

Imagine

Plan a situation that could include the elements listed above. You could choose one of the suggestions below or use your own ideas.

> Two students are explaining to a teacher why they have not done their homework.

> Two criminals are explaining to a police officer why they broke into a bank.

1 Write one or two sentences summarising your ideas.

Plan

2 Plan your two main characters.
   a) What are their names?
   b) How will each of them speak? Note down some ideas about:
   - the kinds of words each character will use
   - the length of the sentences each character will use, considering your use of single-clause and multi-clause sentences.
   c) Note down some ideas about the kinds of things each character will say.

3 Think about how your third character will react as the other two try to explain themselves. Consider whether or not they will:
- react to the explanations similarly or differently
- believe the explanations
- be pleased or annoyed by each explanation
- forgive or punish each of the other characters.

Note down your ideas.

Write

4 Using the notes you have made, write your script. As you write, remember to:
- use the correct layout for a script
- think about how your two main characters will each describe the same event
- think about how vocabulary and sentence length could reveal things about your characters.

This section links to pages 232–235 of the Workbook.

Section 8
Performing

In this section, you will explore how performing a scene in different ways can change your response to characters and events.

This extract is from Shakespeare's play *Hamlet*. Previously in the play, Hamlet's father, the king of Denmark, has died. Hamlet believes he was murdered by his brother, Hamlet's uncle. Hamlet's mother, Queen Gertrude, has now married Hamlet's uncle, making him the new king of Denmark. Hamlet is planning revenge for his father's murder.

In this extract, Queen Gertrude challenges her son about his rudeness to the new king, his uncle. Polonius, the king's advisor, is hiding behind an arras (a heavy tapestry), listening to the conversation.

▼ **Read the extract and then answer the questions that follow it.**

1 Hamlet   Now, mother, what's the matter?

Queen   Hamlet, **thou hast thy**[1] father much offended.

Hamlet   Mother, you have my father much offended.

Queen   Come, come, you answer with an **idle**[2] tongue.

5 Hamlet   Go, go, you question with a wicked tongue.

Queen   Why, **how now**[3], Hamlet!

Hamlet   What's the matter now?

Queen   Have you **forgot me**[4]?

Hamlet   No, by the **rood**[5], not so:
10   You are the queen, your husband's brother's wife;
And, – **would it were not so**[6]! – you are my mother.

Queen   Nay, then, I'll **set those to you that can speak**[7].

Hamlet   Come, come, and sit you down; you shall not budge;
You go not til I set you up a **glass**[8].
15   Where you may see the inmost part of you.

Queen   What **wilt**[9] thou do? Thou wilt not murder me?
Help, help, **ho**[10]!

Polonius   *(Behind)* What, ho! Help, help, help!

Hamlet   How now! A rat? *(**Draws**[11])* Dead, **for a ducat**[12], dead!
20   *(**Makes a pass**[13] through the arras.)*

Polonius   *(Behind)* O, I am slain!

   (Falls and dies.)

Queen   O me, what hast thou done?

Key vocabulary

thou hast thy[1]: you have your
idle[2]: foolish
how now[3]: what's happening
forgot me[4]: forgotten who I am
rood[5]: sacred cross
would it were not so[6]: if only it wasn't true
set those to you that can speak[7]: fetch someone who can talk to you properly
glass[8]: mirror

wilt[9]: will
ho[10]: is there anyone/anything there
draws[11]: takes out his sword
for a ducat[12]: I'd bet
makes a pass[13]: thrusts his sword

Activity 1: Checking understanding

1 At the beginning of the extract on page 246, Queen Gertrude tells Hamlet that he has insulted his father.
   a) Whom does she mean when she refers to Hamlet's father?
   b) Hamlet replies that Queen Gertrude has insulted his father. What do you think Hamlet means?

2 Hamlet assures his mother that he knows who she is, and describes her in **three** different ways. Note them down.

3 Hamlet says that he will bring his mother a mirror. Why does he think she should look at herself in the mirror?

4 Why do you think Queen Gertrude begins to panic that Hamlet will murder her?

5 Why does Polonius call for help?

6 Write **one** sentence summarising what happens in this extract.

Skills Boost: Shakespeare's language

The English language has changed since Shakespeare's time. When reading Shakespeare, it is helpful to remember the following meanings.

- thee = you
- thou = you
- thy = your
- thine = yours

1 Look at the sentences below. They describe the results of a contest. Translate them into Shakespeare's English, using the pronoun 'thee' or 'thou' to replace each instance of 'you'.
   a) You beat him.
   b) I beat you.
   c) She beat you.
   d) You beat me.

Remember

Shakespeare sometimes uses the pronoun 'you' instead of 'thee' or 'thou'. There is a reason: 'thee' and 'thou' can show informal familiarity and affection, and 'you' is more formal and distant.

Pronouns	
Subject	**Object**
I	me
you	you
thou	thee
he	him
she	her

Activity 2: Changing responses

1 Look again at some of the things that Hamlet says in the extract on page 246.

a) Mother, you have my father much offended.   **b)** What's the matter now?

c) And, – would it were not so! – you are my mother.   **d)** How now! A rat? Dead, for a ducat, dead!

Think about how an actor playing Hamlet could say these lines. For each quotation:
- note down **two** words that you think would be effective guides for the actor
- note down **one** word that would definitely **not** be effective.
You could choose from the suggestions below or use your own ideas.

slow | fast | loud | quiet | joking | polite | aggressive | anxious
frightened | uncertain | bored | sneering | smiling

2 Look again at some of the things that Queen Gertrude says in the extract.

a) Hamlet, thou hast thy father much offended.   **b)** Come, come, you answer with an idle tongue.

c) Have you forgot me?   **d)** Thou wilt not murder me?

Think about how an actor playing Queen Gertrude could say these lines.
For each quotation:
- note down **two** words that you think would be effective guides for the actor
- note down **one** word that would definitely **not** be effective.
You could choose from the suggestions above or use your own ideas.

Skills Boost: Reviewing vocabulary choices

When writing a critical response, think carefully before choosing the most accurate vocabulary to express your ideas precisely.

1 Look at the adjectives below.

rude | angry | distressed | aggressive | bold | decisive
obnoxious | argumentative | frightened | violent | daring | impulsive
mean | annoyed | panicked | arrogant | heroic | unpredictable

a) Choose **three** adjectives that could be used to describe the character of Hamlet in the extract on page 246.
b) Use **one** of the adjectives above to write a sentence describing him.
c) Choose three adjectives that could be used to describe the character of Gertrude in the extract.
d) Use **one** of the adjectives above to write a sentence describing her.

Activity 3: Writing a response

You are going to write **one** paragraph about the character of either Queen Gertrude or Hamlet.

Plan

1 Note down which character will be your focus: Hamlet or Queen Gertrude.

2 Note down **one or two** words or phrases that describe **one** possible impression created of your chosen character.

3 Identify **one or two** words or lines from the extract on page 246 that gave you the impression you have noted down.

4 Think about how an actor might say the words or lines you have identified.
a) Note down **two** different ways in which the actor might deliver the lines.
b) How might these two different ways change the audience's impression of this character? Note down **one or two** words or phrases that describe the second possible impression created of your chosen character.

Write

5 Write **one** paragraph explaining the impression that Shakespeare creates of either Hamlet or Queen Gertrude in the extract. In your paragraph:

a) Write one or two sentences that make a key point, stating **one** impression of Hamlet or Gertrude that Shakespeare intended to create.

b) Write another one or two sentences that include a short, focused quotation that gives evidence for your point.

c) Write one or two more sentences to explain how your evidence proves your point, and how the writer's choices help to achieve their intention.

d) Write one or two final sentences to explain how an actor could deliver the words in different ways, and how this might change the impression of the character.

> In this scene, Shakespeare creates the impression that Queen Gertrude is

> For example, when Hamlet first appears, he says

> These words suggest that he feels

> This would suggest she is

> However, the same line could also be spoken as if Hamlet was feeling
> This would create the different impression that

This section links to pages 236–239 of the Workbook.

Section 9
Exploring themes

In this section, you will explore how Shakespeare explores the theme of power in the play *Macbeth*.

This extract is from Shakespeare's play *Macbeth*.

Macbeth is a Scottish thane (a powerful landowner) of regions called Glamis and Cawdor. Previously in the play, he planned to kill the king of Scotland and take his place. However, Macbeth is having second thoughts about the plan. His wife, Lady Macbeth, tries to persuade him to change his mind and achieve his ambition.

▼ **Read the extract and then answer the questions that follow it.**

1 Macbeth   We will proceed no further in this business:
  He hath honour'd me of late; and I have bought
  Golden opinions from all sorts of people,
  Which **would be worn now**[1] in their newest gloss,
5   Not cast aside so soon.

  Lady   **Was the hope drunk**
  Macbeth   **Wherein you dress'd yourself? hath it slept since?**
  And wakes it now, to look so green and pale
  At what it did so freely?[2] From this time
10   **Such I account thy love**[3]. Art thou afear'd
  To be the same in thine own act and valour
  As thou art in desire? Wouldst thou have that
  Which thou **esteem'st the ornament of life**[4],
  And live a coward in thine own esteem,
15   Letting 'I dare not' **wait upon**[5] 'I would,'
  Like the poor cat i' **the adage**[6]?

  Macbeth   **Prithee**[7], peace:
  I dare do all that **may become**[8] a man;
  Who dares do more is none.

20 Lady M.   What beast was't, then,
  That made you **break this enterprise**[9] to me?
  When you **durst**[10] do it, then you were a man;
  And, to be more than what you were, you would
  Be so much more the man. **Nor time nor place**
25   **Did then adhere, and yet you would make both**[11]:
  They have made themselves, and that their fitness now
  Does **unmake you**[12]. I have **given suck**[13], and know
  How tender 'tis to love the babe that milks me:
  I would, while it was smiling in my face,
30   Have pluck'd my nipple from his boneless gums,
  And **dash'd**[14] the brains out, had I so sworn as you
  Have done to this.

  Macbeth   If we should fail?

  Lady M.   We fail!
35   **But screw your courage to the sticking-place**[15],
  And we'll not fail.

Key vocabulary

would be worn now[1]: should be enjoyed now

Was the hope ... so freely?[2]: When hope inspired you, was it like a drunk man who regrets his actions?

Such I account thy love[3]: I judge your love by this

esteem'st the ornament of life[4]: regard as life's most valuable thing

wait upon[5]: be more important than

the adage[6]: the saying 'the cat loves fish, but won't wet her paws'

prithee[7]: please

may become[8]: would be appropriate for

break this enterprise[9]: suggest this plan

durst[10]: dared to

nor time ... make both[11]: you tried and failed to find the right time and place

unmake you[12]: make you weak

given suck[13]: breastfed

dash'd[14]: smashed

screw your courage to the sticking-place[15]: fill yourself with courage

Activity 1: Understanding and responding

1 At the beginning of the extract on page 250, Macbeth clearly states that he no longer wants to kill the king, by saying 'We will proceed no further in this business'. Using your own words, summarise the **two** reasons he gives for this.

2 Look again at Lady Macbeth's first speech in the extract. In just **two or three** words, summarise what she believes is the real reason Macbeth has changed his mind.

3 Look again at lines 20–24 of the extract. Using your own words, summarise the idea Lady Macbeth uses to persuade Macbeth.

4 Later in the extract, Lady Macbeth talks about her child.
   a) How does she use this to persuade Macbeth that he should do what he has 'sworn' to do? Write one or two sentences to explain your ideas.
   b) What does this reveal about the character of Lady Macbeth? Write one or two sentences to explain your ideas.

5 Look again at Macbeth's final line in the extract.
   a) What does the line suggest is a worry for Macbeth?
   b) What does this reveal about the character of Macbeth? Write one or two sentences to explain your ideas.

6 Look again at the whole of the extract.
   a) Which character has the most lines?
   b) What might this suggest about the characters of Macbeth and Lady Macbeth? Write one or two sentences to explain your ideas. You could choose vocabulary from the suggestions below or use your own ideas.

I think it shows Macbeth is

and that Lady Macbeth is

in control | anxious | excited | desperate | happy | overpowered

Activity 2: Selecting evidence

The most effective quotations are short and focused on the point you are trying to prove.

1 Choose **one** of the following quotations as evidence that Macbeth no longer wants to kill the king.

   A   We will proceed no further in this business   **B**   He hath honour'd me of late

   C   I have bought Golden opinions from all sorts of people   **D**   If we should fail?

2 Choose short quotations from Lady Macbeth's lines to support each of the following points.
   a) Lady Macbeth is ruthless.   **b)** Lady Macbeth is manipulative.

Activity 3: Exploring themes

A **theme** is an idea that a writer explores throughout a text. One of the key themes in Shakespeare's *Macbeth* is power.

1 Which **one** word in the following quotation most clearly shows Macbeth trying to assert power?   We will proceed no further in this business

2 Which **one** word in the following quotation most clearly shows Macbeth failing to assert power?   Prithee, peace

3 Which one word in the following quotation most clearly shows Lady Macbeth trying to take control?   From this time Such I account thy love.

4 Which one word or phrase in the following quotation most clearly shows Lady Macbeth taking control?   But screw your courage to the sticking-place,   And we'll not fail.

Skills Boost: Reviewing sentence structures

Look at one student's response to the extract on page 250:

> Macbeth does not want to kill the king so Lady Macbeth tries to persuade him so
> she says 'When you durst do it, then you were a man' and she says that she would
> 'dash' her own baby's brains out if she had promised to, and although Macbeth
> tries to argue back he cannot because she is so persuasive and it is obvious that
> she has great power over him.

1 Is this response clear and easy to read? Award it a clarity mark out of 5.

2 You are going to rewrite the response to make its meaning as clear as possible.
   a) Rewrite the response using only short, single-clause sentences.
   b) Rewrite your sentences to make the response as clear and engaging as possible. You could:
   • use conjunctions to link two or more single-clause sentences
   • leave some sentences as single-clause sentences
   • add adverbials to the beginning of some sentences.

Conjunctions		Adverbials
because	as	However,
when	and	In addition,
although	but	Similarly,

3 Look at the response you have written. Could you make it even clearer? If so, revise your writing.

Activity 4: Writing a response

You are going to write **two** paragraphs in response to the extract on page 250:
- a paragraph about the impressions that Shakespeare has created of Macbeth
- a paragraph about the impressions that Shakespeare has created of Lady Macbeth.

Plan

1 a) Note down **two or three** words that best describe your impressions of Macbeth. You could choose vocabulary from the suggestions below or use your own ideas.

> helpless | powerful | anxious | strong | weak
> persuasive | heartless | aggressive | doubtful

b) Note down two or three words that best describe your impression of Lady Macbeth. You could choose vocabulary from the suggestions above, or use your own ideas.

2 Note down **two or three** short quotations from the extract to show which words or lines gave you those impressions.

Write

3 Write **one** paragraph explaining the impression that Shakespeare creates of Macbeth in the extract. In your paragraph:

a) Write one or two sentences that make a key point, stating **one** impression of Macbeth that Shakespeare intended to create.

> In this scene, Shakespeare creates the impression that Macbeth is

b) Write another one or two sentences that include a short, focused quotation that gives evidence for your point.

> For example, Macbeth says

c) Write one or two more sentences to explain how your evidence proves your point, and how Shakespeare's choices help to achieve his intention.

> These words suggest that he feels

4 Repeat question 3 to write your second paragraph, focusing on Lady Macbeth.

Section 10
Introductions and conclusions

In this section, you will develop your critical writing skills, exploring ways of introducing and concluding your responses.

This extract is from later in Shakespeare's *Macbeth*. Macbeth has taken a step closer to achieving his ambition of replacing King Duncan as ruler of Scotland. Duncan has come to stay at Macbeth's castle, and Macbeth has murdered him. Now Macbeth has blood on his hands and is filled with feelings of guilt.

▼ **Read the extract and then answer the questions that follow it.**

1 Macbeth   **Methought**[1] I heard a voice cry, *Sleep no more!*
                  Macbeth does murder sleep, – the innocent sleep,
                  Sleep that knits up the **ravell'd**[2] sleeve of care,
                  The death of each day's life, sore labour's bath,
5   Balm of hurt minds, great nature's second course,
                  Chief nourisher in life's feast.

   Lady Macbeth What do you mean?

   Macbeth   Still it cried Sleep no more! to all the house:
                  Glamis[3] *hath murder'd sleep, and therefore* **Cawdor**[4]
10   *Shall sleep no more; Macbeth shall sleep no more!*

   Lady Macbeth Who was it that thus cried? Why, worthy thane,
                  You do **unbend your noble strength**[5], to think
                  So brainsickly of things. Go get some water,
                  And wash this filthy witness from your hand.
15   Why did you bring these daggers from the place?
                  They must lie there: go carry them; and smear
                  The sleepy grooms[6] with blood.

   Macbeth   I'll go no more:
                  I am afraid to think what I have done;
20   Look on't again I dare not.

   Lady Macbeth **Infirm of purpose**[7]!
                  Give me the daggers: the sleeping and the dead
                  Are but as pictures: 'tis the eye of childhood
                  That fears a painted devil. If he do bleed,
25   I'll **gild**[8] the faces of the grooms **withal**[9];
                  For it must seem their guilt.

   Macbeth   **Whence**[10] is that knocking?
                  How is't with me, when every noise appals me?

Key vocabulary

Methought[1]: I thought
ravell'd[2]: unravelled
Glamis[3]; **Cawdor**[4]: Macbeth (by his other titles)
unbend your noble strength[5]: weaken yourself
The sleepy grooms[6]: Duncan's drugged guards
Infirm of purpose[7]: Weak and cowardly
gild[8]: cover
withal[9]: as well
Whence[10]: From where

Activity 1: Understanding and responding

1 At the beginning of the extract on page 254, Macbeth believes he heard a voice cry out.

   a) Write **one** sentence summarising what he thinks the voice was telling him.

   b) What might this suggest about Macbeth's state of mind at this point in the play? Write one or two sentences explaining your ideas.

2 Look again at Lady Macbeth's first long speech in this extract.

   a) How does Lady Macbeth describe Macbeth's state of mind?

   b) What **two** things does she tell Macbeth to do?

   c) What impression does this speech create of Lady Macbeth?

3 **a)** When Macbeth refuses to go back to where he left the king's corpse, what does Lady Macbeth say she will do?

   b) What impression does this create of Lady Macbeth? Write one or two sentences explaining your ideas.

4 Note down **two** words to summarise your impressions of Macbeth, and two words to describe your impressions of Lady Macbeth in this extract. You could choose vocabulary from the suggestions below or use your own ideas.

unsympathetic | disturbed | frightened | anxious | heartless | arrogant | relaxed

Activity 2: Planning a response

You are going to plan a response to the following question: How do Macbeth and Lady Macbeth react to their murder of King Duncan?

1 Begin your planning by gathering some key points.
   a) Note down one way in which Macbeth reacts to the murder of King Duncan.
   b) Note down one way in which Lady Macbeth reacts to the murder of King Duncan.

2 Identify a short, focused quotation that clearly supports each of the key points you noted in answer to question 1.

3 Look again at each point and quotation you have noted. What do they suggest about the characters of Macbeth and Lady Macbeth? Note down your ideas.

How do I do that?

Consider everything each of the characters says or might be thinking. Ask yourself: Is this a reaction to the murder of King Duncan? What does it reveal?

Activity 3: Writing an introduction

When you write a critical response to a text, a short introduction can make your writing clearer and more engaging. The introduction should briefly introduce the background of the text you are writing about and indicate your response to the text. You are going to write an introduction to the response you planned in the previous activity, answering the following question: How do Macbeth and Lady Macbeth react to their murder of King Duncan?

1 Begin your introduction by writing one or two sentences that briefly explain the background for the extract on page 254: what has just happened and why?

2 Finish your introduction by writing **one** sentence summarising your ideas about the extract on which the question focuses.

3 Review the introduction you have written. Have you:
   • introduced the background to the extract you are writing about?
   • introduced your response to the extract?

Skills Boost: Proofreading skills

1 When you check your writing for mistakes, it is easy to read what you **think** you have written, and not what you have actually written. The student who wrote the response below did not check them very carefully: there are **three** words missing. What are they?

> Lady Macbeth is not very sympathetic to Macbeth. He is obviously very upset and frightened but she tells him he is 'brainsickly' and gives him lots orders. She tells him to get some water, wash the blood from hands and take the daggers back. She does not try comfort him at all.

2 Another common error is the comma splice (the incorrect use of a comma to link two separate clauses). There are **three** comma splices in the response below. Note down the word just before each comma splice.

> When Macbeth returns from killing the King, he is very anxious and almost hysterical, he thinks he hears a voice saying he will never sleep again, he refuses to go and leave the daggers with the King's dead body, because he refuses, Lady Macbeth tells him he is 'infirm of purpose'.

Activity 4: Writing a conclusion

When you write a critical response to a text, a conclusion can make your ideas clearer and your writing feel more rounded. The conclusion should:
- summarise your ideas
- summarise the impact of the writer's choices.

You are going to write a conclusion to the response you planned in the previous activity, answering the following question: How do Macbeth and Lady Macbeth react to their murder of King Duncan?

1 Begin your conclusion by summarising your response. Look again at the notes you made in answer to Activity 2. Write one or two sentences summarising your ideas about Macbeth's and Lady Macbeth's reactions to the murder.

2 Finish your conclusion by thinking about the impact that Shakespeare may have wanted these reactions to have on his audience. Write **two** sentences summing up how an audience might respond to Macbeth and Lady Macbeth in the extract on page 254. Use the following questions to help you.

a) Copy and complete the following sentences, using the phrases below or your own ideas to replace the **?**.

> Shakespeare intended the audience to feel **?** Macbeth.

> Shakespeare intended the audience to feel **?** Lady Macbeth.

sympathy for | frightened of | worried about | hatred of
disgusted by | jealous of | intrigued by

b) Write **one** sentence expressing a more general comment that responses to the characters would have on the play as a whole.

> These responses would make the play Macbeth

Section 11
Assessment

In this section, you will answer questions on a text to assess your progress in this unit.

This extract is from the final act of Shakespeare's *Macbeth*. Macbeth has become King of Scotland. Desperately trying to protect his position, he has had the thane of Fife's wife and children killed. Now, a concerned doctor and a gentlewoman are watching Lady Macbeth as she walks and talks in her sleep.

▼ **Read the extract and then answer the questions that follow it.**

1	Gentlewoman	Lo you, here she comes! This is **her very guise**[1]; and, upon my life, fast asleep. Observe her; stand close.
	Doctor	How came she by that **light**[2]?
5	Gentlewoman	Why, it stood by her: she has light by her continually; 'tis her command.
	Doctor	You see, her eyes are open.
	Gentlewoman	Ay, but **their sense is shut**[3].
	Doctor	What is it she does now? Look, how she rubs her hands.
10	Gentlewoman	It is an **accustomed**[4] action with her, to seem **thus**[5] washing her hands: I have known her continue in this a quarter of an hour.
	Lady Macbeth	Yet here's a **spot**[6].
	Doctor	Hark! she speaks: I will set down what comes from her, to satisfy my **remembrance**[7] the more strongly.
15	Lady Macbeth	Out, damned spot! out, I say! – One; two: why, then, 'tis time to do't: – Hell is murky! – Fie, my lord, fie! A soldier, and afear'd? What need we fear who knows it, when none can **call our power to account**[8]? – Yet who would have thought the old man to have had so much
20		blood in him?
	Doctor	Do you **mark**[9] that?
	Lady Macbeth	The thane of Fife had a wife; where is she now? – What, will these hands ne'er be clean? – No more o' that, my lord, no more o' that: you **mar all with this**
25		**starting**[10].
	Doctor	Go to, go to; you have known what you should not.
	Gentlewoman	She has spoke what she should not, I am sure of that: heaven knows what she has known.
30	Lady Macbeth	Here's the smell of the blood still: all the perfumes of Arabia will not sweeten this little hand. Oh, oh, oh!

Key vocabulary

her very guise[1]: her usual appearance
light[2]: candle
their sense is shut[3]: they do not see what is around her
accustomed[4]: familiar
thus[5]: like this
spot[6]: mark or stain
remembrance[7]: memory
call our power to account[8]: prove how we got our power
mark[9]: hear
mar all with this starting[10]: ruin everything with this nervousness

Activity 1: Reading

1 The gentlewoman says that Lady Macbeth insists on having a candle beside her 'continually'. What does this suggest about Lady Macbeth's state of mind?

2 Why do you think Lady Macbeth dreams about washing her hands?

3 Look again at lines 15–20 of the extract on page 258. Who is 'the old man'?

4 In lines 15–20 and 22–25, Lady Macbeth talks about lots of different things very quickly. What do these lines suggest about her state of mind?

5 Earlier in the play, Lady Macbeth seemed cold-hearted and cruel. How does this extract change your response to the character of Lady Macbeth? Write one or two sentences explaining your ideas.

Activity 2: Writing

1 Write a response to the following question: In the extract on page 258, what impression does Shakespeare create of Lady Macbeth?

Before you write

Think about:
- what Lady Macbeth does in the extract
- what Lady Macbeth says in the extract
- how your impression of Lady Macbeth has changed, comparing your response to this extract with your responses to earlier extracts.

As you write

Aim to:
- write a short introduction
- write **two or three** paragraphs, including a key point, evidence and an explanation
- write a short conclusion
- express your ideas as clearly and fluently as you can.

GLOSSARY

abbreviation - shortened **word** or **phrase** (e.g. Doctor becomes Dr; Susan becomes Sue; telephone becomes phone)

abstract noun - noun that names ideas you cannot see, hear, smell, taste or touch (e.g. 'happiness'; 'idea')

account - telling or retelling of factual or fictional events (e.g. an account of the football match, or an account of an adventure)

active voice - form in which the thing that is performing the action of a **verb** is the grammatical **subject** of a **sentence**

adjective - word that adds information to a **noun**

adverb - single-word **adverbial**

adverbial - words (adverbs), **phrases** or **clauses** that add information to a **verb**, **adjective** or other adverbial

alliteration - use of one sound to begin two or more **words**

analyse - examine carefully, to improve understanding

analysis - careful examination that improves understanding

antonyms - words with opposite meanings

argument - explanation of an idea with the purpose of changing or guiding someone's **opinions** and/or actions

argument text - text that presents and explains an idea with the purpose of changing or guiding someone's **opinions** and/or actions

article (text type) - usually factual piece of writing about a given topic (e.g. news / magazine / internet article)

autobiography - biography someone writes about their own life

biography - account of someone's life

bullet point - the symbol '•', used to organise a vertical **list** by introducing each new item

capital letter - upper-case version of a letter, commonly used at the start of **sentences** and for proper **nouns**

character - fictional person in a **story**, play or film

chronological - in a manner showing the order in which events happen or happened

clause - group of more than one **word**, including a **verb**

cliché - phrase or idea that is overused and so has lost its impact

climax (in a story) - moment of greatest **conflict**

comma splice - incorrect use of a comma to link two **main clauses**

comparison - looking at similarities and differences between two or more things

conclusion (of a text) - last part, often a result or summary

concrete noun - noun that names a physical thing you can see, hear, smell, taste or touch (e.g. 'cat'; 'tree')

conflict (in a story) - challenge or opposition

conjunction - word used to connect **clauses**, or before the final item in a **list**

connotation - connected idea

consonant - letter of the alphabet that is not a **vowel**

context - situation or **setting** for a **word** or event that helps to explain it

contraction - shortened form of two or more **words**, using an apostrophe to show where letters have been missed out

coordinating conjunction - conjunction used to link two **clauses** with equal importance

counter-argument - argument against a first argument, presenting an objection and/or opposing views

definitive relative clause - relative clause that adds information vital for meaning

description / descriptive writing - writing that aims to create a vivid image in the reader's mind

determiner - word (such as 'the' and 'a') that begins a **noun** or **noun phrase**, indicating whether the noun names something general or specific, and **plural** or **singular**

diagram - simple picture used to illustrate a point or idea, usually in **non-fiction**

dialogue - speech between people or fictional **characters**

direct address - method of speaking directly to the reader or listener

direct speech - words exactly as they are spoken, usually given within **speech marks** and with an **identifier**

embedded quotation - quotation positioned inside a **sentence** and that functions as a part of the sentence

emotive language - words and **phrases** that stir readers' emotions

emphasis - forcefulness of expression that suggests importance

evidence - supporting **facts** or information

example - something with characteristics typical of its type

explanation text - text that makes information and ideas clear and easy to understand

exposition (in a story) - early part of a **story** that introduces the situation, **characters** and/or **setting**

extract - short passage taken from a text or other source

fact - true and proveable idea

fiction - imagined idea, often a **story**

figurative language - words and **phrases** with meanings different from but related to their usual ones, based on their **connotations** (e.g. **similes** and **metaphors**)

finite verb - verb that shows **tense** and **person** (e.g. I saw, he made)

first person - storytelling **viewpoint** where the person doing the action is the writer, **speaker** or **narrator**, using the **pronouns** 'I' and 'me'

flashback - scene that shows events from the past

form (of a text) - shape and **structure**

formal (language) - suitable for an audience that is important, in authority or not known

fronted - positioned at the start of a **sentence**

future - verb tense indicating that actions or events will happen but have not happened yet

heading - main title

homophones - words that sound alike but have different spellings and different meanings

identifier - phrase that tells the reader who is speaking (e.g. 'he said'; 'they shouted')

imperative verb - verb that gives a command or instruction (e.g. 'go'; 'come')

impression - idea or **opinion** (about something or someone)

incidental relative clause - relative clause that adds information not vital for meaning

inference - use of clues to work something out

infinitive - root form of a **verb**, preceded by 'to'

informal (language) - casual; suitable for peers

information text - see **explanation text**

instruction text - text that tells readers how to do something

intention - desired effect

introduction (of a text) - beginning, often establishing **context**

key points - most-important ideas in a text

leaflet - sheet or sheets of paper, sometimes folded, including key information on a topic (often used in advertising)

letter (text type) - written way of communicating with a person or organisation, usually sent using a postal service

line (in a play) - single line of text, or one instance of **words** spoken by a **character**

line (in a poem) - sentence or part of a sentence that finishes at the end of a line

list - sequence of connected items written one after another

main body (of a text) - majority of the writing in a text (as opposed to, for example, an **introduction** and/or **conclusion**)

main clause - clause that makes a main point in a **sentence**, and that could stand alone

metaphor - description of something as though it is something else

modal verb - auxiliary **verb** that expresses possibility or importance

modify (a word) - make small alterations to, by adding to or changing meaning (e.g. with an **adjective** or **adverb**)

multi-clause sentence - sentence composed of more than one **clause**

myth - traditional **story**, often about early history or explaining natural events

narration - description by a **story**'s **narrator**

narrative - account of connected events, often **fiction**

narrator - character who is telling the **story**

non-fiction - factual writing; representing truth

non-finite clause - clause that contains a **non-finite verb**

non-finite verb - verb that does not show **tense**, such as an **infinitive verb** or **present participle**, meaning it does not indicate when something happened

noun - word that names a person, place, object or idea

noun phrase - group of **words** containing a **noun** that name a single person, place, object or ideas

object (of a sentence) - thing that is being acted on by a **verb** or **preposition**

onomatopoeia - technique of using a **word** that sounds like its meaning

opinion - personal ideas that may or may not be based on **facts**

paragraph - group of related **sentences** that develop an idea, presented as a block of text

passive voice - form in which the thing that is being acted on by a **verb** or **preposition** is the grammatical **subject**, rather than **object**, of a **sentence**

past continuous - verb tense indicating that events or actions in the past were still happening when something else happened (e.g. The sun was shining when the elephant came out of the jungle)

past participle - verb form indicating completed events or action (e.g. walked)

past tense - verb tense indicating that events or actions happened in the past

person (of a verb) - manner in which **verb** forms change depending on the person doing the action

personification - metaphor that uses human qualities to describe something non-human

persuasive text - text designed to change or guide someone's **opinions** and/or actions

phrase - group of more than one **word**, without a **verb**

plural - indicating more than one

poetry - stylised text structured by the **rhythm** of language, often used to express ideas or feelings

point of view - opinion, or manner in which events are experienced

preposition - word that expresses how things are connected, for example by place or time (e.g. 'in'; 'with'; 'before')

prepositional phrase - group of **words** that begins with a **preposition**

present continuous - verb tense indicating that events or actions are happening now (e.g. I am walking)

present participle - verb form indicating continuous events or action (e.g. walking)

present perfect - verb tense indicating that events or actions that happened in the past are still having an effect (e.g. I have left: I left in the past, but am still absent)

present tense - verb tense indicating events or actions that are currently happening

presentational features - features used to organise content visually, such as **headings** and **subheadings**

pronoun - word that replaces or stands in for a **noun** or **noun phrase**

proofread - check writing for errors

prose - written or spoken language in its ordinary form - such as in stories or explanations - as opposed to **poetry**

punctuate - give **punctuation** (to)

punctuation - symbols used to assist and alter meaning (e.g. full stops, question marks, exclamation marks, dashes, commas and apostrophes)

quotation - words taken from a text or speech and repeated

quotation marks - see **speech marks**

reasoning - clear, logical explanation or **argument**

register - tone and style of language (see **formal** and **informal**)

relative clause - clause that adds information to a **noun** or **noun phrase**, beginning with a **relative pronoun**

relative pronoun - word that indicates information related to a **noun** or **noun phrase**

repetition - technique of doing or saying something more than once

reported speech - summary or paraphrasing of speech that is included in a writer's or **narrator**'s description

resolution (in a story) - settling and/or explanation of **conflict**

response - reaction; reply

review - evaluate critically

revise - make changes, or recap learning

rhetorical device - language technique that a writer or speaker uses to present ideas persuasively

rhetorical question - question asked when an answer is not expected

rhyme (noun) - similar sounds at the end of two or more **words** or **lines**

rhythm - beat or pulse

scan - look through (a text) for something specific

scene (of a play) - continuous piece of action within a play, often based in a particular **setting**

script - written text of a play or film

second person - storytelling **viewpoint** where the person doing the action is the reader or listener, using the **pronoun** 'you'

sentence - group of **words** that is complete in itself, including a **verb** and a **subject** (sometimes implied): a statement, question, exclamation or command

sequence (verb) - arrange things in a particular order

setting - location

'silent' letters - letters that are not sounded independently when a **word** is spoken aloudsimile - comparison made by using the **words** 'like' or 'as'

simple past - verb tense (see **past tense**)

simple present - verb tense (see **present tense**)

single-clause sentence - sentence composed of only one **clause**

singular - indicating only one

skim-read / skim - look very quickly (at a text) for an idea of its content

slang - informal **words** or **phrases**, often used amongst friends

speaker (in a poem) - see **narrator**

speech marks - punctuation marks indicating **direct speech**

stage direction - instruction to people acting in or producing a play, for example about where to stand or what to do

Standard English - English that is grammatically correct

stanza - group of **lines** in a poem (sometimes referred to as a 'verse')

statistic - fact relating to numerical information

story - retelling of events, either real or fictional

structure (noun) - manner in which parts of something are organised, arranged and related

subheading - smaller **heading** that appears below a main title, used to signal different topics within a longer piece of writing

subject (of a sentence) - noun that is the focus of a **sentence**, usually representing what or who is doing the action described by the **verb**

subordinate clause - clause that adds information to a **main clause** (for example about cause, effect, time, condition or concession)

subordinating conjunction - conjunction used to link a **subordinate clause** to a **main clause**

summary - brief description of the main points

superlative - adjective that shows the highest level of the quality described (e.g. 'biggest'; 'most hungry')

syllable - part of a **word** that makes a single sound

synonyms - words with the same or very similar meanings

synopsis - see **summary**

tense (of a verb) - manner in which **verb** forms change depending on when the action happens

terminology - technical and/or specialised **vocabulary**

theme - overall subject or idea

third person - storytelling **viewpoint** where the person or thing doing the action is not the writer, speaker or **narrator**, using the **pronouns** 'he', 'him', 'she', 'her', 'it', 'they' and 'them'

topic sentence - sentence that clearly states the topic of a **paragraph**

triple structure - persuasive pattern of three ideas

verb - word that names an action or state of being

viewpoint - perspective when telling a **story**

vocabulary - words used

vowel - A, E, I, O or U (letter of the alphabet that is not a **consonant**)

word - arrangement of letters that has one unit of meaning

word class - group of **words** that have similar roles in **sentences**

Published by Pearson Education Limited, 80 Strand, London, WC2R 0RL.

www.pearsonglobalschools.com

Text © Pearson Education Limited 2020
Designed by Pearson Education Limited 2020
Typeset by PDQ Digital Media Solutions Ltd
Project managed by Just Content Ltd
Produced by Just Content Ltd and Danielle Whisker
Edited by Hannah Hirst-Dunton, Liliane Nénot and Judith Shaw
Original illustrations © Pearson Education Limited 2020
Illustrated by David Belmonte at Beehive Illustrations
Cover design © Pearson Education Limited 2020
With thanks to Jenny Roberts and Sarah Ryan

Cover images: Song_about_summer/Shutterstock

The right of David Grant to be identified as the author of this work has been asserted by him in accordance with the Copyright, Designs and Patents Act 1988.

First published 2020

25
10 9 8

British Library Cataloguing in Publication Data

A catalogue record for this book is available from the British Library

ISBN 978 0 435 20072 5

Copyright notice

Printed in Slovakia by Neografia

Acknowledgements

(key: b-bottom; c-centre; l-left; r-right; t-top)
Image credits: 23RF: Scott Griessel/123RF 57, Jacek Chabraszewski/123RF 69, Ian Allenden/123RF 90, Zlikovec/123RF 115cr1, Suwin Puengsamrong/123RF 115cr2, Xiebiyun/123RF 132c, Lightwise/123RF 132cr, Thongruay Jinnaritt/123RF 145, Jakobradlgruber/123RF 172tr2, Barbara Marini/123RF 199tr3, Vasin Leenanuruksa/123RF 203, Anton Sokolov/123RF 212; **Alamy Stock Photo:** Frans Lemmens/ Alamy Stock Photo 148, Granger Historical Picture Archive/ Alamy Stock Photo 196, ITAR-TASS News Agency/Alamy Stock Photo 200; **Getty Images:** John M Lund Photography Inc/ DigitalVision/Getty Images 50, SeppFriedhuber/E+/Getty Images 92, Pick-uppath/E+/Getty Images 134, AFP/Getty images 149, 151, Heritage Images/Getty Images 158, Chris Hyde/Getty Images 162, Chris Hyde/Getty Images 165, Fuse/ Corbis/Getty Images 166br, Wundervisuals/E+/Getty Images 176; **Pearson Education Ltd:** Abhishek Maji/Pearson Management Systems Limited 132b1,Jules Selmes/Pearson Education Ltd 216c; **Shutterstock:** Sergii Gnatiuk/Shutterstock 008, Burnel1/Shutterstock 023, Viktor Gladkov/Shutterstock 023, Mylisa/Shutterstock 052, Anton Starikov/Shutterstock 052, Fizkes/Shutterstock 053, Milos Luzanin/Shutterstock 056, Indypendenz/Shutterstock 058t, NatalieIme/Shutterstock 058b, Syda Productions/Shutterstock 061t, 077, 113, 132bc, Ulegundo/Shutterstock 061b, Palto/Shutterstock 062, Ronstik/ Shutterstock 064, Jiri Pavlik/Shutterstock 068tr, John And Penny/ Shutterstock 068cr1, FocusDzign/Shutterstock 068br,Jean-Michel Girard/Shutterstock 068bl, Georgejmclittle/Shutterstock 069, Durantelallera/Shutterstock 073, Emily frost/Shutterstock 074, Syda Production/Shutterstock 077, Patrizia Tilly/ Shutterstock 078, Pedro Bento/Shutterstock 082, Denis Tabler/ Shutterstock 083, BlueSkyImage/Shutterstock 090tr, Zurijeta/ Shutterstock 090br, Rich Carey/Shutterstock 098bl, 132cl, Tviolet/Shutterstock 098br, SpeedKingz/Shutterstock 100bc, Sebra/Shutterstock 100br, 2728747/Shutterstock 101, Rido/ Shutterstock 102, Oksana Kuzmina/Shutterstock 103, Petr Klabal/Shutterstock; ESB Professional/Shutterstock 106, FloridaStock/Shutterstock 110cl, UbjsP/Shutterstock 110br, Koya979/Shutterstock 112, Maridav/Shutterstock 115cl1, Wavebreakmedia/Shutterstock 115cl2, 138, 161, Africa Studio/ Shutterstock 116, Joker1991/Shutterstock 117, Zakhar Goncharov/Shutterstock 119, Rawpixel.com/Shutterstock 120cr, 134b3, Aliona Rondeau/Shutterstock 120br, MOHAMED ABDULRAHEEM/Shutterstock 123, Tonktiti/Shutterstock 124, Sevenke/Shutterstock 124cr, Fizkes/Shutterstock 127, S.Borisov/ Shutterstock 130, Lamai Prasitsuwan/Shutterstock 132, Kontur-vid/Shutterstock 136, Steve Meddle/Shutterstock 140, Anna Kucherova/Shutterstock 141tr, Vadym Zaitsev/Shutterstock 141cr, Tassel78/Shutterstock 143, Shahjehan/Shutterstock 144cr, BTWImages/Shutterstock 144br, Dainis Derics/ Shutterstock 152br, 153, IPK Photography/Shutterstock 152cr, 208, Shi Yali/Shutterstock 156cr, Windmoon/Shutterstock 159, Fang ChunKai/Shutterstock 159, Stray Toki/Shutterstock 159, Fotokostic/Shutterstock 161, 174, Dallas Events Inc/Shutterstock 161, Ivan Roth/Shutterstock 166cr, LightField Studios/